Sarah Williams, John Chamberlain

Letters Written by John Chamberlain During the Reign of Queen Elizabeth

Sarah Williams, John Chamberlain

**Letters Written by John Chamberlain During the Reign of Queen Elizabeth**

ISBN/EAN: 9783337324148

Printed in Europe, USA, Canada, Australia, Japan

Cover: Foto ©ninafisch / pixelio.de

More available books at **www.hansebooks.com**

# LETTERS

WRITTEN BY

# JOHN CHAMBERLAIN

DURING

THE REIGN OF QUEEN ELIZABETH.

EDITED FROM THE ORIGINALS
BY SARAH WILLIAMS.

PRINTED FOR THE CAMDEN SOCIETY.

M.DCCC.LXI.

# COUNCIL OF THE CAMDEN SOCIETY

## FOR THE YEAR 1861-62.

*President,*
THE MOST HON. THE MARQUESS OF BRISTOL, V.P.S.A.
WILLIAM HENRY BLAAUW, ESQ. M.A., F.S.A. *Treasurer.*
BERIAH BOTFIELD, ESQ. M.P. F.S.A.
JOHN BRUCE, ESQ. F.S.A. *Director.*
JOHN PAYNE COLLIER, ESQ. F.S.A.
WILLIAM DURRANT COOPER, ESQ. F.S.A.
JAMES CROSBY, ESQ. F.S.A.
JOHN EVANS, ESQ. F.S.A.
JOHN FORSTER, ESQ. LL.D.
THOMAS W. KING, ESQ. F.S.A.
THE REV. LAMBERT B. LARKING, M.A.
JOHN MACLEAN, ESQ. F.S.A.
FREDERIC OUVRY, ESQ. Treas. S.A.
WILLIAM JOHN THOMS, ESQ. F.S.A. *Secretary.*
WILLIAM TITE, ESQ. M.P. F.R.S. F.S.A.
HIS EXCELLENCY M. VAN DE WEYER.

The COUNCIL of the CAMDEN SOCIETY desire it to be understood that they are not answerable for any opinions or observations that may appear in the Society's publications; the Editors of the several Works being alone responsible for the same.

# INTRODUCTION.

THE CHAMBERLAIN LETTERS now published are those which were written during the reign of Elizabeth, and, with the exception of a few extracts in Nichols's Progresses, have not hitherto been printed. The nature of Chamberlain's Correspondence is so well known from the letters printed in "The Court and Times of James I.," and in other works, that any comment, either upon his style or the general character of his gossipping letters, is wholly superfluous. There are but sixty-two of the Elizabethan Letters, and all but one are addressed to Dudley Carleton; the single exception is a letter (No. LXIX.) which was begun for Carleton, but was afterwards sent to Ralph Winwood, who was then in Paris with him, and was doubtless handed over by Winwood to Carleton, which will explain its apparently solitary appearance. Chamberlain wrote frequently to Winwood during the sojourn of the latter in Paris, during 1601 and 1602, but I find no trace of any of these letters among the State Papers.

Although Chamberlain's letters are extremely numerous, and are entirely made up of personal allusions and references, little has been known of his own individual history. The importance of the information of which he is the sole chronicler has gained him a niche in Chalmers's Biographical Dictionary, but it is surprising how few details have been collected respecting himself. Even his descent, his parentage, and his family connections, have up to this time been altogether unknown. From his brief allusions to some of these subjects we are enabled to infer that he was born in January 1553-4;[a] that he had brothers named Robert and George; and that after the death of the latter, in February 1623-4, John Chamberlain became the survivor of all his father's children, the last of eight brothers and sisters.

His expression, " our university of Cambridge," used by him in a letter of 17 June 1612, intimates the place of his education, and Messrs. Cooper, the able authors of the Athenæ Cantabrigienses, in a recent communication to the always-useful " Notes and Queries" (2nd series, xi. 296), state that he was matriculated as a pensioner of Trinity College in May 1570, but took no degree. We may probably infer, from the frequency of his visits to his country friends, that he did not follow any profession; sometimes we find him at Rowland Lytton's, at Knebworth; sometimes at Sir Henry Wallop's, at Farley; sometimes at Mr. Gent's, at Ascott (a small parish in the county of Oxford); and at various other places. He seldom went far away from London, with the exception of a " voyage" to Ireland, in 1597 (p. 5), and of a journey to Venice in 1610, in company with Sir Dudley Carleton, whence he returned in November 1611.

In November 1620,[b] " Chamberlain was appointed one of the Commissioners for the repair of St. Paul's." This is his only public appointment of which I have found any trace. Messrs. Cooper,

---

[a] In a letter, dated 25 January 1622-3, he says, that " about the middle of this month" he " began to be *septuagenarius.*"
[b] Birch MS. 4173, f. 46.

in the communication to Notes and Queries before alluded to, state that " he was member for Clithero, in Lancashire, in the Parliament which met 19th November 1592, and for St. German's, in Cornwall, in that which met 24th October 1597;" but, with all deference, I rather incline to think that this must have been another person. Some allusion to such important incidents, if they had really occurred in Chamberlain's usually retired and quiet life, would surely have been found in his voluminous correspondence.

He does not appear to have been married, as there is no reference to wife or children in his letters, with the exception of a playful title which he gave to Winifred Wallop (p. 70). The latest letter in the State Paper Office is one addressed to Sir Dudley Carleton, H. M. Ambassador in Paris, dated March 7, 1625-6, Chamberlain being then in his seventy-fourth year; and in it, after giving the ordinary news, he says, " I have kept house these two days, and taken a little physic, more than I have done in a dozen years before."

From this time all further correspondence appears to have ceased, for, after a careful examination of the Domestic and the French Correspondence, I find nothing whatever concerning Chamberlain, from which I infer that he must have died shortly after writing the above letter. In the Rubens Papers, edited by Mr. W. Noël Sainsbury, a gentleman to whom I have long been indebted for valuable literary information and suggestions, I find a note at p. 9, wherein Secretary Dorchester, writing to Sir Isaac Wake, on the 15th of October, 1630, alludes to " Mr. John Chamberlain, our good friend, who is with God."

All our information respecting him has hitherto stopped a little short of the few facts which I have thus thrown together. But I am enabled to add something more to this meagre narrative.

It has been observed that some of Chamberlain's many letters have remaining upon them an impression of a coat of arms which bears, Quarterly, first and fourth, ermine, on a pale three leopard's faces; and third and fourth, on a chief two crowns; with a mullet for a difference. These arms, with the exception of the mullet, have been found in the Visitation Book of London in 1634, preserved in the College of Arms. They are there stated to have been borne by Robert Chamberlain of London, gentleman, son and heir of Richard Chamberlain late Alderman and Sheriff of London, and of Anne his wife, daughter and heir of Robert Downes of Yalding, in Kent, gentleman.

Following out this piece of information, it has become apparent that the Robert Chamberlain thus alluded to was the brother of John Chamberlain, the letter-writer, and that Alderman Richard Chamberlain, Sheriff of London in the year 1561, was his father. The will of the Alderman has been found in Doctors' Commons, proved on the 20th February, 1566-7. It is in some respects exceedingly minute in its details respecting the family of the testator, and not only confirms in a most singular manner all the personal and family particulars of John Chamberlain, derived from other sources, but satisfactorily establishes his parentage, his family position, his connections, and, in a certain degree, his circumstances. It contains also some personal particulars respecting him, which partly account for the unobtrusive life which he evidently led.

Alderman Chamberlain describes himself as an ironmonger, by which we may understand, I suppose, that he was a member of that distinguished city company, to whom he leaves a legacy of $50l.$ "because," he remarks, "that I heard say that they be at after-dell, [in difficulties, at a disadvantage,] to help them out of debt." The only trace of his own personal trading is in transactions relating to the sale of cloth to certain German merchants which had involved the Alderman in a long and serious litigation. His residence was in the parish of " Saincte Tolloys," meaning, I imagine, " St. Olave's in the Old Jewry," situate in the Ward of Coleman Street, of which it may be inferred, from various passages in the will, that Chamberlain was Alderman. In the church of this parish Chamberlain's first wife was interred, and he directed that he himself should be buried by her side. In the same parish, also, it is probable that John Chamberlain was born, in a mansion purchased and occupied by the Alderman, and respecting which there are some curious particulars in his will.

The first wife just alluded to was Anne Downes, or, as the testator spells the name, Downe, daughter of Robert and Margery Downe, and sister of a younger Robert Downe. She was the mother of the Alderman's eight surviving children.[a] At the making of his will, which is dated on the 18th October, 1558, he had married again to a person whom he describes in terms so often repeated and apparently dwelt upon that we cannot think them otherwise than meant to be strictly indicative of her real character. " My gentle Margaret" is the designation by which he generally distinguishes her, and in one place he describes her more fully as " my good, loving, and wellbeloved gentle and friendly wife, whom I have found very faithful and good in all things." She was a widow when he married her, perhaps had been married twice before, and had nine children living in 1558.

Of the Alderman's own eight surviving children, six were sons and two daughters; the former were named Robert, Thomas,

---

[a] According to his epitaph in Maitland, they had in the whole eight sons and five daughters.

Richard, Alexander, John, and George; the latter were, Elizabeth, the wife of Mr. Hugh Stukely, to whom the testator appeals by their " amity, friendship, and good will, which," he continues, " have been between us since our first acquaintance," and Margery, who was unmarried at the date of her father's will, but was subsequently united to Edmund Windham of Knefford, in the county of Somerset, second son of Sir John Windham, of Orchard, in that county.

The few particulars given of John Chamberlain in the will are worthy of notice. The testator provided for the bringing up of his sons by interesting in their welfare certain of his fellow-citizens, and by specially requesting some one particular named friend to take charge of each of them in the capacity of master or guardian. As to his son John he remarks, " because that he hath been tender, sickly, and weak, I would have him brought up to learning, hereafter when that he comes to some years, either in the university or else in some other place beyond sea . . . . . ; and I will commend him to my loving and friendly cousin, Thomas Goore, that he have the bringing of him up. I shall desire him so." The weakness which is here attributed to the infancy of John Chamberlain probably continued through life. It may have driven him from Cambridge without a degree, and occasioned him to take shelter in the quieter walks of life. It is obvious from his father's will that he inherited means which were sufficient for his support.

Dr. Birch says[a] that John Chamberlain was descended from the Chamberlains of Sherborne in Oxfordshire. The fact may have been so, but I have not found any proof of it. Mr. Clarence Hopper very kindly favoured me with the sight of a pedigree of that family,

[a] Birch MS. 4173, f. 1.

but I was not able to connect them with the Alderman or his descendants. The remainder of Dr. Birch's mention of Chamberlain was no doubt correct. He "was a gentleman," are the Doctor's words, "accomplished in learning and languages, both ancient and modern, and by the advantage of travelling, and an intimacy with some of the most considerable men of his time."

The clue discovered as to his personal history might be easily pursued much further than I have done ; and, although St. Olave's in the Old Jewry was destroyed in the fire of London, I make no doubt that a minute pedigree might be recovered of the Alderman and his descendants. Indisposition compels me to leave the task at present unattempted ; indeed much of what I have stated has been discovered for me by the kindness of friends ; perhaps further research is unnecessary, what is now published being sufficient to fix the parentage and *status* of this admirable letter-writer—the Horace Walpole of his day—and there, for the present at any event, I must leave him.

The excellent pedigree of Sir Dudley Carleton, which I have appended to these remarks, was presented to me by Robert Lemon, esq., a kindness for which I beg to thank him, as also for the uniform courtesy and consideration which I have received at his hands. The pedigree will be found to explain many personal allusions, not only in these letters, but in all other collections of the letters of Chamberlain and Sir Dudley Carleton. With respect to the movements of Dudley Carleton, it will not be necessary for me to follow him beyond the limits of this work. In 1597 he was "Attendant on the Lord Ambassador for H. M. in Paris;" in May 1598 he was "attending on the Lord Governor of Ostend," where he appears to have remained until the autumn of 1599, when he returned to England until the following October; after which he went to the Hague, and stayed there until the middle of 1601, when he went to Paris, where he was serving as secretary to Sir Thomas Parry at the time of Elizabeth's death.

In conclusion, I beg leave to express my very earnest thanks to Mr. Bruce, for the kindly assistance he has given me in the publication of this little volume; to Mr. J. Gough Nichols for his careful supervision of the work during its progress through the press; and to Mr. King, York Herald, for his great kindness in collating the Carleton pedigree with the Books of the College of Arms, and giving me other valuable information from that important repository.

2, *Belgrave Street South, S.W.*
*April 9th*, 1861.

[To follow page xii.

PEDIGREE of Sir DUDLEY CARLETON, subsequently created Viscount Dorchester, originally drawn up by the late ROBERT LEMON, Esq. F.S.A.; with additions made from the books of the College of Arms, by THOMAS WILLIAM KING, Esq., York Herald, F.S.A.

.... Carleton of Lincolnshire=.... dau. of .... Skerne of Lincoln.

6 sons, ob. s. p. | John Carleton of Walton-upon-Thames,=.... dau. and heir of .... Skipwith co. Surrey, esq. of Tettesworth, co. Hunts.

Gerard, 3d son, Dean of Peterborough. | George, 2d son, ob. s. p. | John Carleton of Baldwin=Joyce, dau. of John Welbeck of Oxenheath, Brightwell,co. Oxford, son and heir. | co. Kent, by Margaret, dau. and coheir of .... Culpeper of Oxenheath aforesaid.

Anne, dau. and coheir=Anthony Carleton of Baldwin Brightwell, in com. Oxon. esq. son and heir. | Joyce, 6th dau. of John Goodwin of Winchendon, in com. Bucks, esq. and widow of Robert Saunders of Flore, Northamptonshire. | Other issue.* | George Carleton of Wollaston, co. Northampton. ⚭ issue.†

John, ob. s.p. Joyce, married Edward Denton. ⚭ issue. | Elizabeth, dau. and coheir of Sir John Brockett, knt, buried at Newington, in com. Oxon. | George Carleton of Huntercombe in com. Oxon. esq. Will dated 14 May, 1627, pr. 18 April, 1628. Inq. p. m. 3 Oct. aº 4 Car. | Katherine, dau. of ... Harrison, of the Stable to Queen Eliz. and widow of Thomas Speer of Huntercombe. | Anne, dau. & coheir of George Garrard, 2d son of Sir William Garrard of Dorney, ob. 18 April, 1627, burd in St.Paul's Chapel, Westmr Abbey. | Sir Dudley Carleton, born 10 March, 1573, at Baldwin Brightwell, created Baron Carleton 22May1628, & Viscount Dorchester 22 June following: ob. 15th & buried 19 Feb. 1631-2, in St. Paul's Chapel, Westminster Abbey. Will dated 18 Aug. 1630, Cod. 13 Feb. 1631, pr. 4 April, 1632. | Anne, dau. of Sir Henry Glemham, in com. Suff. ob. and relict of Paul Viscount Bayning. | Elizabeth, wife of Alexander Williams, living a widow 1638. ⚭ issue. Bridget, wife of Sir Hercules Underhill, Knt. Anne, wife of John Dove, D.D. Alice Carleton, died unmarried. Will dat. 3 Dec. 1638, pr. 14 Aug. 1640.

Sir John Carleton of Hallcomb in com. Oxon. & of Chaveley in com. Cambridge, created a Baronet 28 May 1627, æt. 24 ad mort. patris, ob. 5 Nov. 1637, buried at Brightwell, co. Oxon. Will dat. 21 Sept. 1635, pr. 24 Nov. 1637. | Anne, eldest dau. of Sir Richard Houghton of Houghton Tower, in com. Lanc. and relict of Sir John Cotton. | George Carleton, named in the will of his uncle Lord Dorchester in 1630, and in that of his aunt Alice Carleton 1638. | (1 w.)=Sir Dudley Carleton of Imbercourt, in com. Surrey, knt, Resident in Holland in 1630, & Clerk of the Council in 1637. Will dated 28 Feb. 1653-4, pr. 22 March following. | (2 w.) .... dau. of .... | Joyce, dau. of Sir Herbert Croft, knt, Marge lic. dat. in Feb.1632. She then wife of James ob. ante 1653. | Henry, wife of Jno. Harrison of Beechhill, co. Bucks. ⚭ issue. Bridget, wife of James Chambers, M.D. | Frances, died a posthumous dau. died soon after her birth.

Sir George Carleton of Brightwell and of Chaveley aforesaid, Bart. only son, æt. 13 ad mort. pat. Admºon of his effects gr. to his sisters Anne and Katherine, 27 Feb, 1650-1. | (1 w.) Anne, eldest sister & coheir. Marge lic. dat.9June, 1647. She then æt.18; ob.22 Janʸ, 1655-6, æt. 23. | =George Garth of Morden, in com. Surrey, esq. æt. 22 in 1647, ob. 30 Nov. 1676. | (2 w.) Jane, dau. & coheir of Sir Humphry Bennet, knt. Marᵈ 17 June1669, ob.22Jan. 1669.70, æt. 66. | Katherine, 2d and younger sister & coheir. Dorothy, 2d dau. & coheir, wife of William Vanburg of London, Merchᵗ. ⚭ issue. | Anne, eldest dau. and coheir, wife of John Ferrers ofTamworth,esq. ⚭ issue. | Lucy, eldest dau. and coheir, by 2d venter. Livᵍ 1653-4. Mary,second dau. & coheir, by the 2d venter, wife of Edward Pearce of Parson's Green, co Middʸ, gent. Elizabeth, youngest dau. & coheir, by the 2d venter. Wife of Giles Vanbrugh (brother of William, who married her sister Dorothy), by whom she had issue (among others) Sir John Vanbrugh, knt, Surveyor-General and Clarenceux King of Arms. ⚭ issue.

George, ob. inf., buried 14 Oct 1650. | Richard Garth of Morden aforesaid, esq. only surviving son and heir. Died, without issue, 18 July, 1700, æt. 49, burd at Morden. | =Catherine Stone, his wife. Livᵍ 1700. | Anne, Dorothy, & Katherine, all died young or unmard.

* The other issue of John Carleton and Joyce Welbeck are given in Vincent's pedigree.
† The issue of George Carleton of Wollaston are also given in same.

This Pedigree has been collated with several MSS. in the College of Arms, and appears to have been correctly drawn up.
THOMAS W. KING, York Herald.—*March* 23, 1861.

# CHAMBERLAIN'S LETTERS

DURING THE REIGN OF QUEEN ELIZABETH.

## LETTER I.

[Domestic Correspondence, State Paper Office, June 11, 1597.]

GOODE MR. CARLETON,

I know you lookt longe ere this time to have heard from me, and so might you well have don, if Painter the post had not kept your letter of the eight [a] of May a seasoninge till the sixt of this present June. I receved a litle billet before by your sister Williams [b] in the way of an *interim* till you had better leasure, but presently upon it went to Askot, where I met with your brother Carleton [c] (comming from the buriall of your uncle Goodwin [d]), who told me Tobie Mathew [e] had shewed him a letter from you wherin you complained much of want, and what narrow straights you were like to be driven to, marvailing you had toucht no such matter in your letters to him, and therewithall began to dilate to me what he had don and could do for you, but the conclusion was that his abilitie is not to supplie all wants, and therefore you must trust to yourself and make your owne fortune. I replied litle to it but only in generall termes, the rather because I hope it is but a borrowed complaint to distast

[a] The letter referred to is in the French Correspondence, State Paper Office.
[b] Elizabeth, wife of Alexander Williams.
[c] George, son of Anthony Carleton of Baldwin Brightwell.
[d] Brother of Mrs Anthony Carleton.
[e] Son of Dr. Toby Mathew, Archbishop of York; born 1578; knighted 1623; died 1655.

CAMD. SOC. B

younge Mathew from following you into Fraunce then for any true
cause. I am exceeding glad to heare how well you are entertained
by my Lord Ambassador,[a] of whom I presumed no lesse, for though
I alwayes knewe him to be *paucorum hominum*, yet he hath ever
shewed himself an honourable fast frend where he found vertue and
desert. Mr. Evers[b] is in Ireland with the Lord Borrough,[c] between
whom and Sir John Norris[d] there is lately a solemne pacification
made with much counterfet kindenes on both sides. The old
Deputie[e] is come home very fat they say, both in body and purse,
having made a luckie conclusion of his government with the over-
throw and death of Feffe Mackhugh, an auncient and troublesom
rebell; upon which service he made three knightes at his comming
away, viz., Calistenes Brooke,[f] Thomas Maria Wingfield,[g] and one
Trevire,[h] a Welchman. Sir Thomas Norris[i] Lady was lately
brought abed there of three daughters, which the Lord Norris[k]
imputes to the fertilitie of the soile, and exemplifies it by a mare he
sent two yeares ago to his sonne Thomas that brought two foales.
We have great preparation here for a sea viage, which troubles

[a] Sir Anthony Mildmay, son of Sir Walter Mildmay; knighted and sent as resident ambassador to Henry IV. in 1596; died 1617.
[b] Cousin of Lord Evers [See Letter III.]
[c] Thomas, second Lord Burrough, K.G.; succeeded Sir William Russell as Lord Deputy of Ireland in 1597; died Oct. 14, the same year. [Dugdale, ii. 289.]
[d] Second son of Henry 1st Lord Norris of Rycot; Lord President of Munster 1584; died 1597.
[e] Sir William Russell, fourth son of Francis second Earl of Bedford; Lord Deputy of Ireland 1594; recalled 1596-7; created Baron Russell of Thornhaugh 21 July, 1603; died 1613. [Dugdale, ii. 380.]
[f] Sir Calisthenes Brooke of Sutton; knighted May 8, 1597; died at the Hague 1611. [Knights made in Ireland, printed by Sir Thomas Phillipps; and Domestic Correspondence, State Paper Office, October, 1611.]
[g] Knighted May 8, 1597.
[h] Sir Richard Trevor of Trevallin, Denbighshire; knighted May 8, 1597. [Knights made in Ireland, printed by Sir Thomas Phillipps.]
[i] Third son of Henry Lord Norris; Lord Justice of Ireland and Lord President of Munster 1597; died 1599. [Dugdale, ii. 404.]
[k] Henry Lord Norris of Rycot; died 1600. [Dugdale, ii. 404.]

our discoursers how or where it shalbe imployed. The common sort talke of Callais, others of the Islands of Tercera, but the most likelie in mine opinion is to set upon the King of Spaines navie whersoever they can finde it, or to meet with the Indian fleet. Theire whole number consists of fifteen of the Quenes shippes, besides the two Spanish shippes that were taken the last yeare, (which be new fashioned after the English manner,) and of two-and-twentie men of warre of Holland and some fowre-and-twentie flie boats and hoyes that serve for cariage of men and vitailes. They have with them 4,000 prest men, and 1,200 musketticrs that come with Sir Francis Vere [a] out of the Low Countries. The voluntaries are thought will rise towardes 2,000. The Erle of Essex [b] is Generall both at sea and land; the Lord Thomas [c] Vice-Admirall; Sir Walter Raleigh [d] Rere-Admirall, who is newly restored to the executing his place in Court of Captaine of the Garde. The Erle of Southampton,[e] the Lord Mountjoy,[f] and the Lord Rich [g] gô as adventurers, though some say the Lord Mountjoy is to be Lieutenant-generall at land; the Erle of Darbie,[h] the Lord Gray,[i] the Lord Windsor,[k] and Compton [l] pretend likewise to go, but it is thought shall not get leave. The provisions are hastened on very fast, and it is saide the Erle of Essex takes his leave at Court on Sonday next the 12th of this present, and hopes to be gon within

[a] Nephew of John 16th Earl of Oxford, and elder brother to Horace Lord Vere of Tilbury; Governor of the Brill 1598; died 1608.
[b] Robert Devereux, second Earl, 1576-1600-1.
[c] Thomas Lord Howard of Walden; created Earl of Suffolk 21 July, 1603; died 28 May, 1626.
[d] Born 1552; executed October 29, 1618.
[e] Henry Wriothesley, third Earl; died November 10th, 1624.
[f] Charles Blount; created Earl of Devonshire 21 July, 1603; K.G.; died April 3, 1606.
[g] Robert third Baron; created Earl of Warwick 6th August, 1616; died 24th March, 1618.
[h] William Stanley, sixth Earl of Derby, K.G.; died 1642.
[i] Thomas Lord Grey of Wilton; attainted 1604; died 1614.
[k] Henry Lord Windsor; died 1605.
[l] William Compton; created Earl of Northampton August 2, 1618; K.G.; died June 24, 1630. [Dugdale, ii. 403.]

ten dayes after. The presse of gentlemen wilbe very great, but I will not stand to set downe any but one or two of your acquaintaunce, that is, your cousin Mighell Dormer,[a] whom I can by no meanes yet disswade, and Hugh Beston[b] that standes to be Treasurer of the iorney, though I doubt he shall not be troubled with much receit, for I am half of our Doctor's[c] opinion, that warrants him, if he have it, that a well sadled rat may cary all his accompts. But his true errand is to be knighted as sone or before Sir Peter Evers,[d] neither doth he dissemble it greatly to his frends, but sayes merelie he hath ben a scabd squire a great while, and could now be content to be a paltrie knight the rest of his time. Sir John North died[e] here on Sonday last, and is thought to have left his lady[f] but a meane widowe. Sir Thomas Wroughton went likewise much about the same time, and old Duns when I was in Oxfordshire. Sir John Payton is lately made Lieutenant of the Towre, and Sir Henry Cocke either is, or upon the point to be, sworne Coferer of the Quenes houshold. Philip Scudamore[g] is very forward and like to have Mrs. Lovell the last Coferer's widow, to the great dislike of some of his best frendes. And your Lady Umpton[h] is in parlee with Mr. George Sherly of Northampton or Lecestershire. This terme, here was one Longe, a Captaine of Somersetshire, condemned in the Starchamber in 500 markes and to stand on the pillorie, for chopping and making portsale of his souldiers. We have here a new play of humors in very great request, and I was drawn alonge to it by the common applause, but my opinion of it is (as the fellow saide of the shearing of hogges), that there was a great crie for so litle wolle. This is all I can

[a] Knighted April 1st, 1604; died September 1624.
[b] Hugh Beeston of Beeston; knighted May 7, 1603; Receiver General for the Crown in Cheshire and North Wales; died 1626.
[c] Dr. Gilbert, afterwards physician to the Queen; died 1603.
[d] Sir Peter Evers, of Lincolnshire, was knighted May 11, 1603.
[e] Son of Roger Lord North; died June 5th, 1597.
[f] Dorothy; daughter and co-heir of Valentine Dale, Doctor of Laws.
[g] Knighted July 23, 1603.
[h] Widow of Sir Henry Unton, who died Ambassador in France.

bethincke me of for the present, neither can you chuse but be reasonablie satisfied, for what you want in waight you have in measure. Yet is the greatest newes behinde, that I am upon a viage into Ireland with Mr. Wallop,[a] who with his wife,[b] her mother,[c] and your cousin Lytton,[d] have so earnestly intreated me, that partly at theire request, and partly being weary of idleness I have yeelded, and hope to be setting forward within this moneth, and to be here againe before Bartlemew-tide. You be like enough to heare of me before I go, if here be ought worth writing. Your sister Alice [e] is close prisoner at her ladies; the rest of your frends are in state as you left them. And so wishing you all health and goode hap, I bid you farewell.

From London, this longest[f] day of 1597.

Yours most assuredly,
JOHN CHAMBERLAIN.

[*Addressed,*]
   To my assured goode frend
      Mr. Dudley Carleton,
         attendant on the Lord Ambassador
            for her Majestie
               at Paris.

[a] Henry, son of Sir Henry Wallop, Vice-Treasurer of Ireland; born October 18, 1568; knighted in Ireland 1599; died November 15, 1642. [Collins's Peerage, iv. 317-21.]
[b] Elizabeth, daughter of Robert Corbet of Morton-Corbet, esq.; died November 5, 1624. [Ibid.]
[c] Anne, daughter of Oliver Lord St.John, widow of Robert Corbet, and wife of Rowland Lytton; died February 28, 1601-2. [Collins's Peerage, vi. 743.]
[d] Rowland Lytton of Knebworth; knighted May 7, 1603.
[e] Alice Carleton; died unmarried.
[f] From internal evidence, it is apparent that this letter was written between the 5th and 12th; an old indorsement assigns it to the 10th; but I have assigned it to the 11th, which was the 21st N.S.

## LETTER II.

[Domestic Correspondence, State Paper Office, May 4, 1598.]

I am newly returned from Knebworth,[a] whence I made the more haste that I might aunswer your letter from Ostend of the 9th of Aprill. I wrote to you much about the time of your departure, which how it came to your handes God knowes, as likewise what shall become of this, which I write at all adventures, for here is nothing but solitude *ante ostium*, no body at home, neither at your brother Williams,[b] nor my Lady Northes. Your sister Alice, they say, is in the country; belike there is somewhat a brewing, and this is all I can tell you of houshold matters. Now touching your owne commonwealth, I do not greatly like the course you are in, and yet hard beginnings commonly prove best, but still methinckes you are out of your way as longe as you carry but the title of a souldier, and therfore unles your stomacke serve you the better, or that you see great probabilitie of well doing, *cedant arma togæ*, retire in time, and if nothing els will take, reserve that course for *ultimum refugium* at a dead lift. Mr. Secretary[c] returned the first of this moneth somwhat crased with his posting jorny;[d] the report of his father's[e] daungerous estate gave him winges, but for ought I can learne the old man's case is not so desperate but he may hold out another yeare well inough. Most of his followers shipt themselves at Nantes and came away by longe seas, and were well coursed, and almost taken, by fowre or five Spanish shippes of Bluet, but yet arrived safely at Sandwich; himself came overland to Caen, and so to Portesmouth. Dr. Harbert[f] and his train are not yet

[a] The seat of Rowland Lytton, esq. co. Herts.
[b] Alexander Williams.
[c] Sir Robert Cecill.
[d] From Paris, where he had been on a special embassy to Henry IV. of France.
[e] Lord Burghley died August 4th, 1598.
[f] John Herbert, Master of Requests; knighted 1602. [Birch MS. No. 4,173, note to Chamberlain's Letter of May 4, 1598.]

come to towne, but I heare they be in England. The successe of this jorny is not fully knowne, but thus far, that it hath staide the French Kinge from going thorough with Spaine, and made him pause, at least. The States offer to maintaine him 4,000 men in Picardie, which with litle other help will continue the warre there, now that he hath nothing to do elsewhere. They have likewise offered the Quene that whensoever it shall please her to make an invasive jorny into Spaine to assist her with great store of shipping at theire owne charge, some say to the number of 150 saile. Yet for all this it is still in deliberation whether we shall joine with Fraunce in a peace and leave the Lowe Countries or sticke to the Lowe Countries and hold out the warre, and the balaunce swayes not yet on either side, at leastwise that can be discerned. Matters in Ireland are farther out of square then ever, so that there is no other way but to provide the sharper sword. Here is speach of forces to be sent thether, but they cannot yet resolve upon a Deputie, for Sir Walter Raleigh, Sir Robert Sidney,[a] and Sir Christofer Blunt,[b] (as I heare,) have refused it. Here be certain apprehended for a conspiracie against the Quenes person and my Lord of Essex, wherof one shold be a Scottishman or somwhat that way; much buzzing hath ben about it, but either the matter is not ripe or there is somewhat els in it, for it is kept very secret. Alabaster,[c] that was clapt up for poperie, hath broken prison and got away. Snelling, the ruffian that had the brabble with Charles Chester, had not so goode lucke, for on Monday morning he went a mayeng to Tiborne and was hangd there for a robberie committed about Highgate the Tewsday before. I heare that Justice Beau-

---

[a] Appointed Governor of Flushing 1589; created Lord Sidney, Viscount Lisle, and ultimately Earl of Leicester and K.G.; died July 13, 1626. [Dugdale, ii. 412.]

[b] Married the mother of Robert Earl of Essex, and was involved in his conspiracy.

[c] William Alabaster, Chaplain to Essex in the Cadiz expedition, a convert to Rome, but afterwards returned to the Church of England, and became Rector of Therfield, Hertfordshire, and Doctor of Divinity. [Birch MS. No. 4,173, note to Chamberlain's Letter of May 4, 1598.]

mont and Sergeant Drew that rode the northern circuit are bothe dead, upon some infection of the gaile, as is most like.[a] Likewise Dr. Lewin that had the office of Wills is lately dead, and one Dr. Gibson[b] that was Chauncellor of Yorke hath his place. The marchants have newes that the Emperor of Moscovie died in January last, and that his wifes brother that was elected after him shuld be murthered before his coronation, wherupon there is great confusion in those parts. And this being all I can bethincke me of for the present, I will commit [you] to Gods protection. From London, this 4th of May, 1598.

Yours most assuredly,
JOHN CHAMBERLAIN.

[*Addressed,*]
To my very good frend
Mr. Dudley Carleton,
attending on the Lord Governor of Ostend,
geve these.

## LETTER III.

[Domestic Corr. State Paper Office, May 17th, 1598.]

GOODE MR. CARLETON,

You have gotten the start so far before me, that I am almost out of hope to overtake you, and yet I have not bene altogether negligent, for this is my second letter since my comming to towne about the beginning of this moneth, but I doubt mine do not finde such spedy passage as yours do hitherwards, for I receved one of the 10th[c] upon the 13th of this present, and another of the 12th yesterday,

[a] Chamberlain's conjecture was incorrect as to Sir Francis Beaumont, who died at his seat, Grace Dieu, in Leicestershire, on 22 April, 1598. He was the author of Bosworth Field, and father of the dramatist. [Foss's Judges, v. 456.]
[b] John Gibson, D.C.L., knighted July 23, 1603.
[c] I have been unsuccessful in a search for these Letters in the Holland Correspondence of 1598.

I delivered my last at Mr. Williams to be sent with the first opportunitie, but I understand by Mrs. Alice it was there within these three dayes. This (according to your direction) I send by Mr. Clarke, whom I could not heare of at your Lord Governors,[a] but I caused my man to finde him out in Litle Wood Street, but (by his sayeng) he made more questions and examined him upon more interrogatories then the conveyeng of a letter comes to, so that if you have any better meanes let me know it and I will not faile you from time to time while I am here. We are all of opinion that the peace goes forward, and the Lord Buckhurst[b] is appointed to go to Abbeville, or some other place thereabout, to conclude it. Mr. Bodley[c] is named as an assistant, but he will not go if he can possiblie avoide it. There is speach likewise of some greater man for countenance, as the Lord Marquis of Winchester,[d] the Erle of Northumberland,[e] or the Erle of Shrewsburie.[f] Matters in Ireland grow daily worse and worse, so that unles they have round and speedy succoures all is like to go to wracke; the counsaile have consulted about it these three or fowre dayes, but I heare of no resolution but only that 4,000 men shalbe sent at leisure. Here go flienge tales that the Erle of Cumberland[g] hath met with fowre carraques bounde for the Indies, and suncke one of them and taken two, but it is so diversly and faintly reported, that I have no great beliefe in it. We say that the Hollanders have taken a rich ship of treasure comming out of Spaine that past by our loitering sentinells that lie

---

[a] Sir Edward Norris, sixth son of Henry Lord Norris. [Dugdale.]
[b] Thomas Sackville, created Earl of Dorset March 13, 1604; died April 19, 1608. [Dugdale, ii. 400.]
[c] Thomas Bodley, founder of the Bodleian Library; born 1544; appointed Resident with the States General 1588; knighted April 1, 1604; died January 28, 1612-13. [For date of death see Chamberlain's Letter, Domestic Correspondence, State Paper Office, February 4, 1613.]
[d] William; died November 24, 1598. [Dugdale, ii. 377.]
[e] Henry Percy, ninth Earl.
[f] Gilbert Talbot; died 1616. [Nichols's Progresses Eliz. i. 328.]
[g] George Clifford, third Earl, K.G.; died October 30, 1605.

about the Downes. The Countesse of Hartford[a] is lately dead, and mine old frend Tom Powell, whose companie I shall much want for my walke in Powles. Sir Charles Blunt[b] stayed behinde Mr. Secretary in Fraunce about a quarrell he had with a Dutchman that was knighted at Cales, that had challenged him; newes came two dayes since that they have met, and that the Dutchman is slaine. Our good frend Mr. Evers hath at last left Ireland, and came to towne last weeke; within three dayes after, his cosen the Lord Evers,[c] and Sir William[d] his brother, walking the streets with one page after them, were set upon (as they say) by fowre or five of the Witheringtons about a country quarrell, and so overlaide that the Lord was hurt in the hande, and Sir William receved divers sore wounds, as in the hande, in the shoulder, over the face, and quite thorough the body, notwithstanding all which he holdes out yet, being the fift day, and I hope will do. Your Dr. Robinson[e] of Quenes Colledge is made Bishop of Carlile; and I heare that Dr. Edes,[f] preaching at Oxford on Sonday last, was cleane out and could go no farther; but kepe that to yourself. Mr. Edmonds[g] is either gon or presently going into Fraunce with letters to prepare the way for this peace. All that I heare of Tobie Mathew is, that he staide in Fraunce with younge Throgmorton, that fell sicke of the small pockes. Mr. Dormer and his lady wilbe in towne this weeke. Your cosen Lytton went hence yesterday, but wilbe here again within this sevenight; in the mean time he bad me remember his commendations to you. Sir Anthony Mildmay and all the houshold

---

[a] Frances, daughter of William Lord Howard of Effingham.
[b] Sir Charles Blount was not a party to this combat. [See Letter V. p. 14.]
[c] Ralph, son of William Lord Evers. [Dugdale, ii. 386.]
[d] Third son of William Lord Evers, slain in the battle of Marston Moor, 1645. [Dugdale, ii. 386.]
[e] Henry Robinson, D.D., Provost of Queen's College, Oxford; died Bishop of Carlisle, June 19, 1616.
[f] Richard Edes, D.D., Dean of Worcester 1596.
[g] Thomas, son of Thomas Edmondes of Plymouth, knighted 1603; became Treasurer of the Houschold 1618; died 1639.

went on Thursday last into Northamptonshire. Your sister Alice hath lien at your brother Williams in the country ever since St. Georges day, but I thincke she be now with her Lady, for so she told me fowre dayes ago, when I saw her last. And this being all my store either of publike or private newes, with my best wishes I bid you farewell.

From London, this 17th of May, 1598.

      Yours most assuredly,
        JOHN CHAMBERLAIN.

[*Addressed,*]
 To my assured goode frende
  Mr. Dudley Carleton,
   attending on Sir Edward Norris,
    Lord Governor of Ostend.

## LETTER IV.

[Domestic Correspondence, State Paper Office, 20th May, 1598.]

I wrote to you the 17th of this present, since which time I receved yours of the 24th of Aprill, which had playde the truant I know not where, and loitered very longe after his fellowes; yet it brought goode contentment with it to see your state somewhat amended, and your fortune rising, which if you once lay hold on, I make no doubt but you will manage to your best advantage. Your brother Carleton comes not to towne this terme. I had a letter from him on Wensday last to provide two bookes you write for, wherin I have don my best indevor, and with much ado and longe search, found the one, but the other will not be heard of, yet casting about I remembred myself that of mine owne store I had a treatise of the Siege of Paris, written in Spanish by a Spaniard that was all the while in the towne, which if it may serve your turne is at your disposing; otherwise if you have no great use of it (because Spanish bookes are hard to come by), I could be content you send or bring it back when you shall thincke best. Barnevelt,[a] the agent and advocate of the States, is here, and hath had audience these two dayes together, but I feare we are deafe on that side, and no musike will please us unles it be to the tune of peace. One of the cheifest reasons I can heare for it is a kind of disdaine and envie at our neighboures welldoinge, in that we, for theire sake and defence entring into the warre, and being barred from all commerce and entercourse of marchandise, they in the meane time thrust us out of all trafficke, to our utter undoing (if in time it be not looked into), and theire owne advancement, and though the feare of the Spaniards recovering those countries, and increasing greatnes, do somwhat trouble us, yet it is thought but a weake pollicie for feare of future and uncertain daunger (which many accidents may divert) to endure a present and certaine losse. And come what can come, Fraunce and England holding together (as in all probabilitie and reason they are like) they shall alwayes be able to make theire partie goode with Spaine. Another motive to the peace is the troubles of Ireland, which are like to put the Quene to exceding charge, and withall there appeares a blacke clowde in Scotland that threatens a storme. These, amonge many other reasons that I have heard and sene, are in mine opinion most materiall. Together with an offer from the Spaniard (as they say) that, come peace or war with the States, the Quene shall hold the cautionarie townes fowre yeares, in which space if the States do not repay the mony she hath disbursed for them, he upon those townes will see her satisfied, which semes a matter of such importance to some men, that with such a masse of mony they thincke we shalbe able to defend ourselves against the world. Other newes here goes very lowe, only Sir William Harvy[b] is saide to have married the

[a] The distinguished pensionary of Holland; executed in 1619. [Birch's Mem. of Elizabeth.]

[b] Created Baronet May 31, 1619, and Baron, by the title of Lord Hervey of Kidbrook, February 7, 1628; died June, 1642. [Dugdale, ii. 459.]

Countesse of Southamton.[a] Mr. Dormer and his wife came to towne yesternight, and lodge at your brother Williams for some fowre or five dayes. Thus with my goode wishes for your health and welfare I commit you to God. From London, this 20th of May, 1598.

Yours most assuredly,
JOHN CHAMBERLAIN.

[*Addressed as before.*]

---

## LETTER V.

[Domestic Correspondence, State Paper Office, May 31st, 1598.]

Though I have not heard from you since I wrote last, neither have we any novelties greatly worth the writing; yet, being to go out of towne to morrow towards Askot, methinckes I must needs bid you farewell. Your frend Edmonds came out of Fraunce the last weeke, and bringes worde that the peace there is so forward that it lacks nothing but the publishinge, which is thought to be performed by this time, and all the townes upon the point of deliverie. He is like to be tossed to and fro, and brickewald like a tennis-ball, from the one side to the other, till somwhat be concluded, for we have two moneths time to deliberate whether we will treat or no, and three moneths more for the treaty; wherupon we are not yet fully resolved, but consult daily about it, and the further they looke into it the more difficulties appeare, insomuch that the wisest judgements are distracted, and know not what to choose. For mine owne part, having heard what hath bin saide *pro et contra* on both sides, I cannot well discerne whether were better an insidious peace or so faint and weake a warre as we have made hitherto and

[a] Mary, daughter of Anthony Browne, Viscount Montacute, and relict of Henry Earl of Southampton. [Dugdale, ii. 459.]

are like to do hereafter, which doth rather prolonge and drawe on the consumption then remedie the disease. In the meane time the state of Ireland standes in ill termes, for we are so wholly possest with this imaginarie peace that we cannot attend it. Not past eight dayes since it was decreed that Sir Richard Bingham, Sir Samuell Bagnoll, and Sir Henry Docwray shold be sent thether, with ech of them a regiment of 2,000; but that course is altered, and now they talke that Sir Walter Raleigh and Sir George Carew [a] shold undertake it, but how longe that will hold is uncertain. The Lord Zouch, with Dr. Parkins,[b] is going ambassador into Denmarke about certain of our shippes that have ben staide there, which is doubted to be but a beginning or shadow of a farther matter. One Cary,[c] likewise, secretarie to the Lord Keper,[d] is appointed to go into Poland for some such busines. Bluet in Britain is saide to be rased. The newes I wrote of Sir Charles Blunt must be recalled, for it was a mistaking of a combat that passed betwene a Frenchman and a Dutch Baron. Ewens and the bishop of Glocester [e] are lately dead. Sir Francis Vere is to go very shortly with certain secret instructions to the States. All your private frends are as you left them. And so, wishing the continuance of your health and welfare, I commit you to God.

From London, this last of May, 1598.

Your assured frend,

JOHN CHAMBERLAIN.

[*Addressed as before.*]

[a] Created Baron Carew of Clopton June 4, 1605; Earl of Totnes February 5, 1625; died March 27, 1629. [Dugdale, ii. 423.]

[b] Christopher Parkins, D.C.L., knighted July 23, 1603.

[c] George Carew; knighted July 23, 1603; nominated Master of the Wards June 13, 1612; died November 13, 1612. [Polish Corr. S. P. O. 1598; and Chamberlain's Letters, Dom. Corr., June 17 and November 19, 1612.]

[d] Sir Thomas Egerton.

[e] Godfrey Goldsborough.

## LETTER VI.

[Domestic Correspondence, State Paper Office, August 30th, 1598.]

I came out of Oxfordshire on Satterday last, and on Monday came posting to London with your cosen Lytton to be a beholder of the solemne funeral,[a] wherein he and your brother Carleton were actors. They are gon downe together this day since dinner, and have left me to convay theire letters, and to write you such refuse newes as peradventure might scape them; but the worst is I heare your boat goes away the next tide, so that I am forced to make hudling haste, which of all things I love not, and that causes me to tarry behind them for two or three dayes, for I am no frend to sodaine motions, but of a setled constitution and naturally loth to remove. The Lord Treasurers[b] funeral was performed yesterday with all the rites that belonged to so great a personage. The number of mourners one and other were above 500; wherof there were many noble men, and among the rest the Erle of Essex, who (whether it were upon consideration of the present occasion, or for his owne disfavours,) methought carried the heaviest countenance of the companie. Presently after dinner he retired to Wansted, where they say he meanes to settle, seing he cannot be receved in Court, though he have relented much and sought by divers meanes to recover his hold. But the Quene sayes he hath plaide longe enough upon her; and that she meanes to play awhile upon him, and to stand as much upon her greatnes, as he hath don upon stomacke. The Lord Treasurer hath left the Quenes cofers so bare, that there is but 20,000 to be found, and the Quene is faine to demaund in lone of the cittie 40,000, wherof they can presently furnish her but with the one halfe. Of his private wealth there is but 11,000. come to light, and that all in silver, whereof 6000. (with eight or nine

---

[a] Of Lord Burghley.   [b] Died August 4; buried August 29.

hundred poundes land) he bequeathed to his two neeces [a] of Oxford, the rest in other legacies. And his lands some not so great as was thought, for Mr. Secretarie [b] sayes his owne part will not rise to 1,600. a-yeare upon the racke. It is much laboured to make him Lord Treasurer, wherin if he faile, it is assuredly thought he shalbe Master of the Wardes, for of necessitie there must be one, by opinion of all the lawyers. Mr. Maynard [c] is become the Quenes man, and that with such high favor that in goode earnest he is thought to be neerest in election to be Secretarie, and the rather for that Mr. Secretarie is altogether for him. The States are gon away well contented in that they thincke they have tied us fast by offring to pay our men of warre, garrisons and all, and to rembourse 3000 yearlie to the Quene, till the whole debt be run out. Yet for all this it is thought we shall treat, marry so that the States must be included with theire owne conditions. The Lord Cromwell [d] sues hard and makes large offers for the government of the Brill, but it is thought, if the warre go forward, that the Quene, with the States' consent, will translate that garrison to Arnew, therby to have her forces neerer together, and to assure herself the better of Middleburgh and the Ile of Walkeren. It is saide your Lord Governor of Ostend [e] shall continue his place, but most of your companies shalbe called away for Ireland. We say the late Cardinall [f] is sworne and receved Duke of Burgundie, by 14 of the provinces, and that presently he made proclamation that he meant to renounce all his father in lawes [g] quarrells, and to entertain amitie with all his neighbours, specially the aunciente allies and confederates of the house of Burgundie, and that Englishmen, Scottes, and others might

[a] The two granddaughters of Lord Burghley, by his daughter Anne, wife of Edward Earl of Oxford. [Nares's Life of Burghley.]
[b] Sir Robert Cecill.
[c] Henry Maynard had been secretary to Burghley; knighted in the last year of Elizabeth; died May 11, 1610. [Brydges's Collins, vi. 284.]
[d] Edward Cromwell, third Baron; died 1607.
[e] Sir Edward Norris.
[f] The Archduke Albert of Austria. [g] Philip II. of Spain.

safely trafficke in all his dominions, and that the States of Holland might likewise trade, go and come with all securitie during eight moneths, till other order may be taken for continuance; and that all straungers men of warre are to avoide within two moneths. Further, that he is gon into Spaine to fetch his bride,[a] having obtained leave of the provinces to be absent one yeare, when if he returne not, they are discharged from theire oath and obedience. Wherby we gather (as it is likewise reported) that the King of Spaine is certainly dead,[b] but these things must be better knowne to you as being neerer the market. We have lately receved a great blow in Ireland; Sir Henry Bagnoll the Marshall went with 3,500 foot complete, and 300 horse, to relieve the fort of Blackwater, distressed by Tiron,[c] and being come within two mile of it, in a pace or woode, where the ennemie had strongly intrenched himself, was so furiously set upon, that himself was there slaine [d] with 16 other captaines, and above 700 [e] souldiers; the rest retired to Armagh (having left to the ennemie seventeen ensignes), not knowing how to tarry there or remove thence in safetie, the ennemie being betwene eight and ten thousand strong. But newes came yesterday that they had made theire appointment, and that Tiron, out of his merciles bountie, had granted them leave to bury theire dead, and to go away with all they had, so that the fort might be delivered him; to the governor wherof, Captaine Williams, and his souldiers, he wold geve no better conditions, then to depart in theire dubletts and hose only, with rapier and dagger. This is the greatest losse and dishonour the Quene hath had in her time, and yet it seemes we are not moved with it; which whether it proceed more of courage then of wit I know not, but I feare it is rather a careles and insensible dulnes. Sir Samuel Bagnoll went post for Ireland on Satterday last, but his course and plot must be quite altered, for it is to no purpose to go to Lough-

[a] The Infanta Isabella Clara Eugenia. [b] Philip II. died on the $\frac{7}{1}$ of September, 1598.
[c] Hugh O'Neal, made Earl of Tyrone 1587.
[d] August 14. [Irish Correspondence, State Paper Office.]
[e] The loss in killed and run away amounted to 1,800 foot and 10 horsemen. [Ibid.]

foile now that the Blackwater is lost. Sir Richard Bingham hath ten dayes respite to set his thinges in order, and then to go Marshall of Ireland with 5,000 men; but I doubt it wilbe rather in speach then in performance. The Lord Cobham [a] was installed Lord Warden of the Cinq Ports on Bartlemew day at Caunterbury, at which ceremonious solemnitie were assembled almost 4,000 horse, and he kept the feast very magnificently, and spent 26 oxen with all other provision sutable. He, the Lord Thomas Howard, Sir Walter Raleigh, and Sir John Stanhope,[b] are in speach to be sworne shortly of the counsaile. Our marchants have lost two or three ships going to Moscovie, and one is missing that shold come from thence. Sir Charles [c] and Sir Henry Danvers [d] are come. I saw them both yesterday. Sir James Scudamores lady, that was so rich a mariage, is lately dead in childbed. Mrs. Vernon [e] is from the Court, and lies in Essex house; some say she hath taken a venew under the girdle and swells upon it, yet she complaines not of fowle play, but sayes the Erle of Southampton will justifie it; and it is bruted, underhand, that he was latelie here fowre dayes in great secret of purpos to marry her, and effected it accordingly. I thancke you for the letter you wrote me hence, though it were longe ere it came to my hands. I met your Alexander and Bucephalus at Sir William Spencers, and delivered his letter to your brother Carleton, for he challenged it as by your appointment, though he shewed no commission; and thus, having wearied both myself and you, I bid you farewell and commit you to God.

From London, this 30th of August, 1598.

[Addressed as before.]

Yours most assuredly,
JOHN CHAMBERLAIN.

[a] Henry Brooke; attainted 1604; died 1619. [Courthope's Nicolas, 119.]

[b] Created Baron Stanhope of Harrington, May 4, 1605; died 1620. [Courthope's Nicolas.]    [c] Executed for the Essex conspiracy.

[d] Created Baron Danvers of Dantsey July 21, 1603; Earl of Danby February 7, 1626; K.G.; died 1644. [Courthope's Nicolas, 141.]

[e] Elizabeth, daughter of Sir John Vernon of Hodnet; one of Elizabeth's maids of honour. She became Countess of Southampton.

## LETTER VII.

[Domestic Correspondence, State Paper Office, September 17th, 1598.]

I heard not of this messengers being here, nor of his intended jorny to Ostend, t'll he was almost going; and, though I had known it sooner, yet could I not have writ you much more then I am like to do on this sodain, for here growes no newes at Knebworth, unles I shold tell you how well harvest is come home, or some other adventures of hawking, hunting, bowling, or such like. But what I want of mine owne store I will borrow of my neighbours, and for brevities sake in this haste send you a letter I receved fowre or five dayes since, that shewes how the world went at the writing thereof; whereto I can only adde that this day sevenight the Erle of Essex went to the Court, but with what successe, or how matters stand since, I know not. The Quene removed on Wensday toward Nousuch, taking Dr. Cesars[a] in her way, who had provided for her eight severall times. Sir John Brocket lies languishing and is thought will not hold out long, but whether he better for your nephew that he go or tarry is a question. On Thursday your cosen Lytton and I receved your letters of the 29th of August and the 8th of this present, which came so fully furnished with ballads, bookes, and babies, that we cannot overcome them yet, specially Aldegondes tedious discourse. If he were now at home I know he wold send you many thancks, which I wold faine supplie if I were as good at it as himself, but you know my plain dealinge, and therefore I hope will expect no ceremonies. He went yesterday to Bletso[b] to convoy the Lady Pelham,[c] that hath lien here this fortnight, and wold faine

---

[a] Julius Cæsar, D.C.L.; born 1557; Master of the Requests and Judge of the Admiralty; knighted May 20, 1603; Master of the Rolls 1614; died April 28, 1636. The house in which he entertained the Queen was at Mitcham: see Progresses of Elizabeth, iii. 19.

[b] The seat of Oliver Lord St.John.

[c] Judith, daughter of Oliver first Lord St.John, and relict of Sir John Pelham. [Dugdale, ii. 399.]

have drawne me along with him, but by good hap a certain cold and hoarsenes kept me at home, for, how well soever they use me, yet methincks still I am out of mine element when I am among Lords, and I am of Rabelais minde that they looke big *comme un millord d'Angleterre*. I can send you nothing of your privat frends, neither can I tell certainly when I shalbe at London, but toward the Terme have with you to Westminster, till when I bid you farewell, with my best and kindest wishes.

From Knebworth, this 17th of Sept., 1598.

Yours most assuredly,
JOHN CHAMBERLAIN.

[*Addressed as before.*]

## LETTER VIII.

[Domestic Correspondence, State Paper Office, Oct. 3, 1598.]

GOOD M<sup>r</sup>. CARLETON,

I receved two letters from you at Knebworth; to the former I made aunswer from thence by a man of Sir Gerrard Harvies, and now (being called hither by some occasion sooner then I looked for,) I wold fain requite your kindnes and repay you in the same coine, if our market did afford it, but the odds runs too much on your side, and the fertilitie of that soile seemes to flourish with a later springe of pamflets and discourses now that we are here in the dead of winter. The Erle of Essex is at Court in as good termes (they say) as ever he was, but there be no offices bestowed, nor no more shew of bestowing them then the first day the Lord Treasurer died. All men give him theire voices to be Master of the Wardes, and it is thought that, *serius ocius*, it will light upon him. Here hath ben much speach of new Counsaillors, and some have ben very neere it, and appointed to be sworne; but the contrarietie of opinions, the number that stand for it, and the difficultie, or rather impossibilitie, to please both sides, kepes all backe; yet it is certainly thought that Sir John Stanhope shalbe shortly Vice-Chamberlain. Sir Francis Vere, *per tot discrimina*, and with much brave and shove, hath got the government of the Brill. One Stanley,[a] that came in sixteen dayes over land with letters out of Spaine, is lately committed to the Towre. He was very ernest to have privat conference with her Majestie, pretending matter of great importance, which he wold by no meanes utter to anybody els. He affirmes that the King of Spaine was not dead at his comming away, but that he had retired himself, and was drawing on. There hath ben some small bickering of late in Ireland, wherin there were sevenscore rebels slaine (but not of the maine troupes of Tiron), yet the newes is very welcome, and we are glad to make much of a litle. The Erle of Cumberland is come, and some of his shipping; the rest are saide (or rather thought) to be upon the coast, for according to our custome they came scattering, and every man made shift for himself, as though they had plaide at formost take up hindmost. They had goode hap to misse the Spaniards that lay for them with 30 men of warre at the Terceras, and removed from the Iland of Flores but the day before the Erle came thether. The great expectation of this viage is come to this, that they tooke the towne and castell of Porto Ricco, where they found no great riches, for, having intelligence of theire comming, the Spaniards had conveyed away theire chiefe wealth. My lord himself saith that he hath made a saving jorny, but they that understand it better say that all he hath brought (whereof the greatest part is sugar and ginger), will not amount to above fifteen or sixteen thowsand pound, which is not halfe the charge of the setting out, besides the adventure and waste of the shipping and the losse of 600 men, what by sword and sicknes. Some finde great fault, and say his owne wilfullnes and want of

---

[a] John Stanley alleged, October 18, that he had been employed by the King of Spain to kill the Queen of England and fire the Tower. [Domestic Correspondence, State Paper Office.]

direction overthrew the viage, and that if he wold have ben advised he might have don them all goode, but he neglected present profit in hope of greater matters, and so forsooke the substance for the shadow. I thincke the heat of our sea-viages is well alayed by this and the rest, which, being no better conducted, serve rather to fortifie and confirme then hinder the ennemie. I can send you nothing of your privat frends, for I have neither seen nor heard of any of them. I am here all alone till the terme come that we may be *plena curia*. The Court is at Nonsuch, and shold come to Richmond on Tewsday next; if it bringe any thing with it worth the writing I will not faile you—and so God keepe you. London, this third of October, 1598.

Yours most assuredly,

JOHN CHAMBERLAIN.

[*Addressed as before.*]

## LETTER IX.

[Domestic Correspondence, State Paper Office, October 20, 1598.]

M<sup>r</sup> CARLETON,

I wrote to you about the third or fourth of this present, and have now staide the longer to see if this north-easterly wind wold have brought us anything from you, or brought foorth anything at home worth the sending; but we are still at the same stay as when I wrote you last, and are fed on from Sonday to Sonday with expectation from the Court, wherewith I am so weary that I will not tarry nor trifle out the time any longer, but acquaint you with matters as they stand now, though it be certainly thought we shall have some alteration on Sonday next. The voice ran all this weeke with Sir John Fortescue * to be Lord Treasurer, but now it is come about

* Chancellor of the Exchequer.

againe to the Lord Buckhurst,[a] and so every three or foure daies it is tossed from the one side of the Court to the other. The next new Counsaillors are thought shall be the Lord Mountjoy and the Lord Chiefe Justice,[b] who hath plaide rex of late among whoores and bawdes, and persecutes poore pretty wenches out of all pittie and mercy. The Court of Wardes sitts not, for want of a master; and, though the Erle of Essex be alone in election, yet there is still some rub in his way that he comes not on. Some day the Quene meanes to dissolve that Court, and, instead therof, to raise a yearly contribution out of all landes *in capite* or knight service, which wold be more for her profit and lesse grevance to the subject, but this is too goode to be true. Others say he may have it if he will, but because there is a course spoken off to geld and curtail it, he refuseth to accept it unles he may have it whole and unmaimed; and others say he findes some scruple in the strictnes of the othe, and wonders how the late Lord Treasurer could dispense so easilie and so largely with it and his conscience. But this were somewhat too pure and maidenlike, or rather *inutilis verecundia*. The state of Ireland growes dayly *di mal in peggio*, for they begin now to stirre in the province of Munster, where the White Knight,[c] Sir James of Desmond,[d] and one Patricke Condon, a shrewd fellow, are out. Sir Samuel Bagnol is lately slaine there,[e] beinge stabd by St. Lawrence (sonne and heire to the Lord of Nooth), about the lie, or such like brabble. Some thincke the Lord Mountjoy shalbe sent thether deputie; others say the Erle of Essex meanes to take it upon him, and hopes by his countenance to quiet that countrie. Marry, he wold have it under the brode seale of England, that after a yeare he might return when he will. Here is a French Ambassador [f] (a Civilian) come to be Lieger: some thincke he is rather sent at the earnest request of the Spaniard to further a peace then for any great love or busines of theire owne; others say his cheife errand

[a] Thomas Sackville.  [b] Sir John Popham.
[c] Edmund Fitz-Gibbon.  [d] James Fitz-Thomas Fitz-Gerald of Desmond.
[e] Contradicted in Letter X.
[f] M. de la Boysier, arrived at Dover October 14. [Domestic Correspondence, State Paper Office.]

is about matters of piracie, whereof the Frenchmen complaine excedingly. Here is some speach of sending one thether if they could resolve whom. Dr. Harbert, Sir Thomas Parry,[a] Mr. Bodley, and Mr. Nevill [b] of Berkshire are in question. Besides that, somebody must be sent extraordinary to the marriage of Madame the king's sister, wherto Sir Robert Sidney is most named. John Wroth is making redy to go ambassador into Turkie. Sir Francis Vere is comming to the Brill, out of which intertainment he payes yearly 400l. to the Lady Burroughs.[c] There was some snapping of late twixt him and the young Lord Gray, who went about to have a regiment, and to be cheife commander over the English in the Lowe Countries. Sir John Gilbert,[d] with six or seven saile, one and other, is going for Guiana, and I heare that Sir Walter Raleigh shold be so deeply discontented because he thrives no better, that he is not far off from making that way himself. Foure or five more of Stanley's consorts are lately apprehended and sent to the Towre, among whom are, one Rolles, Pates, and Dr. Bagshaw.[e] The King of Poland [f] is saide to be in hard termes, and almost taken in Sweden by his uncle the Duke Charles. There is one at Venice gives himself out to be Sebastian late King of Portingale, and sayes he was not slaine at the battell in Barbarie (as was thought), but taken prisoner, and concealed himself till he might conveniently get away. They make him aunswer that if he be the man, he shall not want maintenaunce, nor theire mediation, but if he be not he must look for what he deserves. We say the younge King of Spain [g] hath altered or augmented his counsaile by taking in eight of the nobilitie, and that the Infanta,[h] either of her owne

[a] Resident ambassador in France August 1602; recalled November 1605; died Chancellor of the Duchy of Lancaster, May 1616. [Dom. Corr. S. P. O.]
[b] Sir Henry Neville, ambassador to France April 1599; died July 10, 1615. [Lodge's Illustrations, iii. 123; Lord Braybrooke's Audley End, p. 103.]
[c] Widow of Thomas Lord Burrough, who had been Governor of the Brill.
[d] Son of Otho Gilbert, esq. and half-brother of Raleigh.
[e] Christopher Bagshaw of Derbyshire, a zealous Roman Catholic, and Doctor of the Sorbonne. [Note to Birch MS. No. 4,173.]
[f] Sigismund III.   [g] Philip III.   [h] Isabella Clara Eugenia.

motion, or by his order keepes in a monasterie of nunnes till the
Archduke\* come to fetch her. I can bethincke me of nothing ells,
unles I shold tell you of certain mad knaves that tooke tabacco all
the way to Tibern as they went to hanging. I have here sent you
some verses that go under the name of the Lord of Essex when he
was in disgrace, but I cannot warrant them to be his, nor made at
that time. Your cousen Lytton was here two dayes at the beginning of the weeke, but is gon downe to the buriall of Sir John
Brocket. I have not heard lately of your brother, nor of any other
of your frends. So that, with a short *bezo las manos*, I bid you
farewell for this time.

From London, this 20th of October, 1598.

Yours most assuredly,<br>JOHN CHAMBERLAIN.

[*Addressed as before.*]

## LETTER X.

[Domestic Correspondence, State Paper Office, Nov. 8, 1598.]

MR. CARLETON,

Your letters of the 23rd of the last came sixe or eight dayes since,
and I have staide the longer to aunswer them in hope somwhat
wold fall out worth the writing, and withall I had another lay on
my hands for want of cariage, for, though with much search I
found out where the post of Sandwich lay, yet not having any body
there to direct it unto, or that wold take care to send it over, I wold
not commit it altogether to hap hasard, and put it out so carelesly
to seeke his fortune. Upon inquiry, I learne there is one Mr. Robinson might do it very conveniently if either of us had any acquaintaunce with him. Our court causes are still *in statu quo prius*, and
no more certainty what will become of any of those places then

---

\* Albert of Austria.

when I wrote you last; only they have resolved upon Mr. Nevill [a] for
Fraunce; and, for all his earnest sute to the contrary, he hath
warning to make himself redy twixt this and Christmas. The
Frenchman [b] that is come is *de robbe longue*, brother-in-law to him
that was here this time twelvemoneth, having maried two sisters,
daughters to the president Harlé. We heare the French king [c] is
sicke of a carbuncle or carnosite in his yard, which is thought wilbe
a very difficult cure. When I wrote you last we did but suspect
the kindling of a fire in Ireland, which is since broken out into an
open flame, so far foorth that, unless there be present help, it is
feared all wilbe gon, for we heare of new conspiracies every day,
and there was a plot laide to betray Dublin; and, besides that the
people are generally (as well in respect of religion as for other alli-
ances) inclined to the rebells, the townes begin to stagger, and
refuse to receve garrison. Those of Mounster have set up a new
Desmond (by the Pope's meanes, as is saide,) and persecute our
English undertakers that were planted in those partes with all
manner of villanie and barbarous cruelty. The Erle of Ormond [d]
hath sent over in post for 2,000 men, which are making redy with
all possible haste, and it is looked he shold do other manner of service then he hath don hitherto, now that it toucheth his freehold,
and that the fire is come so neere him that it hath almost consumed
his countie of Tipperare. It is generally held that the Erle of Essex
shall go thether towards the spring as Lieutenant-generall, and the
Lord Mountjoy as his Lord Deputy, with divers other younge
lordes and noblemen, and that he shalbe açcompanied with the
most part of those knights that be his creatures, for it is thought fit
they shold not come too easilie by theire honor, but that, in this
case, as well as in many others, it should be graunted for service
don and to be don. We looke tomorrow for the arraignment of
Stanley, Rolles, Squire, and the rest of that crue. The report goes

[a] Sir Henry Nevillo; see before in p. 24. He was knighted in 1599. [Morgan's Sphere of Gentry.]
[b] M. de le Boysiez.
[c] Henry IV.
[d] Lord Justice of Ireland.

of very fowle matters discovered, and some part attempted by them; as
theire trialls fall out you shall heare more by my next. The Imperiall
Count Arundell is committed to the keping of Dr. Harbert [a] about
some conferences had with Stanley at his first arrivall. The new
Countesse of Southampton [b] is brought a bed of a daughter; and,
to mend her portion, the Erle, her father, hath lately lost 1,800
crownes at tennis in Paris. Sir Robert Southwell [c] is dead, and hath
left his lady [d] a rich widow. The Quene hath geven the Countesse
of Kildare 700l. a-yeare out of the Exchequer, in recompence of
her jointure lost and spoiled in Ireland. The Warden [e] of Marton
Colledge hath got a great victorie of his fellowes, and raunsommed
and punished divers of them, and, amongst the rest, expelled Mr.
Colmer, who, of greife or curst hart, died within five dayes after.
Dr. Raynolds [f] is head of Corpus Christi Colledge, having exchaunged
his deanery of Lincoln with Dr. Cole.[g] The Kinge of Spaine [h] is
saide to have staide all the Hollanders, and all Irish ships that have
not the Erle of Tirones passe. I had almost forgot to recall the
killing of Sir Samuell Bagnoll, for it falls out to be nothing so, and
yet was it current both in court and countrie above ten dayes
together. Ortelius his Thesaurus Geographicus is too bigg to be
sent by an ordinarie messenger, and therefore it must stay till your
boat come or that you send other order; your cousen Lytton will
needs bestow it on you, wherin I made no longe strife. I
sent your letter to the Lady Northes because she lies far of, and
the wether hath ben so exceding fowle that I stir litle abrode,
neither am I over hastie to come there, they be so apt to take toyes,
and become so humerous, that they send backe your letters when I

[a] John Herbert, Master of Requests.
[b] Elizabeth daughter of Sir John Vernon : see p. 18.
[c] Of Woodrising, Norfolk. With Essex at the taking of Cadiz.
[d] Elizabeth daughter of Charles Howard, Earl of Nottingham. [Dugdale, ii. 279.]
[e] Henry Savile, knighted Sept. 21, 1604 ; Provost of Eton College ; died 1622. [Note to Birch MS. No. 4,173, Nov. 8, 1598.]
[f] John Reynolds, D.D. ; Dean of Lincoln 1598 ; died 1607.
[g] William Cole, D.D., Dean of Lincoln 1599 ; died 1600. [h] Philip III.

desire they wolde convey them, or geve me any direction how I might send my self; but I will find a time to visit them, both because you wish it, and for the auncient goodwill and kindly affection hath past betwene us, in which respect I will alwayes be redy to do them the best service I can. And so, wishing you all health and welfare, I commit you to God.

From London, this 8th of November, 1598.

Yours most assuredly,    JOHN CHAMBERLAIN.
[*Addressed as before.*]

## LETTER XI.

[Domestic Correspondence, State Paper Office, November 22, 1598.]

MR. CARLETON,

This longe and permanent abode of westerly windes bringes us no newes but such as we least desire to heare of. I meane out of Ireland, whence messengers come daily (like Jobs servants) loaden with ill tidings of new troubles and revoltes. The English of Mounster are much blamed for making no better proofe of themselves and geving so easie way to the rebells, and (as goode I tell it you as another,) Sir Thomas Norris hath his part with the rest, and is thought to have taken the alarme too soone, and left his station before there was neede, wherby the ennemie was too much incouraged, and those that were well affected or stoode indifferent forced to follow the tide. The remedies of these mischiefes go as slowly forward as other matters; only it is said the Erle of Essex shall go thether about February or March with as ample commission as ever any had, the conditions wherof were lost labour to set downe, because they varie and alter every weeke; and withall his going is not resolved so fully but that once in ten dayes it is in question. The day that we looked for Stanleys arraignment he came not himself, but sent his forerunner, one Squire, that had ben an under purvayer of the stable, who, being in Spaine, was delt withall by one Walpoole, a Jesuite, to poison the Quene and the Erle of Essex, and

REIGN OF QUEEN ELIZABETH. 29

accordingly came prepared into England, and went with the Erle in his owne ship the last jorny, and poisoned the armes or handles of the chaire he used to sit in, with a confection he had receved of the Jesuite, as likewise he had don the pommell of the Quenes saddle, not past five dayes before his going to sea; but because nothing succeded of it, the priest thincking he had either chaunged his purpose or bewraied it, gave Stanley instructions to accuse him, therby to get him more credit and to be revenged of Squire for breaking promise. The fellow confest the whole practise, and, as it seemed, died very penitent. The seventh of this moneth the Quenes Atturney[a] married the Lady Hatton,[b] to the great admiration of all men, that after so many large and likely offers she shold decline to a man of his qualitie, and the world will not beleve that it was without a misterie. The day before Sir John Packington[c] maried Mrs. Barnham,[d] one of our London widowes. The Erle of Southampton is come home, and for his welcome committed to the Fleet, but I heare he is alredy upon his delivery. The Quene came to Whitehall the last weeke, being receved a mile out of towne by the Lord Mayor[e] and his bretheren, accompanied with 400 velvet cotes and chaines of gold; her day[f] passed without any extraordinarie matter more then running[g] and ringing. Your brother Carleton hath ben in towne most part of this terme, but is now gon. Other newes we have none, so that, with my best wishes, I bid you farewell. London, this 22th of November, 1598.

Yours most assuredly,

[*Addressed as before.*]      JOHN CHAMBERLAIN.

[a] Edward Coke, born Feb. 1, 1552; appointed Attorney-general March 24, 1594; knighted May 22, 1603; died September 3, 1634.

[b] Elizabeth, daughter of Thomas Cecill, Earl of Exeter, and widow of Sir William Hatton. [Dugdale, ii. 407.]

[c] K.B. See Nichols's Progresses James I. i. 192, and the valuable new particulars respecting Sir John Pakington and his connection with Bacon, in Dixon's Personal History of Lord Bacon, p. 135.

[d] Widow of Benedict Barnham, Alderman of London.   [e] Sir Nicholas Mosley.

[f] 17th November; the day of her accession.   [g] Running at the ring.

## LETTER XII.

[Domestic Correspondence, State Paper Office, December 8, 1598.]

GOODE MR. CARLETON,

I wrote last by the post of Sandwich, but what meanes it made to get over I know not. Your skipper brought me yours of the 25th of the last, for the which I thank you, but specially for the translated letter, so full of perticulers which are *mon gibier*. This winter weather affoordes no great novelties; only we talke of provisions for Ireland, but the whole plot is so uncertain and unsetled that I feare we shall only talke it out. The rebells grow daily both in hart and strength, and (which is worst) the great ones of that countrie, and those that have ben alwayes thought soundest, use the matter so that they be not out of suspicion; for neither do they any service themselves, nor assist those that wold do it, as in a case of apparent advantage it happened to Sir Thomas Norris to be hindered by those that are put most in trust. The Erle of Essex jorny thether is neither fast nor loose, but holdes still in suspence, by reason the proportions thought fit for such an enterprise are daily clipt and deminished, for it was first set downe that his number (with those that be there alredy) shold be 14,000, and so to be continued from time to time, with full allowaunce of vitaile, mony, and other things aunswerable; but, whether they thincke the matter may be compassed with lesse charge, or that we be not able to beare such a burthen, these rates are brought lower, wherewith he is nothing pleased; and on these termes it standes. For eight or ten dayes the souldiers flockt about him, and every man hoped to be a colonell at least; and, to content theire humors somwhat, it was said there shold be petty regiments raised of 500 and 300 men. The Erle of Southampton was named to be Generall of the Horse, Sir Robert Sidney to be Lord Marshall, and I know not how many more to other places. But now all is husht again, and only Sir

Arthur Savage is going thether with a thowsand men, and the Erle of Tomond, with some other small forces, to be Governor of Limricke. Here is order geven for 2,000 men to be sent out of Kent, Surrey, and Sussex into the Lowe Countries, and so many to be drawne from thence out of the garrison for Ireland. And for horsemen to that service, the justices of peace thoroughout England must be intreated to furnish them; but the greatest difficultie is mony, which goes so lowe that for all the subsidies comming on, the privy seales that are past, and the loane of 20,000*l.* the other day, the Quene is now in hand to borrow of the Citie 150,000*l.* more, offering to lay 500*l.* of her land in morgage and the Customes of the citie of London for the repayment of it; and the marchaunts and aldermen of London are sent for and dealt with all severally, and urged to lend some 3,000*l.*, some 2,000*l.*, some more, some lesse; but howsoever it fall out, yea, though they were willing, I hardly think it is to be had, for the citie is much decayed by reason theire trafike is greatly impaired, and the marchant adventurers were almost upon dissolving, being hindered in theire trade by certain enterlopers (as they call them), against whom they could have no remedy. Many men muse how the Quene, being discharged of the burthen of the Lowe Countries, and having no other charge but Ireland, shold be driven to these straights, and unles there shold be exceding urgent need indeed, it is thought a straunge pollicie to discover our want so far to the world, whereat our ennemies abrode will take no small hartening. The Lord Buckhurst is now in full cry to be Lord Treasurer, and it is thought the Wardes in the end will fall to Mr. Secretary[a]; yet some say the Quene will bestow it upon some meane man, who for a pension shall execute the place to her best advantage. It was said awhile that the Erle of Essex shold have 6.000*l.* yeerely out of it, otherwhile that he shold have 20,000*l.* toward the payment of his debts, and so to leave his hold; but we see neither come on very fast. He kept a

[a] Sir Robert Cecill.

kinde of Marshalls Court of late, where the title of Nevill,[a] that
claimes to be Lord of Abergeny, and the title of Sir Henry Leonard [b]
that wold be Lord Dacres of the South, was argued, but after divers
hearings he left the matter as he found it, and so it is referred to the
Quene. We heare that Sir Anthony Shirley [c] hath ben at Constantinople, and there wrounge out of our marchants 400*l*., and from
thence he went to Aleppo, and there scraped together 500*l*. more,
wherewith he hath charged the Lord of Essex by his billes, and so is
gon on God knowes whether to seeke his fortune. Sir Richard
Lewsen hath lately staide 17 saile of Easterlings and Hollanders in
the narrow seas that were going for Spaine; in the mean time his
father, Sir Walter,[d] is staide in the Fleet, being faln into hucksters
handes (I meane his old creditors), who laide a traine for him and
caught him at Lambeth. The Lord Marquis [e] is lately dead, having
left his sonne [f] to succeed him, who is like to prove as sufficient a
nobleman as none of them all. Mr. Parker, brother to the Lord
Morley, was slaine the last weeke by a man of Sir Thomas Gerrards,
about a brabble for the way, wherof the fellow is acquitted, being
found he did it in his owne defence. The French Inventairie [g] is not
come foorth, the author [h] being saide to be dead, but there is hope
it wilbe found among his papers. Here is nothing come out this
last mart worth the looking after; I do not thincke but you may
fit your self better at Middleburg, for that many times thinges are
current there that be here forbidden. You shall receve by this

[a] Edward Neville had the title of Baron of Abergavenny confirmed to him May 25, 1604; died 1622. [Courthope's Nicolas, 17.]
[b] Became Lord Dacre on the death of his mother, Lady Dacre, in 1611; died 1616. [Courthope's Nicolas, 138.]
[c] Son of Sir Thomas Shirley of Wiston, Sussex; born 1565. [Shirley's Memoir of the Shirley Brothers, p. 2.]
[d] Died in the Fleet, 1602.
[e] William Marquis of Winchester; died November 24, 1598. [Dugdale, ii. 377.]
[f] William, died February 4, 1628. [*Ibid.*]
[g] Inventaire générale de l'Histoire de Fance, illustré par la Conférance de l'Eglise et de l'Empire. Paris, 1597. [Biographie Universelle, xlii. 101.]
[h] Jean de Serres; died at the end of the year.

bearer your Thesaurus Geographicus, which may well serve your turn for old authors, but for the late writers and discoveries I thincke it will stand you in litle stead. I send you likewise such pedlarie pamflets and three-halfpeny ware as we are served with; make the best use you can of them, and use your owne censure, but if I be not deceved some of the satires are passable. Our Mrs. Anne [a] is become a widow before she was wife, an old Doctor of Law, that hath held her long in hand to marry her, being dead yesterday, wherupon she hath taken her chamber and mournes out of measure. I doubt not but you have heard that Mr. Sherley [b] hath at last married the Lady Umpton, and made her his deere wife: for mine owne part, as poore a man as I am, I wold not buy such another of the price. Doctor Parkins is come out of Denmarke, and says he hath brought a goode aunswer. And thus wishing you all health and welfare, I end for this time.

From London, this 8th of December, 1598.

Yours most assuredly,
JOHN CHAMBERLAIN.

[*Addressed as before.*]

LETTER XIII.

[Domestic Correspondence, State Paper Office, December 20, 1598.]

MR. CARLETON,

The world is litle or nothing chaunged here since I wrote last; only the Quene is resolved to kepe Christmas at Whitehall; and the matters of Ireland stand at a stay, or rather go backward, for the Erle of Essex jorny thether that was in suspence is now, they say, quite dasht; not that there is any other order taken, but only that

[a] Daughter of Rowland Lytton, esq. [Birch MS. No. 4173.]

[b] George Shirley, esq. created a Baronet in 1611, and ancestor of the Earls Ferrers. His second wife was Dorothy, eldest daughter of Sir Thomas Wroughton, and widow of Sir Henry Unton, who died ambassador in France. See The Unton Inventories, 1841, 4to.

things shall still drive on there as they may, and perhaps they hope *cunctando restituere rem;* which all men take to be a wronge course in *deplorata valetudine,* and so desperate a disease. From Tewsday last till Sonday it held fast and firm that the Erle of Essex was to go, and all things were accordingly setled and set downe, but a sodain alteration came on Sonday night, the reason wherof is yet kept secret: some say the Quene had promised to forgeve him twelve thowsand pound debt due by his father, and 20,000*l.* he ought her himself for cochenilla since his last jorny, which belike was mistaken, for the Quene sayes she meant but the forbearance of it, and that it shold not be called upon in his absence; but whether it were that or some other matter, all is turnd upside downe, and he and Mr. Secretarie [a] have so good leisure that they plie the tables hard in the presence chamber, and play so round game as if Ireland were to be recovered at Irish.[b] The rebells in the meantime have don many outrages, and slaine lately Sir Thomas Moore (surnamed the lying Knight) and his Lady, and one Capt. Gifford, and hurt his wife, that was Sir Henry Dukes daughter, and the properest gentlewoman of Ireland that I saw. They have likewise overthrowne or defaced fowre or five and twenty strong places, or castles, as they call them. Sir Richard Bingham with 800 men went to scowre the country about Dublin, but before he came to the Nasse, which is not past ten or twelve miles, he was so incountred and beset that he was fain to retire without attempting further, and fell sicke at Dublin, where some say he is dead. Dr. Parkins,[c] at his first comming out of Denmarke, made his bragges that he had brought matters there to a goode passe, but all he hath don is only a promise of 40,000 dollers to be restored on condition his subjects may be satisfied for such injuries as they have receved; and to that purpose he sent an ambassador [d] along with him, who had audience on Sonday last; but

---

[a] Sir Robert Cecill.
[b] "A game differing very slightly from backgammon."—Nares's Glossary.
[c] Doctor Parkins arrived in England Dec. 6, 1598. [Danish Corresp. S. P. O.]
[d] Nicholaus Cragius, Legate of Christian IV. [Ibid.]

his message was nothing pleasing. as being for the most part a complaint of our piracies. And, as Dr. Parkins returned with half an aunswer, so they say Mr. Cary[a] is come out of Poland with none at all, nor could get no audience. The ships that were staide by Sir Richard Lewson stole away most of them the night following, and I left him *con tanto di naso*, as the Italian saith, so sutable is the managing of our affaires both at home and abrode. Fowre or five shippes of your Dunkerke neighbours gave a great alarme lately to Yorkshire, and made them fire theire beacons; but that was all the harme they did them. It is thought they meant to have landed and taken some prisoners to help to redeem theire governor. We heare the States make huge levies of mony, and meane to be masters of the feild the next sommer whatsoever it cost them. The French king is sending to the Pope to determine the controversie of the Marquisat of Saluces, for in the treaty of peace that was referred to his arbitrement. The loan of 150,000l. makes many of our citizens shrincke and pull in theire hornes, but yet it goes forward, and they must furnish it; and some whispering there is that when that is don we shall heare of a benevolence. If we be driven to these shifts alredy, God knowes how we shall hold hereafter; and I marvaile that they which knew these wants did hearken no more after the peace when they might have had it with goode conditions. You see how confidently I write to you of all things, but I hope you kepe it to yourself, and then there is no daunger, and I am so used to a libertie and fredome of speach when I converse or write to my frends that I cannot easilie leave it. Your brother and sister Williams marvaile they heare not from you. I have had much ado to excuse myself this Christmas from Knebworth and Askot, but specially from Knebworth, the rather because Wat Cope[b] and his wife, Hugh Beeston, and Mr. Evers, go thether; but upon some

[a] Mr. George Carew.
[b] Walter Cope of Oxfordshire; knighted April 20th, 1603; died Master of the Wards July 31st, 1614. [Chamberlain, Domestic Corresp. State Paper Office, Aug. 4th, 1614.]

occasions I am growne so privat that I stirre not abrode, nor mean to do, but to live at home like a snaile in the shell. And so, wishing you a goode new yeare and many, I end.

From London, this 20th of December, 1598.

Yours most assuredly,
JOHN CHAMBERLAIN.

[*Addressed as before.*]

LETTER XIV.

[Domestic Correspondence, State Paper Office, Jan. 3, 1598-9.]

GOODE Mr CARLETON,

I receved your letter of the 18th of the last on Christmas day, and had aunswered it sooner if these holy dayes had affoorded any matter to worke on. Only the wind is come about again for Ireland, and the *disgusto* that made stay of the Erles going for awhile is sweetned and removed, so that now he prepares with all diligence, and hath 12,000*l.* delivered him to raise five or sixe hundred horse. I cannot come by his particular proportions, but, as far as I can learne, he is not to have hence above 2,000 besides the 2,000 that are to come out of the Lowe Countries, which together with 10,000 (in name) that are saide to be there alredy, must make up his nomber. He is so ill satisfied of some that have government there alredy, as namely of Sir Thomas Maria Wingfield and others, that it is thought he will make a cleane riddaunce, and displace most of them. Sir Thomas Norris hath lately relieved Kilmallocke, a towne in Mounster, that was beset and distressed by the ennemie, and Sir Samuel Bagnoll hath don some small peece of service upon Tiron, and brought away three or fowre score cowes. But the rebells are growne so bold that not long since they fetcht away the Lord Chauncellors [a] cattell out of his yarde close by St. Patricks

---

[a] Dr. Adam Loftus, Archbishop of Dublin.

church in the suburbs of Dublin, so that it were more then time the Erle were there, and yet some doubt he shall hardly get hence before St. Georges day. Sir Robert Mansfeld goes shortly with three shippes to lie upon that coast. The citie went on reasonable roundly with theire taske, and paid in 50,000*l.* the last weeke; the rest is comming after, and it is thought they shalbe excused with as much more, or litle over. Now they are to furnish out 600 men for the Lowe Countries within these five or sixe dayes, but that seemes but a flea biting after the great blowe. The 21st of the last the Quene signed the patents of Fulke Grivell, Sir Henry Palmer, and Mr. Trevor (the Lord Admirall's secretarie), for the office of Treasurer, Controller, and Surveyor of her Navie, and the same time it is said she cancelled a bonde of 21,000*l.* of the Erle of Essex, wherin he and a dousen marchants were bound for cochinille. One Peter Browne, a French post, is clapt up in the Gatehouse for jugling with the French Ambassadors[a] letters, who complaines that his masters letters and his are usually opened before they come at them. It was expected that the Treasurership shold have ben bestowed on the Lord Buckhurst for a new yeares gift, but it succeeded not, so that he must tarry the time, and it may chaunce light on him on the sodain when he doth least look for it, according to the custome of the court, that commonly knowes not over night what shalbe don in the morning. I can bethincke me of nothing els uules it be the death of Judge Owen,[b] who was in some speech to be Master of the Wardes. And so I commit you to God.

From London, the 3ᵈ of January, 1598.

Yours most assuredly,
JOHN CHAMBERLAIN.

[*Addressed as before.*]

---

[a] M. De le Boysiez. Edmondes, in writing to Cecill Jan. 26, 1598-9, mentions a conversation he had with M. de Villeroy on the subject. [French Correspondence, State Paper Office.]

[b] Thomas Owen, made a Judge of the Common Pleas 1593; died 1598.

## LETTER XV.

[Domestic Correspondence, State Paper Office, January 17, 1598-9.]

M<sup>r</sup> CARLETON,

Though I look in a manner daily for your comming over, yet, because many accidents may chaunge your course, or defer your passage for a time, I will not omit this present occasion to salute you after my accustomed manner, the rather because I have neither heard of you nor written since the end of Christmas; and, to begin with the best first—the Quene, on Twelvth day, to close up the holy dayes, and, do the Danish Ambassador[a] honor, daunct with the Erle of Essex very richly and freshly attired. Since, there fell out a great unkindnes twixt the Erle and the Lord Admirall,[b] and some high wordes passed. The matter was about Sir William Woodhouse,[c] that was to have a companie in the Lowe Countries, in Sir Thomas Knolles[d] regiment. I do not heare the matter is yet taken up, but that they continue to speake hardly one of another. The Erles jorny for Ireland is somwhat prolonged; for his vitailers, that had order to make theire provisions for February, are now put over till March. He shall cary a great troupe of gallants with him if all go that are spoken of, as the Erles of Darbie,[e] Rutland,[f] and Southampton; the Lords Windsore, Gray, Audeley,[g] and Cromwell,[h] who standes to be Lord Marshall of the army, besides knights sans nomber, wherof Sir Ferdinando Gorge is named to be Sergeant

---

[a] Nicholaus Cragius.      [b] Charles Howard, Earl of Nottingham.
[c] Knighted 1591. [Nichols's Progresses of James I. ii. 25.]
[d] Son of Sir Francis Knolles. [Dugdale, ii. 413.]
[e] William Stanley, K.G.; died 1642. [Courthope's Nicolas, 154.]
[f] Roger Manners; died 1612. [Ibid. 409.]
[g] George Tuchet, Lord Audley; created Earl of Castlehaven Sept. 6th, 1617; died 1617. [Ibid. 35.]
[h] Edward Cromwell; died 1607. [Ibid. 131.]

Major, Sir Henry Davers to have the leading of 300 horse, Sir Charles Davers, Sir Charles Percy, Sir Charles Blunt, Sir Thomas Egerton, Sir Thomas Germin, Sir Alexander Ratcliffe, and I know not how many more to be Colonells; and yet Sir Christofer Blount, Sir Edward Wingfield, and ten or twelve others of that standing, looke to be served too. But it is said the Erle geves few places nor bestowes offices to any as yet, because he will hold his followers in hart till he have them there. Many that wish well to the jorny have no great conceit of it, seing so many raw youthes prease for the greatest charges. Here was speach that the Erle of Kildare and the Lord of Delvin began to stand upon termes, and to geve doubtfull annswers, and that the cheife rebells in Munster began to put water in theire wine, and to proceed with more temper. Those shippes that stole away from Sir Richard Lewson at their comming on the coast of Portingale understoode of the embargo and arrest of theire fellowes, the Hollanders, and other Lowe Countrie men, wherupon they came backe, and were by weather put into Plimmouth, which comes well to passe for the vitailing of Ireland. The Duke of Florence hath barred our nation from traffícke in his territories, and it is feared the Venetians and the French king will serve us in the same sort. The Queue is very angry with Sir Thomas Gerrard for the escape of one Blackwell, an arch-priest, out of the Marshalsea. There was a plot laide by certain Jesuites and preistes to murther or poison the Scottish kinge, as it is confessed by some that are taken. Here be many Englishmen come out of Spaine that were delivered at the younge kinges [a] comming to the crowne. They say that the king had a sore bruise with the fall of an horse in running at the ring, for the which he was let bloude fower times. It is said likewise (how truly I know not) that the very same day his Quene was so skarred with a fire that tooke place in the house where she lay in Milan that she was driven to run into the street in her petticote. The newes comes now very

[a] Philip III.

hot that Sebastian the king of Portingale, that was said to be slaine in the battell in Barbarie, is at Venice, and hath made so goode triall of himself that the Venetians allowe him, and maintaine almost fowrescore persons about him at theire charge. They say he tells very straunge stories, how he with fowreteene more escaped from the battaile, and got up into the mountaines, and so, by many adventures, he went and he went till he came into Ethiopia, or Prester Johns lande, meaning from thence to have gon into the East Indies, but, understanding that they were yeelded and sworne to the King of Spaine, durst not proceed, but turned backe again, and *per tot discrimina* in this longe pilgrimage (wherin he hath ben taken, bought, and sold twelve or thirtene times), got at last to Venice, where he tells them all that was negotiated twixt him and them either by Letters or Ambassadors since he was of any goode remembraunce, and that with so many particulers as are thought infallible testimonies. Besides it is saide that his confessor is come out of Portingale, and, upon conference with him, avoucheth all to be true that he saith, touching what passed betwene them in confession, both at other times, and specially the day before the battell. We run away with all, as though all were our owne, and are easilie persuaded to believe that we wold have. What will come of it God knowes, but it were a happy turne for Christendome if it were true, and so beloved; but it will by no meanes sincke down with me, but that still I feare he wilbe cousened and trussed up in the end. The King of Spaine is said to be going into Portingale with a 1,000 horse and 3,000 foote upon this rumour; but I rather thincke it is to be receved there and crowned. Sir Dru Drury [a] is in his old remitter, and commaunded to wait in his place of Gentleman Usher of the Privie Chamber. There is a marriage spoken of twixt the Lord Cobham and the Countesse of Kildare, and betwene his lame

---

[a] Sir Drue Drury, in conjunction with Sir Amyas Paulet, had the custody of the Queen of Scots from 1584 till her death; sworn Lieutenant of the Tower 1595. [Birch, Mem. i. 342.] Died 1617. [Chamberlain, Dom. Corr. S. P. O. May 10, 1617.]

brother, Mr. George Brooke, and the Lord Borroughs eldest daughter. It is saide likewise that Sir William Woodhouse hath married ⁿ the Lady Southwell,[b] and the Lord Marquis[c] woman or concubine (before he is buried) hath married a youth not full eightene yeares old, younger sonne to Mr. Fleetwoode, Recever of the Court of Wardes. Sir Mathew Arundell died these holy daies, and hath left much to goode uses, as 2,000*l.* to the making of a cawsey about Sherborne, and 2,000*l.* to the poore, and many other legacies of like nature. The Lady Cope,[d] your cousen, and mine old mistris, left the world (as I heare) on twelvth even; and Spencer,[e] our principall poet, comming lately out of Ireland, died at Westminster on Satterday last. Mr. Nevill goes within these eight or ten dayes into Fraunce, and hath won Mr. Winwode,[f] at my Lord of Essex commaud, to beare him companie, and be about him. If I had more, you see I am no niggard, and therefore without further ceremonies I bid you farewell.

From London, this 17th of January, 1598.

Yours assuredly,

[*Addressed as before.*]   JOHN CHAMBERLAIN.

## LETTER XVI.

[Domestic Correspondence, State Paper Office, Jan. 31, 1598-9.]

MR. CARLETON,

I receved your letters of the first and ninth of this present very lately, and marvaile you had not heard of your skipper before that

---

ⁿ Contradicted in Letter XVIII.   [b] Widow of Sir Robert Southwell.
[c] Of Winchester.
[d] Frances, daughter of Sir Robert Lytton of Knebworth, and wife of Sir Anthony Cope of Hanwell; knighted 1590; created a Baronet 1611; died 1614.
[e] Edmund Spenser; born 1553; died Jan. 16, 1598-9. [Chalmers's Biographical Dictionary, xxviii. 292.]
[f] Ralph Winwood, knighted June 28, 1607; Secretary of State 1614; died Oct. 27, 1617. [Chamberlain Letter, Domestic Correspondence, State Paper Office, Oct. 31, 1617.]

time. I pray God all be well with him, and that he have not miscaried, for you had a rich adventure in him of Thesaurus Geographicus sent by your cousen Lytton, who is now in towne, and commends him to you. Your brother Carleton is not yet come; and for your other private frends, here is no chaunge. The Erle of Essex commission for Ireland is at length, after many difficulties, agreed on, though not yet signed. He hath the name of Lieutenant, may returne at pleasure, make Barons, and dispose of such landes as shalbe won from the rebells, at his goode liking, and many other such points are spoken of, but how truly *viderit successus:* he makes great provision for horses, and many are presented him. They talke likewise of carrienge over two or three hundreth mastives to werry the Irish, or rather (as I take it) theire cattell. The preasse of his followers wilbe much abated by reason the Quene countermaunds many, as namely, and first, all her owne servants, the Erle of Rutland and the Lord Gray, Sir Nicolas Parker, Sir Ferdinando Gorge, Sir Edward Yorke, Sir John Barclay, Sir John Brooke, Sir Charles Blunt, Sir Thomas Egerton, Sir Thomas Germin, Sir Charles Davers, and divers other that come not now in my way. Some suspect it is his owne doing, because he is not able to geve them all satisfaction; but I am not of that opinion. He hath dealt well aforehand with Cap. John Davis,[a] and put him in possession of Survayor of the Ordinaunce, which is a place will sticke by him howsoever this jorny succeed. The unkindnes twixt him and others is not yet reconciled, which no doubt will much hinder this action that had need of all furtheraunce. Newes came lately thence that Sir Richard Bingham is dead, and that the Erle of Ormond hath geven the rebells a blow in relieving a fort, and slaine 3 or 400, in which incounter Sir Henry Poore receved a shot in the head, which remaines there, but it is thought without daunger. Here is a great and curious present going to the Great Turke, which no doubt wilbe

[a] Implicated in the Essex conspiracy, and tried March 5, 1601. [Camden's Annals, 199.]

much talked of, and be very scandalous among other nations, specially the Germanes. Upon the Duke of Florence embargo and complaint of our piracies, here is order taken, upon paine of death, that no prises be taken in the Levant seas. We are like enough to fall at some odds with the French king about his trafficke into Spaine, for of late (meaning to set his people on worke, and make them industrious) he hath forbidden all manner of wrought silkes to be brought into his dominions, or any worke made of wollen (which is contrary to our former contracts of entercourse), and withall doth incourage his people all he can to build and buy shippes, thereby to get the whole trade of Spaine, wherin if he be not prevented, he will sone begger both the Hollanders and us, and hereafter we shall have more ado with him and his then ever we had with the Spaniard. Here hath ben much contesting about it with his ambassador, and that hotly inough; but we have the wolfe by the eares, and know not how to hold him, nor how to let him go. The Quenes want of mony is not yet so fully supplied, but that they are faine to descend to mean men, and pick up here and there as they can get it; and you must thincke they were neere driven when they found out me as a fit man to lend mony; but I thincke I aunswered them sufficiently that, where nothing is to be had, the Quene must loose her right. There is a sale in hand of 3,000*l*. of the Quenes land, which is thought will help well to stop a gap. It is geven out that the Lord Compton shall marry our Sir John Spensers [a] daughter [b] of London, on these conditions, that he geve him 10,000*l*. redy mony with her, and redeeme his land that lieth in morgage for 18,000*l*. more. Sir William Harvies marriage with the old Countesse of Southampton, that hath lien smothering so longe, comes now to be published. I send you here certain olde epitaphes and epigrammes that go under the name of pasquills.

[a] Lord Mayor 1594; died March 30, 1610. [Nichols's Prog. of James I. i. 159.]
[b] Elizabeth. There is an amusing letter from her to Lord Compton in Goodman's Court of James I. ii. 127.

Touching Flushing, I heare of no alteration. And thus, with my harty commendations, I commit you to God.
From London, this last of January, 1599.

Yours most assuredly,
JOHN CHAMBERLAIN.

[*Addressed as before.*]

LETTER XVII.

[Domestic Correspondence, State Paper Office, February 15, 1598-9.]

GOODE MR. CARLETON,

Because it is long since I heard from you, I did verely thincke when I saw Sir Gerrat Harvy in Powles that your Lordship had ben arrived; but, understanding by him that your *congé* was not come from the Haghe at his departure, I made account we may looke after you a moneth more at the least, if not longer. I am going to Knebworth (I know not how soone) and mean to tarry there all Lent. If you come over in this interim let us intreat your companie, if it may be spared. Our provisions for Ireland go forward with leaden feet, and the Erle of Essex commission is no neerer signing (in shew) then when I wrote last. The jarres continue as they did, if not worse, by daily renewing, and our musicke runs so much upon discords that I feare what harmonie they will make of it in the end. Many thinges passe which may not be written; but, in conclusion, *Iliacos intra muros peccatur et extra*, there is fault on all sides, and, *quicquid delirant reges plectuntur Achivi*, whosoever offends the common wealth is punished. Here is a benevolence demaunded of the lawyers, not only of the Innes of Court, but of all manner officers and clarks of the Exchecquer, Chauncery, Star Chamber, Kinges Bench, Common Pleas, Court of Wardes, Duchy of Lancaster, auditors, receivers, and the rest, not forgetting the poore Doctors of the Arches. There was some curtesie made at the first, but in the end they must geve downe theire milke; and, whether from them it shall proceed over all England, it is doubtfull. Two dayes since we had a proclamation that no Englishman going to sea shold, upon paine of death, et cet. take any that were in amitie with her majestie, either Italians, French, Lowe Countrie men, Danes, or of the Haunse Townes, but only meere Spaniards, or subjects to the King of Spaine. I heare that the Erle of Essex is much offended with Sir Francis Vere for refusing the Captaines that were lately sent over into the Lowe Countries. The Quene removed to Richmont on Satterday last, and on Monday we had a great marriage in towne of younge Terringam with a daughter of Sir Thomas Gorge by the Lady Marquesse,[a] and the next weeke we shall have another of younge Duns with a daughter of Sir Henry Cromwells, and I heare the match is concluded for younge Vane [b] (that standes to be Lord of Abergevennie) with the daughter of Sir Antony Mildmay.[c] Thus, you see, for want of better marchandise, this pettie ware must serve the turne. And so I bid you farewell with my best wishes and commendations.

From London, this 15th of February, 1599.

Yours most assuredly,

JOHN CHAMBERLAIN.

[*Addressed as before.*]

[a] Of Northampton, whose second husband was Sir Thomas Gorges. [Birch MS. No. 4173. Note to Chamberlain's Letter of Feb. 15, 1599.]

[b] Francis Fane; created Earl of Westmoreland Dec. 29, 1624; succeeded to the barony of Despencer 1626; died March 23, 1628. [Courthope's Nicolas, 507.]

[c] Mary, daughter and heiress of Sir Anthony Mildmay. [Brydges's Collins, iii. 295.]

## LETTER XVIII.

[Domestic Correspondence, State Paper Office, March 1, 1598-9.]

GOODE MR. CARLETON,

I receved both your letters of the 12th and 20th of the last, full fraught both with theire owne store and much other goode matter that came in theire companie. We kepe still at a stay and do neither *movere* nor *promovere*, but drive on with the weather to see what time will bringe foorth. The Erle of Essex is erased, but whether more in body or minde is doubtfull. Thinges do not succede as he wold wish them, but new difficulties arise daily about his commission, as touching the time of his abode, touching his intertainment, and touching the disposing of places and offices, upon which points and some others he is so litle satisfied that many times he makes it a question whether he go or not. Sir George Carie[a] of Cockington (by Plymouth) is named to be Treasurer of Ireland in Sir Henry Wallops[b] place;[c] but whether he be to my lords liking or no I know not. The rebells of Mounster and Connagh are not so united but that they have many jarres among themselves, and of late a bickering, wherin Patricke Condon (a cheife ringleader) is saide to be slaine or sore hurt. Here was newes that Capt. Simmes and his companie were cut a peeces by the enuemie, but, as far as I heare since, it was but a private quarrell, in which Simmes miscaried. On Satterday last Sir William Woodhouse, accompanied with fowre hacksters, understanding that Sir Robert Drury was to come from Totnam toward London, waited for him in the way, and set upon him as he was comming out of his coach, wounding him in three or fowre places, and, thincking they had dispatcht him, left him for dead, but it falles out better with him, for he is like to recover;

---
[a] Cary.
[b] Son of Sir Oliver Wallop; died April 14, 1599. [Brydges's Collins, iv. 317.]
[c] Lord Ormond succeeded Sir Henry Wallop as Treasurer of Ireland.

marry, his man that offred himself in his masters defence was slaine outright in the place. Upon the first alarme at the Court there was commaundment from the Counsaile for a privie search all over this towne to apprehend them, but within two howres after (upon what reason I know not) it was countermaunded. Some geve out that Sir William Woodhouse shold be likewise hurt in the face and in the hande, but I thincke it is rather geven out to move pitie than otherwise, for I cannot learne he was neere daunger, and the match was very uneven, of five to two, and they taken on the sodain. The Lady Drury (Sir Roberts mother) died some ten or twelve dayes since, and hath left Sir John Scot a fresh widower. I wrote you in one of my letters that Sir William Woodhouse had maried the Lady Southwell, but the matter was mistaken, though it were generally bruited. One Doctor Ledsam, sometimes the Queues Chaplain, but allwayes a giddibraind fellow, hath lately stab'd and made away himself here in towne. The match is made up twixt younge Norris[a] and the Lady Briget, second daughter to the Erle of Oxford. We are still fed with fresh rumors of Don Sebastian, that he is *ipsissimus*, and that the Venetians have sent ambassadors to the King of Spaine to signifie so much unto him; and that there have ben some great men executed of late in Portingale about this busines, and many others trauslated into Spaine; but I will lay no wager of all this. For lacke of better matter, I send you three or foure toyes to passe away the time. The letter of Squires conspiracie is well written, but the other of Dr. Dee is a ridiculous bable of an old imposturing jugler. The Silkeworme is thought to be Dr. Muffetts,[b] and in mine opinion is no bad piece of poetrie. The treatise of Henry the Fourth[c] is reasonablie well written. The author

[a] Francis, afterwards Lord Norris of Rycot; created Baron Thame and Earl of Berkshire Jan. 28, 1620; died Jan. 30, 1622. [Dugdale, ii. 405.]

[b] Probably Dr. Moffatt, a physician, and native of London; the "Silkworm" is not included in the volume of his poems preserved in the British Museum.

[c] "The first part of the Life and Raigne of King Henrie IIII. extending to the end of the first yeare of his raigne." 4to. London, 1599. Written by John, afterwards Sir John Hayward.

is a younge man of Cambridge toward the civill lawe. Here hath ben much descanting about it, why such a storie shold come out at this time, and many exceptions taken, especially to the Epistle, which was a short thing in Latin dedicated to the Erle of Essex, and objected to him in goode earnest, wherupon there was commaundment it shold be cut out of the booke; yet I have got you a a transcript of it that you may picke out the offence if you can; for my part I can finde no such buggeswords, but that everything is as it is taken. I am going the next weeke (God willing) to Knebworth, in which consideration I am not greatly sory for your stayeng at Ostend, for I shold have injoyed but litle of your company, which perhaps will come better to passe at some other time. And so, wishing you all contentment both here and there, I commit you to God.

From London, this first of March, 1599.

Yours most assuredly,
JOHN CHAMBERLAIN.

[*Addressed as before.*]

LETTER XIX.

[Domestic Correspondence, State Paper Office, March 15, 1598-9.]

GOODE MR. CARLETON,

I have tarried longer in towne (upon some occasion) then I made account of, but now am packinge away out of hande. This is therefore to salute you at parting, thinking it longe since I heard from you, especially the winde serving so well. The last I wrote you was at the beginning of this moneth, which came short but two howres of the boat that was dispatcht to you in such haste, so that I was faine to send it by the poste of Sandwich, and wold gladly heare the safe arrivall of it, because it was accompanied with some other letters and bookes that I wold be very loth shold miscarie. Your brother Carleton was here yesterday, and went downe into Hartfordshire, where I make reckoning to finde him at my comming. *Tandem aliquando* this great commission for Ireland is dispatcht, and the Erle[a] hath all his demaundes, the Quene showing herself very gracious and willing to content him. Marry, the clause of liberty to returne at pleasure is not inserted in the patent, but must pass under the brode seale by itself. He gives out that he will be gon the 19th of this moneth, and all thinges are hastened accordinglie. There be fowrescore horse laide at every poste twixt this and Chester, and so to Holyhead, for him and his followers, and as many by the way of Bristow. The Erles of Southampton and Rutland (who hath lately married the Countesse of Essex[b] daughter), the Lords Gray, Audeley, and Cromwell, do accompanie him, and Sir Christofer Blunt is named Mareshall of Ireland, though the Quene had a goode meaninge to Sir Henry Broncker. His whole forces are saide to be 16,000 foote and 1,400 horse, but when they shall come to the polle I feare they will fall short. In the meane time we heare that Tiron is growne into a vaine of fortification, and deviseth by all the meanes he can to defend himself: and, to furnish him the better, there be fowre ships come out of Spaine that have brought him 120,000 crownes and great store of munition. This unluckie brawle and revolte of Ireland doth so pinch us that we are apt to entertaine any ouverture of peace though it hold but by a heare; and even now there is somewhat a working, for here be certain close fellowes of Antwerp and Brussells about such a matter. The plague is saide to be very great at Lisbon, and to have consumed allredy towardes 80,000 persons. I thincke your Dunkerkers are on our Western coast, for we heare of five or sixe saile that scowre up and downe there, and have lately taken a man of warre. It was saide here the last weeke that there were 400,000 crownes sent out of Spaine in a French ship, which, for feare of the Hollanders, were

[a] Of Essex.
[b] Elizabeth only daughter and heir of Sir Philip Sidney, by Frances daughter of Sir Francis Walsingham, afterwards Countess of Essex.

landed at Diep. and so convayed into the Lowe Countries overland. And this morning I heard there shold a frigate arrive there lately that brought some man of great account (as shold seme by his traine) who tooke post from thence to Brussells. It may be you have not heard that the Duke of Joyeuse is once more become humerous, and, surrendring all his state into Montpensier (his sonne and lawes) handes, is returned again to be a Capuchin. The Lord North is come from the Court, being taken with such a deafness that he can scant heare though they crie never so lowde in his eare. The matter betwene Sir Rob. Drury and Sir William Woodehouse falles not out altogethere so fowle as was reported at first, for it is saide he undertooke him single and is himself hurt in two or three places; but the lying in wait with such cutters, and, when they saw him hurt, the setting upon Sir Robert and slaying his man, cannot be coloured; himself is in the custodie of Sheriffe Hamden, and what will come of it is not yet knowne. Our Sir John Spencer, of London, was the last weeke committed to the Fleet for a contempt, and hiding away his daughter, who, they say, is contracted to the Lord Compton; but now he is out again, and by all meanes seekes to hinder the match, alledging a precontract to Sir Arthur Henninghams sonne. But upon his beating and misusing her, she was sequestred to one Barkers, a proctor, and from thence to Sir Henry Billingsleyes[a] where she yet remaines till the matter be tried. If the obstinate and self-willed fellow shold persist in his doggednes (as he protests he will) and geve her nothing, the poore lord shold have a warme catch. The Erle of Lincoln hath bought Chelsey of Mr. Secretarie,[b] and the Lord Mountjoye, Wansted, of the Erle of Essex. And thus, wishing you all health, I commit you to God. From London, this 15th of March, 1599.      Yours most assuredly,

[*Addressed as before.*]          JOHN CHAMBERLAIN.

[a] Alderman of London; Lord Mayor in 1596. [Nichols's Prog. of James I. ii. 666.]

[b] Sir Robert Cecill is supposed to have rebuilt the manor-house at Chelsea, once the residence of Sir Thomas More. [Lysons, Env. of London, 1795, ii. 86.]

## LETTER XX.

[Domestic Correspondence, State Paper Office, June 28, 1599.]

GOODE MR. CARLETON,

Because I have so litle time to stay in towne, I meant to have plied you, and written the last weeke, but an extraordinarie accident came in the way. Now I am in such haste of going to the commencement at Cambridge with Mr. Bodley, that it is odds but I shall forget somewhat that I wold have remembred, and yet I will search every corner to make up goode measure, because I am not certain whether I come to towne again before Michaelmas. Out of Fraunce we heare nothinge, and from Spaine as litle, saving that here is a flienge tale that the Holland fleet hath taken Lisborne, which was almost utterly dispeopled by the plague. Sir Samuell Bagnoll hath don some small service in Ireland, at leastwise if that may be called a service, to defend himself when he was assaulted by the ennemie. But the case is so altered there, and we come to such an afterdeale that we are glad of anything, and take all in goode part. Yet Sir Thomas Norris hath gon further, and geven the rebells a blow wherein he hath slaine above 200 and killed theire leader (which was a Burcke) with his owne handes, which service is much magnified by her Majestie herself to the old Lord and Lady Norris, with so many goode and gracious words to them in particular as were able to revive them if they were in swoune or halfe dead. The Erle of Rutland is returned out of Ireland upon commaundment, and they say the Erle of Southampton is either come or comming, having his place of generall of the horse taken from him by order from hence. The Quene is nothing satisfied with the Erle of Essex manner of proceding, nor likes anything that is don; but sayes she allowes him 1000*l.* a day to go in progresse. He is saide to be returned to Dublin, and tarries for more men to go toward the North. The Quene is geven to understand that he hath geven Essex house to Antonie

Bacon, wherwith she is nothing pleased; but as far as I heare it is but in lieu of 2000l. he meant to bestow upon him, with a clause of redemption for that summe by a day. We have yet no Chauncellor of the Duchie; there be so many competitors that they hinder one another, and there be three that pretend an absolute promise—Sir Edward Stafford, Sir John Stanhope, and Dr. Harbert. It is thought, verely, that the Lord Burleigh[a] shall shortly be Lord President of Yorke. The Scottish King is highly offended with Sir William Bowes, our Ambassador, for conveyeng cunningly away one Ashfeild,[b] a dangerous fellow, to Berwicke, and sweares if any harme come to him, or that he be not restored, he will be revenged on his head. On Monday was sevenight Tom Compton and Mackwilliams went into the feild upon an old quarrell, where Mackwilliams was left dead in the place, and Compton came away sore hurt. The Lady Cheeke[c] and her frends follow the matter with great extremitie, and will not be perswaded but that he had help, which for ought I heare will not be proved. The same day in Nottinghamshire John Stanhope assaulted Sir Charles Candish[d] very fowly, the whole manner wherof I have here sent you,[e] as I had it from my Lord of Shrewsburie. The fable of Don Sebastian is once more afoote, and our great ones at Court talke of it as freshly as if it were a new matter. On Monday last the Quene dined here in towne, at the Countesse of Darbies,[f] the widow; and

[a] Thomas Cecill; Lord President of York October, 1599; created Earl of Exeter May 4, 1605; K.G.; died February 7, 1622. [Courthope's Nicolas, 85.]

[b] Sir William Bowes, writing to Sir Robert Cecil, affirmed that Asbfield escaped by using his coach without his privity or consent. [Scotch Corr. Eliz. June, 1599.]

[c] Elizabeth, daughter and heiress of Richard Hill, serjeant of the winecellar to Henry VIII., was married to the learned Sir John Cheke, schoolmaster and secretary of state to Edward VI., and, having been left his widow in 1557, was remarried to Henry M'Williams, esq. and survived until 1616. The present passage relates to the fate of one of her sons by this second marriage. [See Athenæ Cantab. i. 168.]

[d] Sir Charles Cavendish, of Welbeck Abbey, Notts; son of Sir William Cavendish; died 1617. [Dugdale, ii. 421.]    [e] See No. XXI.

[f] Alice, daughter of Sir John Spencer of Althorpe; widow of Ferdinando fifth Earl of Derby, and subsequently married to the Lord Keeper Egerton. [Dugdale, ii. 251.]

we have speach of a progresse intended this summer into Warwick and Oxfordshire. There were two knights made at Court on Sonday, Sir John Savage and Sir Richard Haughton of Lancashire. Booth, that married the Lord Andersons[a] daughter, was appointed to stand with them, but on the sodain was countermaunded; some guesse it was because that Drue, my neece Stukeleys father-in-law (that had a great office in the Common Place) dienge two nights before, the Lord Anderson had geven the place, and sworne an officer before eight aclocke the next morning, and within an houre after came the Quenes letters for another, which by that meanes were frustrate. Sir William Fitzwilliams,[b] after a longe lingering sicknes, is gone at last. Sir Robert Remington hath married the Lady Savage, and Sir James Scudamore the younge Lady Baskarvile. The Bishop of Winchester[c] hath printed his two sermons, about which there was so much stirre two or three yeares ago. Your brother Carleton is yet here, and followes his busines hard with Mr. Secretarie, wherein he hopes of good successe. I have many thanckes to geve you for the French Bible you left behinde, which I have bestowed on your cousen Lytton in your name. And thus, wishing you all health and goode hap, I commit you to God.

From London, this 28th of June, 1599.

Your ever assured,<br>
JOHN CHAMBERLAIN.

[*Addressed as before.*]

[a] Sir George Booth, ancestor of the Earls of Stamford and Warrington, was knighted this year (1599); created a Baronet at the first creation in 1611; died 1652, aged 86. His second wife was Katharine, daughter of Sir Edmund Anderson, Chief Justice of the Common Pleas.

[b] Lord Deputy of Ireland 1560.

[c] Thomas Bilson; translated from Worcester, April 29, 1597; died June 18, 1616.

## No. XXI.

[Domestic Correspondence, State Paper Office, June 18, 1599, Inclosure in Letter of June 28.]

### INTELLIGENCE OF AN ENCOUNTER BETWEEN SIR CHARLES CANDISH[a] AND JOHN STANHOPE.

About nine aclocke in the morning, Sir Charles Candish being at his new building, which is some quarter of a mile from his litle house where he and his Lady do lie, and going from thence to a bricke kill, as far distant from that building as that is from his house, being attended by these three persons only, Henry Ogle, Launcelot Ogle his page, and one horse-keeper, he discerned to the number of about 20 horse on the side of a hill, which he thought to be Sir John Biron with companie hunting, but sodainly they all gallopping apace towards him, he perceved he was betrayed; wherupon, being upon a litle nagge, he put spurres to him, thincking to recover the new building, but the titt fell with him, and before he could recover out of the stirrop, he was overtaken, and before he could drawe his sworde, two pistolls were discharged upon him, and one of them with a round bullet hit him in the inner side of the thighe, but missed the bone and lies yet in the flesh nere the point of his buttocke. He hath also divers small shot in severall parts of his thighe and body thereabouts, which are thought came out of the same pistoll. Notwithstanding, so stronge was the hande of God with him as, after this wound receved, he and his two poore men and boy unhorsed sixe of them and killed two in the place, a third fell downe in the forrest and is thought dead also, and the fourth was left behinde in the same place, so sore hurt as it is not thought he can recover, and lieth in the village adjoining. Upon this some of the workmen came towards them, being without weapons. John Stanhope, who was the hindmost during all the fight, was now the formost in running away, carieng all the rest of his hirelings with

[a] Cavendish.

him. Sir Charles is hurt also in the head and in the hand, but those two are but small hurtes, and the surgeons do assuredly hope that there is no great daunger in the other wounds with the pistoll, though by incision they intend to take out the bullet, which is within an inch and a half of the skinne. Sir Charles and his three had rapiers and daggers only. They left behinde them six goode geldings, whereof some are worth twenty pounds a peece, two or three cloakes, two rapiers, two pistolls, one sword and dagger, and some of theiro hattes, all of which are safely kept by Sir Charles. All this companie did all the morning before lie in the forrest, seming as though they had ben a hunting; one of them that were killed was a keper, whome Stanhope that morning tooke with him, as he found him in his parke without bootes or weapon, but a pike staffe which he had, and, as the fellow confessed before he died, he knew not whether he was caried, or what to do, untill he came to the hill-side where they staide so longe.

This is the truth of that accident.

[*Endorsed.*]

1599. Mr. Stanhope with 20 men falling upon Sir Charles Candish by surprise, onely with 2 and a page, and worsted.

## LETTER XXII.

[Domestic Correspondence, State Paper Office, August 1, 1599.]

GOODE MR. CARLETON,

I wrote to you at my going to Knebworth about the ende of June, and had no sooner sealed it up but I receved one from you, and now about three dayes since at my comming thence I receved another of the 18th of the last, and the day before my comming away your cousen Lytton had one from you of the 22th of July, which found speedy passage, as you shall perceve by his annswer hereinclosed, wherwith I send you the fruits of our Cambridge commencement, for want of better occurrents I could meet withall in those partes, presuming that (although *inter arma silent leges*) yet perhaps verses and schollerlike exercises may be welcome in the middes of warres, the alarme wherof begins to ringe in our eares here at home as shrill as in your beseiged towne. For, upon what grounde or goode intelligence I know not, but we are all here in a hurle as though the ennemie were at our doores. The Quenes shippes are all making redy, and this towne[a] is commaunded to furnish out 16 of theire best ships to defend the river, and 10,000 men, whereof 6,000 to be trained presently, and every man els to have his armes redy. Letters are likewise going out to the bishops and theire clergy and all the noblemen and gentlemen hereabout to prepare horses and all other furniture, as if the ennemie were expected within fifteen dayes. Here is likewise speach of a campe to be raised at Tilburie, the Lord Admiral[b] to be general, and the Lord Thomas Howard to have charge of the navie. But that which makes me doubt most and thincke all is in goode earnest, is that Sir Francis Vere is certainly sent for out of the Lowe Countries with 2,000 of his best souldiers. All this noise riseth upon report that the Adelantado hath an armada redy at the Groine of 30 gallies and 70 ships (though some say more) which makes us misdoubt that the besieging of your towne is but in shew, to drawe their men downe to the sea side and this navy to convay them over hither. Howsoever it be, I wold we were well rid of this brunt, in hope we shold be better provided hereafter not to be thus taken *tardè* on the sodain. The Holland fleet is saide to have taken the grand Canarie and Tenariffe, and to have used great crueltie and spoile in revenge of 300 of theire conntry marriners lately hanged up in Spaine. It is thought they will passe on to Brasil in hope to finde great store of sugars and small resistaunce, and so to possesse themselves of the country, thereby to intertaine trafficke and maintaine theire navie.

[a] London.   [b] Charles Howard, Earl of Nottingham.

We have almost nothing out of Ireland, and many men marvaile that my Lord[a] hath spent so much time and don so litle; he is now at Dublin, but yet hath one fortnights jorny more about those partes before he draw toward the North. There is a meaning that Sir Coniers Clifford shold go to Loughfoile with 3,000 men, and Sir Thomas Norris with as many to Balyshanon, and so to hedge in Tiron on all sides, who fortifies himself altogether in his paces, and they say hath quit the Blackewater. My Lord hath lately made 16 new knights, for what service I know not, but belike it is *de bene esse*, in hope they will deserve it hereafter: I send you here a list[b] of theire names. My Lords decimating of Sir Harry Harringtons companies is much descanted of, and not greatly liked here, though in mine opinion never men deserved it better, for first they were more then double the number of the rebells; then the ennemie left his strength and assaulted them in the plaine, which in all reason was our advantage; lastly, we had horse and they none. Sir Henry himself is referred over to be censured here. We are not without suspicion of some tempest brewing in Scotland, the rather for that the Kinge of Denmarke[c] pickes quarrells, and went latelie in his owne person and tooke five of our shippes[d] as they were fishing on the coast of Norway, and his brother and he with theire owne hands beat and misused our men very unprincely, geving prowde and contumelious words against our whole nation. The Quene removed from Greenwich the 27th of the last moneth, and dined the same day at Monsieur Charons,[e] and so to the Lord Burleighs at Wimbleton, where she tarried three dayes, and is now at Nonesuch. The younge Lord Harbert,[f] Sir Henrie Carie,[g] and Sir William Woodhouse are all in election at Court who shall set the best legge

---

[a] Of Essex.   [b] This list has not been found.   [c] Christian IV.
[d] See Norway Corr., State Paper Office, July 30, 1599.
[e] Noël de Caron, the Dutch Ambassador. His house was at South Lambeth : see Progresses of Queen Elizabeth, iii. 440.
[f] William, afterwards Earl of Pembroke.
[g] Cary, afterwards Viscount Falkland.

formost. The Lord Treasurer[a] hath ben very sicke of the stone, but is now upon recoverie. Doctor Bennet,[b] Deane of Windsore, is thought shall presently be made Bishop of Ely. Scory hath ben so long tampering for the philosophers stone, that he is faln into the way of all alchimists, and committed to the Gatehouse for a coiner. I thincke to go the next weeke into Oxfordshire. I have sene none of your frends since my comming, nor had no leasure to seeke after them. So that with mine owne best salutations and wishes, I commit you to God. From London, this 1st of August, 1599.

Yours most assuredly,
JOHN CHAMBERLAIN.

[*Addressed as before.*]

## LETTER XXIII.

[Domestic Correspondence, State Paper Office, August 9, 1599.]

Though here be litle happened since I wrote last, but only scambling provisions and preparations for warre, yet because I cannot tell when I shall write again if any sodain alarme call us away, I thincke it not amisse to let you understand what was and is intended to be don. The newes increasing daily of the Spaniards comming, and advertisements concurring from all parts, of theire desseigne for London (whereof the Adelantado himself gave out proude speaches), and the day of theire departure from the Groine being saide to be appointed at the uttermost as Sonday last, order was geven for a campe to be raised, wherof the Lord Admirall to be generall, the Lord Mountjoy lieutenant, Sir Francis Vere marshall, the Erle of Northumberland generall of the horse, the Erle of Sussex[c] colonell generall of the infantarie, Sir William

---

[a] Lord Buckhurst.
[b] Dr. Bennet was not preferred to the bishopric of Ely, but to the bishopric of Hereford on January 7, 1602; died October 25, 1617.
[c] Robert Radcliffe, K.G.; died 1629.

Russell his lieutenant (but he refused), Sir Thomas Wilford sergeant-major, Sir Edward Wotton* treasurer, and Mr. Maynard secretarie. The rendezvous for Hertfordshire men was to be at Tottenham, the 12th of this moneth, and so forward to Tilburie, or somewhether els, as shold be injoined them. Your cousen Lytton hath the leading of 300 men, and came up to make his provisions, whome I meane to accompanie, and (though I were never professed souldier) to offer myself in defence of my country, which is the best service I can do it. Twelve or thirtene of the Quenes shippes are preparing in all haste, whereof the Lord Thomas Howard to be admirall, Sir Walter Raleigh vice-admiral, Fulke Grivell rere-admirall. Sir Thomas Gerrard was appointed colonell of the Londoners, but for an old grudge since the last Parliament they wold none of him; wherupon the Erle of Cumberland was geven them, to have charge of them and the river, which he undertooke with great confidence, meaning to make a bridge somwhat on this side Gravesend, after an apish imitation to that of Antwerp, and to that end got together all the lighters, boates, Westerne barges, cables, and anchors that were to be found, geving out that with 1,500 musketters he wold defend that bridge or loose his life upon it (but God forbid he shold have bene put to it); but whether upon triall they finde it not faisible, as bearing another manner of bredth and billow then the river of Antwerp, or upon what other reason, I know not, yesterday, after much turmoile and great charges bestowed, it was quite geven over, and now they have an imagination of sinking certain hulkes in the channell, if need shold be. Upon Monday, toward evening, came newes (yet false) that the Spaniardes were landed in the Ile of Wight, which bred such a feare and consternation in this towne as I wold litle have looked for, with such a crie of women, chaining of streets, and shutting of the gates, as though the ennemie had ben at Blackewall. I am sory and ashamed that this weakenes and nakednes of ours on all sides

* Made Comptroller December, 1602. See Letter LXVIII.

shold shew itself so apparently as to be carried far and neere, to our disgrace both with frends and foes. Great provision is made for horse, as being the best advantage we are like to have if the ennemie come. And the noblemen about Court have rated themselves at round proportions, as the Lord Admirall a 100, the Erle of Shrewsbery 100, the Erle of Pembroke [a] 200, the Erle of Worcester [b] 100, the Erle of Northumberland 100, Mr. Secretarie 100, the Archbishop [c] 100, Sir William Russell 50, and all the rest, both court and countrie, according to theire abilitie. But now, after all this noise and blustering, methinckes the weather begins to cleere somwhat, for our preparations begin to slacke and go not on so hedlong as they did, so that there may be hope all shalbe well; and our rendezvous at Totenham is put of for five dayes. Out of Ireland we have uncertain reportes of divers featcs don, as that the Lord Cromwell hath overthrowne 6,000 of Tirons companie, but I cannot learne when nor where; that the Erle of Essex hath likewise defeated 1,500 in Ofalie, layenge 140 of them alonge, and bringing away 1,000 cowes and more; that Captain Masterson and Sir Francis Darcy shold be slaine; that there shold be a new supplie of eight or ten knights made. Sir Gilly Merricke,[d] they say, is newly come over, by whom we shall understand some more certaintie. The last that came report that they left Sir Henry Norris[e] in hard case, and make account his life will not long tarry after his legge. The world comes very fast upon Mr. Wallop,[f] who going into Ireland to burie his father,[g] within five daies after his arrivall his mother [h] died also, so that he shall put them both into one account. The Lord Burleigh is made President of Yorke, and makes provision to

[a] Henry Herbert, K.G., died 1601.  [b] Edward Somerset, K.G.; died 1628.
[c] John Whitgift; died February 29, 1604.
[d] Hanged for the Essex conspiracy, March 13, 1600-1.
[e] Son of Henry Lord Norris of Rycot.
[f] Henry Wallop, knighted in Ireland, by Essex, 1599.
[g] Sir Henry Wallop senior, Vice-Treasurer and Treasurer of the wars in Ireland, died at Dublin April 14, 1599.
[h] Katharine, daughter of Richard Gifford, Esq. [Brydges's Collins, iv. 317.]

go thether shortly. The Quene, at her being at Wimbleton, made two knightes, Withipoole[a] of Suffolke, and one Lassells[b] of Yorkeshire. The Court continues at Nonesuch, where I wish it may tarry longe. And so, commendinge myself to your goode affections, I bid you farewell. From London, this 9th of August, 1599.

Yours most assuredly,

JOHN CHAMBERLAIN.

[*Addressed as before.*]

## LETTER XXIV.

[Domestic Correspondence, State Paper Office, August 23, 1599.]

GOODE MR. CARLETON,

Having written twise since the beginning of this moneth and hearing nothing from you, it makes us thincke that either you are hard set aworke or els that you are so blockt up that letters can finde no passage. The world is well amended here since I wrote last, and the storme that seemed to looke so blacke almost quite blowne over; yet our navie is gon to sea prettilie stronge and in goode plight for so short warning, conteining 23 shippes and pinnasses of the Quenes, 12 good marchant shippes provided by the citie, and 6 more hired by her Majestie, with 14 hoyes well furnished with ordinaunce and made for fight. Our land forces are dayly discharged by litle and litle, and this day I thincke wilbe quite disolved. The Hartfordshire men were sent home first, and so by degrees one after another; yet they all receved pay more or lesse, some for fowre, some for five dayes, and some for a whole weeke. On Friday there mustered 1,600 horse by St. James, and the next day 400 for the clergie in St. Georges feild. Yet none of the noblemen have shewed theire troupes, which together with other voluntaries are thought wold double that number. If occasion had

---

[a] Sir Edmund Withipole.  [b] Sir Thomas Lascelles.

ben to draw forces to a head or into campe, it is thought the first proportion wold have risen to 27,000 foote and 3,000 horse. I assure you they were very well provided for the most part of horse armor and apparaile, and wanted not theire setting forth with feathers, skarfes, and such other light ware. The Lord Generall,[a] with all the great officers of the field, came in great bravery to Powles Crosse on Sonday was sevenight and dined with the Lord Mayor,[b] and then was the alarme at hottest that the Spaniards were at Brest, which was as likely and fell out as true as all the rest. The vulgar sort cannot be perswaded but that there was some great misterie in the assembling of these forces, and because they cannot finde the reason of it make many wilde conjectures, and cast beyond the moone; as sometimes that the Quene was daungerously sicke, otherwhile that it was to shew to some that are absent that others can be followed as well as they, and that if occasion be, militarie services can be as well and redily ordered and directed as if they were present,[c] with many other as vaine and frivolous imaginations as these. The forces in the West country are not yet dismissed, for there if anywhere may be some doubt of daunger. Sir William Russell was sent thether to be generall and to take order for all things as he thought best. And now in the middest of all this hurle burle here is a sodain sound of peace, and that certain fellowes are come from Brussells with commission from Spaine. The Lord Cromwell and Sir John Davies are newly come out of Ireland; the ones errand is thought to be about Sir Coniers Cliffords government and so to returne; the other, some say, hath that he went for. Sir Coniers Cliffords defeat was very fowle, at a place called the Curlewes in O'Donnells country, for besides himself and Sir Alexander Ratcliffe there were eight or nine commaunders lost and above 240 men. There is great fault laide in one Capt. Cosbie

---

[a] The **Earl of Nottingham.** See Letter XXIII.
[b] Sir Nicholas Mosley.
[c] An explanation of this allusion to the Earl of Essex will be found in Dixon's Personal History of Lord Bacon.

that wheeled about and caused the first disorder, but some say Sir
Coniers himself went not souldier-like to worke, and when he saw
his error, though he might have escaped, wold not outlive such a
losse. Here was newes a while that Sir Thomas Norris and Sir
Harry shold be both dead of theire hurtes; but I saw a letter of the
14th of this present that only makes mention of Sir Thomas his
weakenes without any shew of extremitie, and for Sir Harry it is
saide he wilbe here shortly. The Erle of Essex hath made many
new knights, but I cannot yet come by the bead rolle; marry for a
taste you shall have as many as I well remember, as first Sir Henry
Lindley.[a] Sir Harry Cary[b] (that was Sir Francis Veres lieutenant),
two Lovelaces,[c] Sir Ajax Harrington,[d] Sir Jacke Heydon,[e] Sir
Dick Morrison,[f] *cum multis aliis*, English and Irish, to the number of 59 in the whole, since his first arrivall. It is much marvailed
that this humor shold so possesse him, that, not content with his first
dosens and scores, he shold thus fall to huddle them up by halfe
hundreds, and it is noted as a straunge thinge that a subject in the
space of seven or eight yeares (not having ben sixe moneths together
in any one action) shold, upon so litle service and small desert, make
more knights then are in all the realme besides, and it is doubted
that if he continue this course he will shortly bring in tag and rag,
cut and longe taile, and so draw the order into contempt. The
Lord Burleigh hath his patent and is by this time halfeway at Yorke.
The Lady Hatton is brought a-bed of a daughter,[g] which stoppes
the mouth of the old slaunder, and about ten dayes since it was
christened with great solemnitie, the Quene (by her deputie the

---

[a] Knighted July 30, 1599. [Knights made in Ireland, published by Sir Thomas Phillipps.]     [b] Knighted July 12, 1599. [Ibid.]

[c] Sir William Lovelace, knighted July 30, 1599, and Sir Richard Lovelace, knighted August 5, 1599; [Ibid.] died 1612.

[d] Sir John Harrington, knighted July 30, 1599; [Ibid.] died 1612.

[e] Sir John Haydon, knighted August 5, 1599. [Ibid.]

[f] Sir Richard Morison, knighted August 5, 1599. [Ibid.]

[g] Elizabeth, eldest daughter of Lady Elizabeth Hatton by Sir Edward Coke, died young. [Collins's Peerage, 1741, iv. 355.]

Lady of Oxford[a]) and the Countesse Dowager of Darbie being godmothers, and the Lord Treasurer[b] godfather. I had almost forgot the greatest newes of all, that Dicke Fowler[c] was committed to the Towre the last week for no lesse matter then suspicion of practise against her Majesties person; but I hope it will fall out better with him upon examination, for, though I alwayes thought him foolish enough, yet I did not looke he shold prove devilish. Capt. Chute (that shold or wold have ben knight in Fraunce) is in likewise about some such matter. And Alablaster that escaped out of the Clinke is brought in *coram* again, being sent from Rochelle. Your brother Carleton hath ben almost this sevenight in towne to offer his service with two horses to Mr. Secretarie,[d] but yet could never find him at leisure, so that I doubt he will come too late when the play is don. This is all we have unles I shold tell you that last weeke at a puppett play in St. Johns Street, the house fell and hurt betwene thirty and forty persons, and slew five outright, wherof two (they say) were goode handsome whoores. Mr. Dormer was in towne yesterday, and came to accompanie Sir Harry Lee[e] to the Court. Sir Anthony Mildmay is come to towne with a cornet of his owne of 60 horse. I thincke to go into Oxfordshire very shortly, and God knows how long I shall tarry there, but I imagin there and at Knebworth till toward Michaelmas. In the meane time, with my best wishes, I betake you to God.

From London this 23th of August, 1599.[f]

Yours most assuredly,

JOHN CHAMBERLAIN.

[*Addressed as before.*]

[a] Anne, daughter of William Lord Burghley, and wife of Edward de Vere, 17th Earl of Oxford. [Dugdale, ii. 406.]

[b] Lord Buckhurst.

[c] See Domestic Correspondence, State Paper Office, August 17, 1599.

[d] Sir Robert Cecill.

[e] Son of Sir Anthony Lee; elected K.G. April 23, 1597; died 1611. [Nichols's Prog. of Elizabeth, iii. 44.]

[f] The answer to this letter is in Holland Corr. S.P.O. September 24, 1599.

## LETTER XXV.

[Domestic Correspondence, State Paper Office, Feb. 22, 1599-1600.]

MR. CARLETON,

You left us here with so faire weather, and with so confident an opinion that all shold go well with my Lord of Essex, and that we shold see him a-cockhorse again, that I know it wilbe straunge newes to you to heare that all was but a kinde of dreame, and a false paradise that his frends had fained to themselves, giving theire hopes and discourses libertie to outrun theire wit, for the bright sunshine that seemed so to dasell them was indeed but a glimmering light that was sodainly overshadowed again, and the skie as full of cloudes as before; and, though they thought they saw a reconciliation twixt him and Mr. Secretarie,[a] (wherupon they built many idle fancies and liberall discoursings,) yet either theire eyes were not theire owne, or els they had false spectacles that made everything that was don seeme more then double; for Mr. Secretarie never spake with him since he was committed, but only carried his letter of submission that kept him from the Star Chamber, so that my lord continues where he was, and, for ought I heare, is like enough to tarry there still. The Lady Rich[b] hath ben called *coram* again about her letter, but she excused herself by sicknes, and (as the Scottishman sayes) did not compeere. The Lord Cobham is contracted to the Countesse of Kildare[c] before the Quene, but is thought will not marry till he be a Counsaillor. Some say he is appointed a Commissioner with the Lord Treasurer, Sir John Fortescue, Mr. Beale,[d] and Dr. Dun,[e] for this peace; but the Lord Treasurer makes some difficultie, and sayes it is without example for a man of his place[f] to be employed

[a] Sir Robert Cecil.
[b] Penelope, daughter of Walter Devereux, Earl of Essex; married to Robert Lord Rich, afterwards to Charles Blount, Earl of Devonshire.
[c] Before mentioned in p. 27, the widow of Henry FitzGerald, 12th Earl of Kildare, who died in 1597; now remarried to Henry Lord Cobham (attainted in 1603), and died 1628.
[d] Robert Beale.
[e] Daniel Dunne, D.C.L., made Master of the Requests 1602, knighted 1603.
[f] That of Warden of the Cinque Ports.

out of the realme. The Archdukes Ambassador [a] came hither on Monday, accompanied only with eight or ten, whereof three be gentlemen, the rest servants. He is lodged at Alderman Bannings, and went yesterday to the Court, being to have audience this afternoone. All the counsaile and lords about this towne are gon thether to give theire attendaunce. Tiron is gon with 2,000 foote and 200 horse into Mounster to confer with Desmond and the other rebells, and to wrecke himself upon the Erle of Ormonds countrie for cutting of some of his followers this last winter. If the Erle had sufficient forces, or wold make the best use of those he hath, it is thought he might geve him a blow in his returne backe, and teach the foxe not to forsake his hole, nor go so far from home. Litle Sir Edward Denny is dead in Ireland. The Scottish nobilitie find themselves greeved that theire Kinge is no more respected, and have lately made an association among themselves against all those that shall hinder his right and succession. The Duke of Savoy is gon from Paris, some say homeward, and some into the Lowe Countries; having only gotten thus much by his jorny as to have two moneths respite to take or leave the offers the Kinge hath made him. The French King [b] is looked for at Callis, where he meanes to settle a staple or mart to serve the Lowe Countries. The fort of Bommell, wherin were 17 companies, is come into the States handes [c] by composition, upon a mutinie [d] that fell among them for want of pay; and, some small store of mony being sent by the Archduke to content the Spaniards only, the Wallons tooke such indignation that they were no more regarded, that they turned them out of doore and delivered the place. There hath ben a set combat (upon divers quarrells and challenges) twixt twenty French horse of the garrison of Gertrudenberg, and as many of one Grobendoncks of Sartogenbosch, wherin, besides other fowle play, and odds of weapon more then was agreed, Durant, Captain of the French, being taken prisoner, was kild in cold blond, contrary to covenant. The gallies

[a] Louis Verreyken.   [b] Henry IV.   [c] Contradicted in Letter XXVI.
[d] An account of this mutiny at Bommell is given by Gilpin in a letter to Cecil, Feb. 9, 1599-1600. See Holland Correspondence, State Paper Office.

of Sluce have lately taken three shippes of Holland that were driven upon theire coast in a fogge and could not be rescued, one laden with salt, another with wine; the third was one of the best and richest shippes that returned from the viage at sea. It is written out of Spaine that the Adelantado is in disgrace and committed to his house for letting the Hollanders passe away so easilie. If it be so, we lacke but a Plutarch to make him and my Lord of Essex paralells, for I thincke they and theire fortunes may be compared in many thinges. I know not whether Mr. Edmonds [a] were returned before you went; else he came presently after, and is much used in the intertainment of this ambassador.[b] If any thing fall out worth the writing, you shall heare of me next weeke; in the meane time I wish you all health and welfare.

From London, this 22th of February, 1600.

        Yours most assuredly,

[*Addressed,*]       JOHN CHAMBERLAIN.

 To my assured good frend
  Mr. Dudley Carleton,
   geve these,
    at Ricot.

## LETTER XXVI.

[Domestic Correspondence, State Paper Office, Feb. 29, 1599-1600.]

MR. CARLETON,

But for my promise, I shold scant kepe touch with you now, this weeke hath ben so barren. The Archdukes Ambassador,[b] that shold have had audience this day sevenight, was put of till Satterday, by reason the Quene was somwhat ill at ease; but then he had it with all the ceremonies and compliments that could be devised, to crie quittaunce for the honor don to Mr. Edmunds. The like respect was geven him at the Lord Treasurers [c] on Monday and Wensday,

[a] The Mr. Edmondes here frequently alluded to, was the subsequent Sir Thomas.
[b] Louis Verreyken.        [c] Lord Buckhurst.

when he sat in counsaile there with the Lord Treasurer, Lord Admiral,[a] Lord Chamberlain,[b] Mr. Secretarie,[c] and Sir John Fortescue. The negotiation is kept very close, yet some will needs beleve that he hath stoode only yet upon the time, place, and the commissioners for the treatie. It seemes we seeke to prolong the time, and to reduce the meeting to Caunterburie. Some say he sollicits his dispatch, others that he hath sent away one of his companie for further direction in some point, and must attend his returne. Our discoursers shoote many boltes in this busines, which to them seemes so intangled and intricate that, in seeking to undo one knot they make two, and therefore geve it over in the plaine feild as not faisible. Whatsoever the reason is, methincks we are not so hot on this peace as we were, and the least stop in such a cause may turn the tide. It may be we feare the French will fall in with the States if we leave them in this extremitie; and yet on the other side some say that the States, for all theire bragges, hath left themselves and theire cause wholy to the Quenes wisdome to be comprised in this peace as she shall thincke best for herself and them. The French Ambassador[d] had audience on Sonday; and we heare there is some great man comming out of France, in shew about the Kinges installation at Windsore, whatsoever other errand he may have in secret. Some geve out it shold be the Duke de Mayen, and that Somerset House is preparing for him, but I thincke it very unlikely. The fort of Bommell is not come into the States handes as was reported, but only continues still in mutinie. The Grave Maurice is saide by a *trattato doppio* to have overthrowne 14 ensignes of the ennemie that had a practise in Wachendoncke. The Lord Burke and his brother are both slaine in Ireland in the Quenes service; and one Florence Maccartie, that was latelie here well used and much made of, is fallen away in Mounster, and made himself Maccartie Moore (a great title in those parts), and is thought will do much harme. Seven or eight of our best marchants ships and theire goods are

[a] Earl of Nottingham.  [b] George Lord Hunsdon.
[c] Sir Robert Cecil.  [d] Mons. de la Boysiez.

staide at Venice upon divers quarrells, but specially upon a prise of theires lately taken by Sir John Gilbert to Sir Walter Raleighs use. I am sory we shold have any difference with a commonwealth so generally estemed for justice and wisdome. The Bassa of Caramania, revolted from the Turke, that kept so much stirre all the last yeare, hath latelie overthrowne the Bassa of Aleppo, and taken the towne, and raunges over all Siria, as they write from Tripoli. On Monday there was a great assemblie of men and women of this towne at the Marshalsee to heare a Scottish Frier Capuchin preach; where they were staide and kept all night, to the number of three or fowre score, and afterwards examined by the Bishop of London,[a] Dr. Stanhop,[b] and others. Some were dismissed payenge theire chardges, some bound over, and some committed.[c] The Erle of Essex hath ben somwhat crasie this weeke. The Lord Keeper[d] was sent for yesterday to the Court, wherupon his followers feed themselves fat with hope in this leane time of Lent. I heare that Sir Henry Nevill is become deafe since his going over, and therfore makes meanes to be called home. Litle Britain is left desolate, and the whole household translated into Essex. I know not how my last came to your hands, nor how this shall finde the way, but you see what shift I have made to peece out a letter more then I meant in the beginning. And so in haste I commit you to God.

From London, this last of February, 1600.[e]

Yours most assuredly,

[*Addressed*,]            JOHN CHAMBERLAIN.

   To my assured goode frend
      Mr. Dudley Carleton
         geve these, at Rycot,
            or elswhere.

---

[a] Richard Bancroft, elected 1597; translated to Canterbury 1604; died 1610.
[b] Edward Stanhope, D.C.L., knighted 1603.
[c] A list of the persons taken at the Friar's Sermon on Monday, Feb. 25, 1599-1600, is in Domestic Corresp. State Paper Office, Feb. 26.     [d] Sir Thomas Egerton.
[e] The answer to this letter is in Dom. Corr. State Paper Office, March 2.

## LETTER XXVII.

[Domestic Correspondence, State Paper Office, March 5, 1599-1600.]

MR. CARLETON,

This is now my third letter since I saw or heard of you, and I write in the more hudling haste because I thincke to go to Knebworth very shortly, where I meane to tarry till toward the terme, when my wife[a] promiseth to come and fetch me home. Your cosen Lytton wisheth me to intreat your companie, and to bringe you alonge with me, but I returne his writ with *non est inventus*. You may do well, if you have any idle time, to play the goode fellow and come and see our matches at football, for that and bowling wilbe our best intertainment. Yet, if this letter come to your hands in any time I wold have you know that Mr. Edmunds is bound for another viage to the Archduke and Infanta, and makes account to be gon toward Satterday or Sonday[b] (peradventure a day or two more will break no square), so that if you have any minde to the jorny, and can be redy in time, or presume you may be admitted, you have all the helpe I can afoord you, which is to geve you notice of as much and with as much speede as in me lies. Our peace goes but slowly on, and when all is don, it is thought it will prove but a cessation or truce for seven or ten yeares at most. Neither do I thincke any great persons shalbe imployed in the treatie when Sir Walter Raleigh is like to be second in the commission, as himself sayes, in secret. He attends the ambassador[c] much, by the Quenes apointment, and carries him up and downe to see sights and rarities hereabout. He hath had him at Powles, at Westminster, at Whitehall, and where not?

[a] The lady whom Mr. Chamberlain in this and other letters calls his wife, was Winifred, daughter of Sir Henry Wallop, who died in 1599; she was unmarried at this time, but subsequently, in 1601, married to her cousin, Sir Richard Gifford. See Letter XXXIX.
[b] His passport is dated March 9. [Dom. Corr. State Paper Office.]
[c] Louis Verreyken.

This day he is feasted at the Lord Treasurers,[a] and to-morow at the Lord Chamberlaines,[b] where me thinckes it shold be somwhat straunge to see carowses to the Kinge of Spaines health. Here is a flieng tale that he shold be dead, but no man geves eare to it. The Marquis of Denia governes there soveraignly, and his wife is entred into like credit with the younge Quene. The Adelantado is prisoner at Madrid in his owne house, not for any matter of state, but for a processe of some importance commenced against him. The Count de Fuentes is made one of the Grandes of Spaine, and Governor of Milan. The French King is saide to be gon toward Lyons, and so to Marseilles to meet his new bride[c] (the Duke of Florence neece) that comes thether by sea. His former marriage[d] is annullated by the Pope, upon very fickle points, as supposall of force, feare, and compulsion, and affinitie or kindred not lookt into, nor dispensed withall. His mistress, Mademoiselle Dentragues, is with child, but yet possesseth not his affections in such superlative sort as his last love.[e]

The Duke of Savoy is gone from Paris, having gotten nothing by his longe jorny and large expence but that which is thought he might have had better cheape if he had staide at home; that viage hath stoode him in fowre or five hundred thowsand crownes, having presented the King and his sonne, the Duke of Vendosme, very richly, but specially the Kinges mistress, and almost all the Court; and the Kinge was so miserable that, though he lodged him in the Louvre, yet he gave him leave to finde his owne diet and all his traine. Capuchin Joyeuse preacheth all this Lent with great concourse and admiration of all who love him. The Duke of Wittenberg (a Protestant, as I take it) went to the Jubile at Rome upon curiositie, in the beginning of the yeare, and is returned. Some of our Englishmen are clapt up there in the Inquisition, and among the rest a younger sonne of Sergeant Heales.

[a] Lord Buckhurst.  
[b] Lord Hunsdon.  
[c] Marie de Medicis.  
[d] With Marguerite de Valois.  
[e] " La Belle Gabriello."

The Duke of Parma hath married the daughter of Aldobrandini, brother to the Pope and Gonfaloniere della Chiesa. His brother, the Cardinall Farnese, is become protector of the English Seminarie, by the death of Cardinall Caietan. Here is an ambassador come out of Denmarke,[a] but I know not for what purpose. The Erle of Essex hath ben lately troubled with his old disease of loosenes, but yet tarries still by it where he was, as a man quite out of minde: and yet Babbington,[b] Bishop of Worcester, preaching at Court on Sonday last, made many profers and glaunces in his behalfe, as he was understoode by the whole auditorie, and by the Quene herselfe; who, presently calling him to a reckoning for it, he flatly forswore that he had any such meaninge. And now that I have drawne myselfe drie, and have no store left, I will bid you farewell without further ceremonie.

From London, this 5th of March, 1600.[c]

Yours most assuredly,
JOHN CHAMBERLAIN.

[*Addressed,*]
To my assured goode frend
Mr. Dudley Carleton,
geve these,
at Ricot, or elswhere.

---

[a] There is no indication, in the Danish Corr. State Paper Office, of an ambassador's having come to England at this time; but it appears that Danish Commissioners came to Embden, and in March, 1600, Richard Bancroft bishop of London, Dr. Parkins and Dr. Swale, doctors-at-law, were sent to meet them there.

[b] Gervase Babington; translated from Exeter August 30, 1597; died May 17, 1610.

[c] The answer to this letter is in Dom. Corr. State Paper Office, March 29, 1600. It is addressed to Chamberlain at Knebworth.

## LETTER XXVIII.

[Domestic Correspondence, State Paper Office, May 10, 1600.]

Mr. CARLETON,

This is only to salute you, being alredy booted and bound for Knebworth. I litle thought of this jorny yesternight when I went to bed; but your cousen Lytton will needes have it so, though I refused his importunitie in as goode sort as I could to himself, but for all that he hath adventured to send horses, and sayes he is sure I will not send them empty away. I will make as litle stay as I can, and hope to find you here at my returne. Our commissioners[a] shold take theire leave at Court on Tewsday; those of the contrarie side[b] are expected at Callis towardes the end of the weeke; and our Lord Ambassador[c] makes account to be at Bollen much about that time. Here is newly come out of Ireland the Lord of Upper Osserie. I heare of nothing he bringes but that the Erle of Ormond is not delivered,[d] as was reported, but cousigned over to the Desmond. We have a flienge tale that O Conor Sligo hath taken O Donell, but there is no great credit geven to it. Nine or ten goode marchant ships are come out of the Levant, wherof the owners are not a litle glad, because they heard they were strongly layde for in the streights and in the sleve twixt England and Fraunce. Not far from the North Cape they met two of the King of Spaines armadas or gallions,

---

[a] John Herbert, Robert Beale, and Thomas Edmondes received their instructions May 12, 1600 [Spanish Corr.], and arrived at Boulogne May 16. [French Corr. State Paper Office.]

[b] The Commissioners appointed on the part of the Low Countries were Jehan Richardot, and Louis Verreyken; those for the King of Spain were Don Baltazar de Cuniga and Don Fernando Carillo. [Spanish Corr.]

[c] Sir Henry Neville, the Ambassador in Paris.

[d] "Ormond could not be released on the terms proposed by the O'Moors; he was then in the woods of Leix, removed every three hours." [Irish Corr. State Paper Office, May 9, 1600.]

and after some fight suncke the one and were possest of the other, but having taken out some few men, shot, and powder, with some other thinges they wanted, they let her go, because they knew not how to bestowe her men, which were almost five hundred; and withall the Spaniards gave out that the peace was concluded twixt England and Spaine, which made them the more mercifull. I have some papers of yours which I meane to leave at your sister Williams. I cannot send you Grobendones booke, for I presently restored it to Blacke Milles, of whom I borrowed it. Thus in haste I bid you farewell.

From London, this 10th of May, 1600.

Yours most assuredly,
JOHN CHAMBERLAIN.

[*Addressed,*]
To my assured goode frend
Mr. Dudley Carleton,
geve these,
at Ricot.

## LETTER XXIX.

[Domestic Correspondence, State Paper Office, May 28, 1600.]

MR. CARLETON,

I wrote you at my going out of towne what Scarborough warning I had to prepare myself. At my comming backe on Friday last with your cosen Lytton and Will Cope, I found yours of the 14th[a] of this present, whereby I see we are like to want your companie this terme to help to furnish our walke in Powles. Your brother Carleton and I met here the first day of the terme, but I had no leisure to aske how longe we shold injoy him. Mrs. Lytton and

[a] In the letter alluded to, Carleton says, " By reason of my goode cosen Gilpins trifling and delays in the business he undertooke for Sir Ed. Norreys, I am appointed to goe into the Low Countries." [Domestic Correspondence, State Paper Office, May 14, 1600.]

her litle ones come up on Monday next, when I could wish your companie, because here wilbe *plena curia* of your frends and kindred. There came a large packet this day out of Ireland, the contents whereof are not yet come abrode. But it was saide before that the Lord Deputie[a] was gone towards Tiron, to kepe him occupied, whiles Sir Harry Docwray shold plant himselfe at Lough Foile, where O Donell and Ore Orgh are redy with forces to withstand him. One Don Hispagno hath utterly burnt and wasted the country of Wexford, saving one house and castle of Sir Henry Wallops that was able to make resistance. There be two ships come out of Spaine with mony and munition to the rebells in the north. Sir George Carew[b] doth reasonablie well in Mounster, and hath brought in Florence Maccartie and the White Knight.[c] Here goes a speach that Grave Maurice is gon with 200 flat-bottomed boats into Flaunders with intent to besiege Sluce, but some thincke it rather to build a fort in the mouth of the haven or other convenient place to kepe in the gallies. The Lord Gray and Sir Robert Drury are gon over with twelve or fowretene horse to serve the States, but it is geven out under hande that the Lord[d] meanes to make a start into Ireland to meet with the Erle of Southampton in Mounster, whether he called him, but me thinckes it were very far set and might be dere bought to take such a compas. Our Bishop of London[e] and his associates came to Embden just as the Danish Ambassadors were departing, because they pretended the date of theire commission was expired, so that our men are to stay there till they have further advise what to do.[f] Secretarie Harbert (or, as some malapert fellowes call him, Secondarie Harbert, because in his patent he is not termed *principalis secretarius*, but *secundus*,) and his collegues arrived the same day at Bullen that our Ambassador[g] came thether from Paris, being

[a] Lord Mountjoy.  [b] Lord President of Munster.
[c] Edmund Fitzgibbon.  [d] Grey.
[e] Richard Bancroft.
[f] There is a long account of this matter from the Commissioners at Embden in the Danish Correspondence, State Paper Office, May 13th, 1600.
[g] Sir Henry Neville.

two dayes before the Spanish agents appeared. Hetherto they have don litle but examine* ech others commission, upon view whereof ours at the first sight made shew to be more ample, but yet upon further consideration from hence they be advised to proceed. They lodge all in the base towne, wherein our men please themselves in thincking they be more respected and better provided then the other side.

There is a meaning to call the Erle of Essex before the counsaile and other noblemen assistants, on Satterday next, at the Lord Kepers,[b] where, according to his aunswers to such matter as shalbe objected by the Quenes learned counsaile, there is hope he may have further inlargement. His apologie was lately printed with the Lady Riches letter in the end, and some few of them sold, but they were presently suppressed, and upon search found not to be don so much upon frendship or faction as upon hope of gaine. The poore Lady is like to have the worst of it, being sent for and come up to aunswer and interpret her riddles. Here is one Ashfield, a gentleman, dead of a light hurt geven him by some servants or followers of Mr. Pope of your country,[c] and by his procurement as is suggested, which, if it prove so, is like to turne him to much cost and trouble. This is all I can remember for the present, saving that your frends in Litle Britain are all well, and marvaile they heare not from you; and so, with my best wishes, I bid you farewell.

From London, this 28th of May, 1600.

Yours most assuredly,<br>
JOHN CHAMBERLAIN.

[*Addressed as before.*]

---

[a] The examination took place on the 19th and 20th of May. [Spanish Correspondence, State Paper Office.]

[b] Sir Thomas Egerton.   [c] Oxfordshire.

## LETTER XXX.

[Domestic Correspondence, State Paper Office, June 13, 1600.]

GOODE MR. CARLETON,

I thancke you for your letter and the inclosed papers, which together with those you left behind I have bequeathed to your cousen Lytton, who according to his old custome carries all to his nest. This hath ben a day of great doings in seing him and his troupes well set out of towne, and in the armies removing from Clarkenwell, whence they are all dislodged this afternoone towardes Hamshire, and your brother[a] with his pettie regiment marched away much about the same howre, so that I was greatly distracted to supply all places, wherby I could not do my wife[b] the honor (as was my meaning) to conduct her some part of the way, though she were otherwise sufficiently accompanied; but that error will easilie be pardoned with my spedy repaire to them after I come to Askot, where I hope to be soone after Midsommer. In the meane time you were not forgotten at the farewell, but had many goode wishes from all sides. I was yesterday at the Star Chamber upon report of some speciall matter that shold be delivered touching my Lord of Essex, where the Lord Keper[c] made a very grave speach in nature of a charge to the Judges, to looke to the overgrowinge idle multitude of justices of peace, to maintainers and abettors of causes and suites, to sollicitors and pettifoggers, to gentlemen that leave hospitalitie and housekeping and hide themselves in cities and borough townes, to the vanitie and excesse of womens apparell, to fore stallers and regraters of markets, to drunckards and disorderly persons, to masterles men and other companions that make profession to live by theire sword and by theire wit, to discoursers and medlers in princes matters, and lastly to libellers; upon occasion whereof he fell

[a] George Carleton.
[b] Winifred Wallop. [See Note to Letter XXVII.]
[c] Sir Thomas Egerton.

to a digression how mercifully her Majestie had dealt with the Erle of Essex in proceeding with him so mildly and by a private hearing, whereas if he had ben brought to that place he could not have past without a heavie censure, the avoiding wherof must only be imputed to God and her Majesties clemencie, upon an humble letter he wrote the night before he was to appeare that she wold be pleased to let that bitter cup passe from him; but yet, to satisfie the world and to stop the slaunders that gave out he was condemned *causâ inauditâ*, she was to justifie her proceedings and call him before her counsaile and others of her auncient nobilitie to aunswer his contempts and misgovernment; where he behaved himself so wisely and so humblie confessing his errors with teares (and sayenge that the teares of his heart had quenched all the sparkles of pride that were in him), that it was great satisfaction to the assistaunce and no doubt wold procure her Majesties further favor towards him. This was the substance and in part the very wordes of that was delivered more at large. So that now we looke every day when he shall have the libertie of Barn Elmes, for I thincke his first step wilbe no further, whatever he do afterward. Faire Mrs. Fowlers[a] cause held us on the same day till almost five a clocke, the conclusion whereof was that she is to be carted to Bridewell and there whipt, her mignon Captaine Heines[b] to stand on the pilloric and imprisoned; her brother Harry Boughton[c] to pay 100*l.*, and be imprisoned till he find sureties for the goode behaviour: and Gascoin a souldier to ride with his face to the horse taile, to stand on the pilloric at Westminster and in Cheapside, and to be marked in the face with a hot iron, and imprisonment during life. The greatest burthen lighted on him because he was the principall actor and best

---

[a] The wife of Richard Fowler, who was committed to the Tower on suspicion of practising against the Queen's life. [See Letter XXIV.]

[b] Hanged at Smithfield, in 1602, for killing his fellow-prisoner in the Fleet. [See Letter XLVI.]

[c] Henry Boughton, who served the Archbishop of Canterbury, was killed by the Archbishop's page. [See Letter XLVI.]

proofe came against him; whereas for the rest, though every man that heard it might justly condemne them *in foro conscientiæ*, yet the case was not altogether so cleere *in foro judicii*, but there is hope she may finde favor and be dispensed withall, though (as my Lord Keper saide) she be *hæc Helena*, the cause of all the evill, carrieng the right picture of a courtisan in her countenaunce, and having rather *frontem meretriciam* (as he called it), then any such delicate feature as I looked for. And now, to the purpose of the varietie of mens tast and likinge, I will tell you while I remember it, I met with your Lady Norris[a] this other day at my Lady Wallops, who in my judgement doth no way aunswer the report I have heard of her, but only in stature. We heare nothing from our commissioners[b] but that they begin to accost one another, but the two principalls make curtesie who shall begin. There is an uncertaine speach that they have a meaning to remove to Paris. The States are very stronge and it is thought have a desseigne upon Gravelinge or Sluce, but I incline to the latter. It is reported underhand that the Lordes of Delvin and Louth are gon into rebellion and carried a great part of the Pale with them; wherupon the Lord Deputie[c] shold be come backe from the Newry towardes Dublin. We shall have the great marriage on Monday at the Lady Russells,[d] where it is saide the Quene will vouchsafe her presence, and lie at the Lord Chamberlains,[e] or the Lord Cobhams, whose mariage[f] is thought likewise shalbe then consummated if it be not don alredy. The Judges are all staide here, and willed to be at Court on Sonday. Will Cecil[g] is returned out of Italie, and could not finde such a mistris as his owne wife[h] in all his travels. Wright

---

[a] Wife of Sir Edward Norris, Governor of Ostend.
[b] To the Archduke Albert.   [c] Lord Mountjoy.
[d] The marriage alluded to was that of Lady Anne Russell to Henry Lord Herbert, son of the Earl of Worcester.
[e] Lord Hunsdon.   [f] With the Countess of Kildare (see p. 65).
[g] Afterwards Earl of Exeter, K.G.; died 1640.
[h] Elizabeth, daughter of Edward Manners, Earl of Rutland. [Dugdale, ii. 407.]

the seminarie priest, that brake from Wisbich, is taken again, and I thincke wilbe tied up shorter. Wat Cope tells me that he is nominated one of the commissioners for the finding of my Lady Norris[a] office, but he could not tell when the day shold hold. I heard there yesternight that Sir Anthony Paulet was drawing on and in so weake case that it was thought he could not live till this morning. I have sent you here a passionate letter of my Lord of Essex, the last he wrote to the Quene out of Ireland; and thus you see what a bundell I have made of all that comes to hand, and perchaunce wearied you as much as myself, and therefore without further ceremonies I will bid you farewell.

From London this 13th of June, 1600.

Yours most assuredly,
JOHN CHAMBERLAIN.

[*Addressed*,]
    To my very goode frend
        Mr. Dudley Carleton,
            geve these,
                at Witam.

## LETTER XXXI.

[Domestic Correspondence, State Paper Office, June 24, 1600.]

MR. CARLETON,

Since my last to you of the 13th of this present, I heard not of you till this day (of your being at Oxford) by Mr. Gent. I hope to see Oxfordshire about the later end of next weeke, if his comming hether or some other unknowne accident do not hinder me. In the

---

[a] Lady Norris was suitor to the Council for 2000*l*., which she alleged to be due to her husband Sir Edward. [Dom. Corr. State Paper Office, Carleton to Chamberlain, June 22, 1600.]

meane time this comes as a forerunner, to know where I may see you or heare what becomes of you. Sir Geffray Fenton [a] is at Court, informinge and solliciting the causes of Ireland. The Lord Deputie had not sufficient forces to front Tirone, and therefore was faine to retire, *plus que le plus*, and to seeke new wayes and force certain passages by moonelight. He is now at Dublin, and hath sent for new supplies to renforce his companies. Order is taken for 2,000 to be sent away presently, for the leading of whome there be above fowrscore captaines, suitors at Court. Mr. Winwod came from Bolloigne the 14th of this present, and Mr. Edmunds on Satterday last; they both bringe one newes, that the difficultie of precedence continues. The Spaniards shold have geven theire resolute aunswer about it on Tewsday last, which they protracted two or three dayes and then demaunded 14 dayes more, till they could send Vereiken [b] to Brussells to know theire finall resolution, and requested that Mr. Edmunds might be sent over to informe and satisfie her Majestie. We cannot aime at the depth of this delay, unless it be that those of Flaunders and Hainhault are in conference with the States about a peace, and do meet in a certaine iland neere Dort. If anything come of it, there were never men plaide theire game better then the Hollanders, to make such a bravado and vie it so franckly as they do at this instant; for the Grave Maurice is past over into Flaunders with 12,000 foote and 1,600 horse (though common report double the number), accompanied with Sir Francis Vere, Sir Robert Sidney, the Lord Gray, and 24 ensignes of English. They were saide to have 2,700 saile, great and small, to transport them, and yet they lost 300 horse, that were smothered and stifled with pestering and heat. They landed most by Beirefleet and Sas, and marched along under the walls of Bruges. The ennemie forsoke his forts before Ostend, and the whole army sat

---

[a] Knighted in Ireland by the Lord Deputy Fitzwilliams, 1583. [Knights made in Ireland, published by Sir Thomas Phillipps.]

[b] Louis Verreyken.

downe at Nieuport; whence if they can dispatch quickly, they
meane to besiege Dunkerke, whether many of our gallants prepare
themselves, and wilbe gon about the beginning of the next weeke,
as the Erles of Northumberland and Rutland, the Lords Harbert,
Windsore, and Mountaigle,[a] with many more that pretend to go
over to that service: there be 200 saile that follow the army with
vitaile and provisions, but so ill guarded that one night the gallies
came forth and burnt and spoiled three or fowre and twenty saile,
and so beat a man of warre of Flushing that he was scant able to
crawle away, having lost his captaine[b] (a man of great worth), and
all his men save eight. Sir Robert Sidney lost his tent, and all his
other provision and furniture in one of those ships that were spoiled,
and Sir Francis Vere some part of his stuffe. The gallies grew bold
upon this success, but within three dayes after they met with eight
men of warre that bent and battered them well favouredly. The
Grave Hollocke is left in Gelderland, with six or seven thowsand
men, to see if the ennemie make any head that way, and if he draw
all towards Flaunders, then he is to follow and come to the campe.
The Grave William is building a cittadell at Gronning. There was
a plot laide by the ennemie to have slaine Grave Manrice, but it
missed, and the parties were taken and confesse the practise. The
French king is still at Paris or thereabout till his mistris[c] be
brought abed, and makes no haste to meet his bride till toward
September. There was a conspiracie plotted by a meane woman [d]
(to whom he ought mony) to poison him, but it was discovered by
the Count Soissons, and she burnt. Our Commissioners are come
away from Embden *re infecta*, and the Bishop[e] comes along through

[a] William Parker, fourth Baron; died July 1st, 1622. [Dugdale, ii. 307.]
[b] Sir William Browne, in relating this occurrence to Cecil, says, "the Captaine was usually called the Yonnger Banker." [Holland Corr. State Paper Office, June 11, 1600.]
[c] Mademoiselle d'Entragues, afterwards Marquise de Verneuil.
[d] An innkeeper's wife of St. Denis, who had supplied the army with wine, and had long been an unsuccessful suitor to the king for payment. [French Corr. State Paper Office, June 5th, 1600.]
[e] Of London, Richard Bancroft.

Holland unknowne. There be three or fowre of the Quenes ships going to sea, but whether, or to what purpose, *ignoramus*. We have six marchant ships newly come from the Levant, which were met with all in the Streights by five ships of war and some gallies, and yet escaped reasonablie well. I doubt not but you have heard of the great mariage [a] at the Lady Russells, where the Quene was present, being caried from the water side in a curious chaire and lodged at the Lord Cobhams; and of the maske of eight maides of honour and other gentlewomen in name of the Muses that came to seeke one of theire fellowes, and of the knighting of Sir Fetipher [Fettiplace?] with many goode wordes more then God knowes he was worthy of. And this being *summa totalis* of that I have to say, I commend you to the protection of the Almighty.

From London, this 24th of June, 1600.

Yours most assuredly,

JOHN CHAMBERLAIN.

[*Addressed,*]
   To my very goode frend
      Mr. Dudley Carleton
         geve these,
            at Ricot, or elsewhere.

## LETTER XXXII.

[Domestic Correspondence, State Paper Office, July 1, 1600.]

MR. CARLETON,

Your letter [b] of the 22th of the last came yesternight late; if mine make no more haste thitherward they bringe but stale newes,

[a] Of Anne Russell to Henry Lord Herbert, son of Edward Earl of Worcester. Other accounts of this marriage masque, from the letters of Rowland Whyte, will be found in the Progresses, &c. of Queen Elizabeth, iii. 498, 499.

[b] The letter referred to is in the Domestic Correspondence, State Paper Office, June 22, 1600.

as I doubt this I send now will come a day after the faire, when you are alredy full of the great fight that happened on Sonday [a] was sevenight neere Nieuport. Yet, because the particulars are not yet thoroughly knowne, but growe daily as letters come, it may be I shall send you somewhat you knew not before ; though peradventure not all gospell, yet with the best choise I could make amonge such varietie of reports. Here is one Edmunds [b] (the translator of Cæsars Commentaries) come from Sir Francis Vere with letters [c] to the Counsaile, but his relation (to my understandinge) is so partiall, as if no man had strooke stroke but the English, and among the English no man almost but Sir Francis Vere. The truthe is he plaide his prises, and Barnevelt hath written to the Quene in commendation of our nation, but specially of his great service that day. The States, no doubt, were over reacht in theire discourse, and meant not to play so great game, and the Archduke [d] thought to catch them in a pit fall, for, having reclaimed his mutined Spaniards, and gathered out of his garrisons and other places a sufficient army, he left the Infanta [e] at Gaunt, and marched after them with all possible speede, meaning to overtake them before they should take in all the forts before Ostend ; but they were set downe the 20th of the last before Nieuport, and the next day, hearing of his approach, sent 22 ensignes of Scottes and others to kepe a passage about Oldenburgh, and so to hinder his comming on till they might consult what were best to be don, but he, marching all night, was alredy possessed of the passage, and, finding the Scotts at advantage, cut them all in pieces (as we say) and upon that successe came on towards Nieuport, whereupon Grave Maurice rose, and drawing toward Ostend, not past fowre English mile from Nieuport, met them upon the sands ; then, taking the leading of the horse from the young Prince his brother, committed them to Sir Francis Vere,

[a] June 22.
[b] Mr. Clement Edmonds; knighted 1617; died October 12th, 1622.
[c] Sir Francis Vere's letter is in the Holland Correspondence, June 26.
[d] Albert of Austria.                                [e] Isabella Clara Eugenia.

as likewise the ordering and disposing of the whole army, reserving the artillerie to himself. The armies stoode more then two houres in view one of the other; at last 700 horse of the ennemie offring to charge (after the artillerie had plaide) were invested in the very tumult and smoke by Sir Francis Vere with 300 horse and beaten up to their squadrons, in which incounter Sir Francis receved three hurts by shot, in the thighe, in the legge, and in the side (as I remember), and his horse slaine under him, but being mounted behinde Sir Robert Drury, came of againe, having left some of his followers behinde him, and the Lord Gray hurt in the mouth. Then came on the Spanish regiment toward the English with such a fury that after a while, leaving their pikes and falling to the sword, our men (some say) began to recale, but by the extreme courage and labour of theire leaders (Sir Francis himself, for all his hurtes, planting himself among them) they were brought on againe, and after three howres fight utterlie defeated them, and had the chasing of them fowre mile. They say we have lost above 500 [a] English and five or sixe captaines, as Yaxeley, Honiwoode, Purton, Tirrell, and I know not who els, besides Charles Drury, brother to Sir Robert, and 16 gentlemen of Sir Francis companie. The ennemie is saide to have lost at least 6,000 [b] men, and among them the Count Busquoy governor of Arras, the Count Barlaimont, the Count Fredericke Van Berghe, Rivas governor of Flaunders and Sluce, the governor of Dunkirk, Llandriani generall of the Italians, La Berlotte, and Sir William Stanley (who was seen to geve great direction that day) are saide to be slaine. The Ammirante of Arragon, the Count de la Fere, the Count de Salines, Don Louis de Veillar, and Don Carlo de Sapina, masters of the campe to the

---

[a] The English lost 2,000, and had 2,000 wounded: *five* captains were slain; Yaxley, Honeywood, Duxberry, Purlen [*sic*], and Tyrrell. [Holland Correspondence, State Paper Office, June, 1600.]

[b] Captain Scott, in his letter to the Lord Treasurer, dated at Ostend, June 26th, says, "There were 4,000 of the enemy slain, and 1,000 taken prisoners." Sir Robert Sydney writes to the same effect. [Holland Correspondence, State Paper Office, June, 1600.]

Spaniards, with many other, are taken. In a worde, it is saide there was not any commaunder of note but is either taken or slaine, saving the Archduke himself (who is hurt in the face), the Duke d' Aumale, and Velasco, generall of the artillerie. Yet some will nedes have it that the Archduke himself is lost, and that his horse is taken, and a page of his who sayes he saw him fall from his horse and never saw him after. But the general opinion is that he escaped very narrowly, and was pursued till he was seen let in by a postern at Bruges. It may be much of this wilbe countermaunded, in the mean time you have it as goode cheape as I. But sure it is the greatest battaile and best fought that hath ben betwixt two disciplined armies in our time in Christendome. There was almost no oddes in number (saving that the States had advantage of almost 500 horse), theire foote were about 9,000 a peece. The Ammirante at supper told Grave Maurice that the game was faire enough on theire side in the beginning of the day, who answered him that was nothing, for he that wins in the end carries away the mony. Sir Robert Sidney, I know not how nor wherefore, was not at this bickering. They speake of more then a hundred ensignes and cornets taken; and so much of that matter till you heare it more at large in some pamflet. The Lord Deputie of Ireland is gon with 1200 men to pacifie the countie of Wexford. The Lord President of Mounster hath taken the Erle of Desmond by a practise, and brought in some other rebells, so that there is hope of better quiet in those partes. The Quene was very vehement the last weeke to disgrade some of my Lord of Essex Irish knights, specially such as were made after a certain letter she wrote, that he shold make no more, which arise to some 39, and would touch some of our frendes freehold. It shold have ben don by way of a proclamation, which was signed on Wensday last, but Mr. Secretarie made great meanes to diswade her Majestie from that course, by many reasons, but specially that she shold wrestle with the Great Seale of England, and bringe the authoritie therof in question; wherupon it was suspended, and lies still in the docke, and so like to lie;

for I heare this afternoone that the Erle of Essex is gon to the Lord Kepers, at Yorke House, to appeare before him, the Lord Treasurer and Mr. Secretarie, and there to be discharged of his keper; but yet to kepe his house, and have no more accesse then of his owne people. Mrs. Elizabeth Russell[a] lies at the last cast, and is either dienge or dead. The Lady of Warwick[b] and Cumberland[c] have watched with her by turnes, and geve her over as past hope. If she go she will mend the new brides[d] marriage. I have not seen Wat Cope since I received your letter, and therfore know nothing more of the commission. I presume you shall find him indifferent, for I remember that, upon a word cast out by myself at the first mention of it, he protested that no respect shold carie him beyond his conscience. I heare nothing out of Oxfordshire, nor from Mr. Gent; if I heare not the sooner I may chaunce take another way, for Sir Harry Wallop[e] is in towne, and very earnest to carie me along with him, but I will hold out one weeke longer at least. And so, wishing you more preferment then all the act can afoord you, I take my leave for this time.

From London, this 1st of July, 1600.

      Yours most assuredly,
         JOHN CHAMBERLAIN.

[*Addressed,*]
  To my very goode frend
    Mr. Dudley Carleton
      geve these,
        at Witam, or Englefield.

---

[a] Daughter of John Lord Russell; a god-daughter of Queen Elizabeth. She died the day after the date of this letter.

[b] Her aunt Anne, daughter of Francis Earl of Bedford, widow of Ambrose Dudley, Earl of Warwick.

[c] Margaret, sister to the Countess of Warwick, and wife of George Earl of Cumberland.

[d] Anne (Russell) Lady Herbert, sister to Elizabeth; see p. 83.

[e] Before noticed in pp. 5, 60.

## LETTER XXXIII.

[Domestic Correspondence, State Paper Office, October 10, 1600.]

GOODE MR. CARLETON,

I have missed you so often and so narrowly in the country that I made sure account to have better fortune, and to have founde you here at my comming to towne about the beginning of this weeke, but here I am worse then before, for I cannot learne where nor when to looke after you. This towne is as empty as if it were dead vacation, no body at the Doctors,[a] nobody in Powles, *solitudo ante ostium* in Litle Britain, and all as close and quiet as if it were midnight. I could be melancolike but for certain reliques of a merry progresse that run up and downe in my remembrance, and will not out till they be committed *tutis auribus* and laide up in safe custodie, and therefore I longe for your comming as well for your goode companie as to disburthen my self of many odde stories and adventures. You have ben wisht for more then once, and in more then one place where I have ben, but specially at Knebworth and Farley. Here is litle forrain newes, but only speach of a great blow the French king hath receved in Savoy, but the particulars are not yet knowne. The fable that Sebastian King of Portugall shold be alive is revived and as freshly talked and beleved in the Exchaunge as ever it was, and they say further that the King of Spaine[b] hath lately don great execution in Portugall. The carraques are come home very rich from the East Indies, and so are the Quenes ships that lay for them at the Ilands poore enough. Our marchants are in hand to send fowre very goode ships and two pinnasses to seeke traffique in the East Indies. One Benwoode, an adventurer that hath bath ben out these fowre yeares, and hath

---

[a] Doctor Gilbert; Chamberlain's letters were usually addressed to him at Dr. Gilbert's house, which was on St. Peter's-hill, between Upper Thames-street and Little Knight-Rider-street.
[b] Philip III.

taken great riches in the South Sea, to the value of two millions and better, in his returne homeward was driven to that want that they were faine to eat one another, and forced at last to put into Porto Ricco, where all that were left are taken and theire wealth lost. Out of the Lowe Countries we have nothing at all, but that we wold faine kepe the treaty of peace on foote which otherwise were like enough to fall to the ground. Here is a great ambassador[a] come from Moscovie, who hath not yet had audience, but shall shortly, now the court is settled at Richmond, whether, they say, it came yesterday. The Erle of Essex is here, and at Barne Elmes his frends make great meanes that he may run on the Quenes day,[b] and are very confident to see him shortly in favour; you may beleve as much of it as you list, but I nere a whit; for, till I see his licence for sweet wines renewed (that expired now at Michaelmas), or some other substantiall favour aunswerable to it, I shall esteem words as winde and holy water of court. The Erle of Southampton and the Lord Gray are come out of the Lowe Countries unhurt, though it were constantly reported they had fought and spoiled ech other. We heare that Sir Robert Mansfeld and Sir John Heydon, two Norfolke knights, have slaine[c] one another in the feild. It shold seem by the number and the manner of theire hurts (the one having sixe and the other foure) that they ran at tilt with theire rapiers. It is every day expected that Sir John Stanhop shalbe made Chancellor of the Duchie. Sir W. Raleigh hath ben in Gersey to take possession of his newe government. His lodgings at Durham House were almost burned the other day with fire that

[a] Gregory Ivanowich Meklin arrived in London September 18, 1600, received audience October 14; took leave at Court May 13, 1601. [Nichols's Prog. of Queen Eliz. iii. 515; and Letter XXXIX.]

[b] November 17th, the day of Elizabeth's accession, when there was always a Tilt, or Running at the Ring.

[c] They were not mortally wounded: see Letter XXXIV. p. 92. The full particulars of this duel will be found in the Gentleman's Magazine for 1853, vol. xxxix. pp. 481—483, vol. xl. p. 51. Sir William Heydon was afterwards called "Heydon with one Hand," and his dissevered hand is still preserved in the public museum at Canterbury.

began in the stables. A peece of the south battlements of Powles fell downe lately and kild a carmans horse without doing more harme. Here were five or sixe souldiers hangd the last weeke in divers quarters of this towne for running from their captaines. Sir Antony Sherly with his Persian ambassage is gon into Germanie to the Emperor and other Princes to sollicite a legue against the Turke. I can bethincke me of nothing els, so that with my best wishes I commit you to God.

From London this 10th of October, 1600.[a]

Yours most assuredly,

JOHN CHAMBERLAIN.

[*Addressed,*]
 To my very goode frend
  Mr. Dudley Carleton
   geve these,
    at Ricot or elsewhere.

---

LETTER XXXIV.

[Domestic Correspondence, State Paper Office, October 15, 1600.]

GOODE MR. CARLETON,

It seemes you had ben kept longe fasting that could finde such taste in those poore occurrents I sent you. At my first comming hither all was fish that came to net, and I bestowed it as freely as it came, which, seing it was so welcome, I wold faine second with the like; but, whether it be that I am not so sharp set as I was, or that the market affoords it not, methinckes, though here be more store of companie, yet here is lesse provision in that kinde, and therefore you must be content with a shorter pittaunce. The Moscovie Ambassador went yesterday to Court; I cannot learne

[a] The answer to this letter is in Dom. Corr. State Paper Office, October 13, 1600.

yet what passed; but the hall and chambers were very richly hanged, and great preparation made to receve him royally. The Barbarians[a] take theire leave some time this weeke to go homeward, for our marchants nor marriners will not carrie them into Turkie, because they thincke it a matter odious and scandalous to the world to be too frendly or familiar with infidells; but yet it is no small honor to us that nations so far remote and every way different shold meet here to admire the glory and magnificence of our Quene of Saba. Mr. Edmunds[b] man is come out of the Lowe Countries with letters, but yet I heare not whether our peace halt or walke upright. There is a speach that the King of Spaine is sickly and unlike to have children, and that the Archduke[c] shold go into Spaine. The Duke of Savoyes two eldest sonnes are sent thether already to be brought up. We wold faine persuade ourselves that Fraunce and Spaine are falling out, and devise many tales and reasons to confirme it, but I doubt those old fencers had so late triall one of another that they will brawle a goode while before they fall to blowes, specially the Pope interposing himself (as he doth) with all earnestness to compound this difference of Savoy; and the patriarch or generall of the friers (that patcht up the peace at Vervins) running so often betwene them. The French King sent Mons. Le Grand, with 50 gentlemen of marke and 50 ladies, to fetch his bride,[d] who is thought to be arrived in Fraunce longe ere this time. Sir Harry Nevill[e] hastened to go thether again, and it is thought some greater man shalbe sent shortly to congratulate these nuptialls. Mons. de Rohan,[f] a great man in Britain and heire to the kingdom of Navarre, *cum pertinentiis*, (if

---

[a] Muly Hamet Xarife, ambassador from Abdola Wayhet Anowne, King of Barbary, arrived at Dover August 8, 1600, and received audience on the 20th. [Nichols's Prog. of Queen Eliz. iii. 516.]
[b] Thomas Edmondes.   [c] Albert of Austria.
[d] Marie de Medicis.   [e] The Ambassador to the King of France.
[f] The Viscomte de Rohan, and his brother, Mons. de Soubise, applied for their passport October 29. [Dom. Corr. State Paper Office.]

the King and his sister die without issue,) is come hither out of the Lowe Countries in his way homeward. Sir Noell Charon[a] is likewise returned thence, being sent thither by the Quene, either with some project touching this peace, or, as others say, to pacifie certain differences and dissensions that were saide to be among the States. They devise many shiftes there to make money, and among the rest an imposition by polle of a guilden *pour teste*. The ennemie hath increased his gallies to the number of eight, and the States have built a galeasse, a great slugge to lie like a bulwarke in the channell before Sluce. The Erle of Essex kepes much here in towne, fed with hope that somewhat will follow, but the licence for sweet wines lies at anchor aloofe, and will not come in. They say the Lord North is once more shakinge handes with the world. Sir Arthur Gorge[b] had a shrewde windfall the last weeke: his daughter, the great heire, (for whom he shold have had eight thousand pound of the Erle of Pembroke, or, as others say, ten thousand of the Lord Thomas,[c]) died on Friday, and the land returnes to the Viscount Binden.[d] Word comes now that our Norfolke knights are scant dead, though they had double the number of wonndes that I wrote you.[e] It is written out of Ireland that the Lord Deputie hath taken the fort of the Moirie, and is not yet returned from the North. The Lord President of York[f] lies here still, and hath leave to tary all this winter. I understand that Litle Britain must lie desolate, like a place for owles and ostriches, all this term. Your brother Williams told me yesterday that M<sup>rs</sup>. Alice[g] hath ben lately in Oxfordshire, and newly returned. I had almost forgot to tell you (if you knowe it

[a] Noël de Caron; returned on the 12th. [Domestic Correspondence, State Paper Office.]
[b] Married Douglas, daughter and heiress of Henry Howard, second Viscount Bindon. [Dugdale, ii. 275.] A daughter of this marriage is the lady whose death is here referred to.
[c] Howard.
[d] Thomas Howard, third Viscount Bindon, K.G.; died 1610.
[e] See Letter XXXIII. p. 89.
[f] Lord Burghley.            [g] Alice Carleton.

not alredy) that Mr. Gent is gon over for three or fowre monethes into Fraunce. And so I commit you to God.
From London, this 15th of October, 1600.

Yours most assuredly,
JOHN CHAMBERLAIN.

[*Addressed*,]
To my assured frend
    Mr. Dudley Carleton
        geve these,
            at Englefield.

## LETTER XXXV.

[Domestic Correspondence, State Paper Office, October 21, 1600.]

GOODE MR. CARLETON,

I had aunswered your letter* this morning, but for your cousen Lytton, who, being to go out of towne, not only trifled out the time himself, but made me such a trifler that I doubt I shall come short of your messenger. Your cousen wilbe here again on Monday, and bringes his sonne William to see my Lorde Mayors pageant and these uncouth ambassadors. The Barbarians were yesterday at Court to take theire leave, and wilbe gon shortly; but the eldest of them (which was a kind of priest or prophet) had taken his leave of the world and gon to prophecie *apud inferos*, and to seeke out Mahound their mediator. Here is no forraine newes at all, but a saying that Ostend shold be besieged and two forts built upon the water to take away the haven, and that Grave Maurice shold geve great wordes that he will visite Flaunders once more and venture to relieve it, but the time of the yeare (besides other circumstances) make it unprobable. The world sayes Sir Edward Norris foresaw these tempests, and, like a wise pilot, provided to kepe himself and

* Of October 19. See Domestic Correspondence, State Paper Office.

his in safe harbour, for, as the matter is used, the towne is now held scant tenable. Sir Henry Nevill[a] is urged to returne into Fraunce, but he makes many excuses and so resolute resistaunce that he pretends he will not backe again unles he be sent *pieds et poings lier*. The Lord Deputie of Ireland[b] makes great meanes to be revoked, which is thought shalbe the sooner graunted to make roomme for Sir George Carie[c] to succeed him. We have a constant report that the Lord Keper[d] shall marrye or (as some say) hath maried the Countesse Dowager of Darbie[e] on St. Lukes day last, (God send him goode lucke!) and that his sonne[f] shall marrie the second daughter, or as others say the Lady Straunge,[g] which were a straunge match. Dr. Cæsar was in full cry for three or fowre dayes to be Master of the Rolles,[h] but now the voice runs with Serjeant Heale. Belike the Lord Keper mistrustes the holding of it and wold make frendes with the meetest mammon. The Chauncellorship of the Duchie likewise is not setled as it was, for now Secretarie Harbert and Sir Edward Stafford are in the same balance. Thus hoping to see you shortly, I take a short leave.

From London, this 21th of October, 1600.

Yours most assuredly,

[*Addressed,*]   JOHN CHAMBERLAIN.

To my very goode frend
   Mr. Dudley Carleton
      geve these,
         at Englefeild.

[a] The ambassador to the King of France.   [b] Lord Mountjoy.
[c] Carew, President of Munster.
[d] Sir Thomas Egerton.
[e] See Note to Letter XX. p. 52.
[f] Sir John Egerton; created Earl of Bridgewater May 27, 1617; died December 4, 1649. [Dugdale, ii, 414.] He married Frances, daughter of Ferdinando Stanley, fifth Earl of Derby. [Ibid. 251.]
[g] Anne, oldest daughter of the Earl of Derby; married Grey Brydges, fifth Lord Chandos. [Ibid.]
[h] He was not appointed to that office until September, 1614.

## LETTER XXXVI.

[Domestic Correspondence, State Paper Office, Dec. 22, 1600.]

GOODE MR. CARLETON,

The letter you left for me was not delivered till Thursday at night, too late to send the inclosed for Mr. Allen by the way of Askot as you wished, so that I thought best to convay it the next morning by the carrier of Oxford. The French King[a] kept the solemnitie of his marriage[b] at Lions the 23th of the last, and saw not the great Duchesse nor the Duchesse of Mantua, who went into Lorraine another way, because they espied his humour that he lingered at the campe for the nonce only to avoide charges and geve them no presents. His miserie and ambition is much misliked of all, and the clergie will in no wise be well perswaded of him. He was so desirous and hastie to see his Quene, that he went disguised as a private gentleman with others (that he had appointed) to see her dine, and caused a letter from himself to be delivered her in his presence (unknowne yet), which she receved with such humblenes that it was praised of every body and pleased him not a little. He could not tarry the solemnity, but went that night to her unknowne, and one of his minions demaunding what he meant, told him he went to do that he never did in his life, to lie that night with an honest woman. But wold you thincke that precedence[c] for place is as much esteemed by women in Fraunce as in England, and that Madame de Fresné and Madame de Chambourg, two great ladies, at theire first enterview before the Quene fought and scratcht one another cruelly? The King is in a manner possest

[a] Henry IV.
[b] With Marie de Medicis.
[c] Carleton made this note on the margin:—"They were to take place *selon la date de leur impression.*"

of all Savoy; the last place he tooke was St. Cateline, a fort built to bridle Geneva, whether Beza came to see him, in hope he wold have left the fort to the towne; but the King meant no such matter, yet used him well and gave him 300 crownes. The Duke of Savoy is retired into Piedmont to stay the inroads there, which the King hath procured by sending 3,000 French to harrie the country and fortify some small places for this winter time. The Pope labours by all meanes to make a peace for the Duke of Savoy, and is thought will effect it in this sort, that the King shall have 800,000 crownes for his charges, and render Savoy, and the Pope will become paymaster for the mony, having (they say) contrived a marriage for his niece with the Dukes eldest sonne. It may be you have heard all or the most part of this alredy, but I measure you by myself that am never cloyed with particulars. We heare out of Poland that the Chauncellor with an army of 20,000 choise men shold be *casus ad internecionem* by the Vaivode of Walachia, and not above eight escaped of all that number. The Moscovite Ambassador hath buried one of his men and sent him with a letter to seeke St. Nicolas. Here is a whispering that Don Sebastian, the revived King of Portugall, shold be secretly at the coort, but *credat Judæus Apella*. The Lord Deputie of Ireland is gon Northward, either to revitaile his new fort or upon some other goode intelligence. He lately made three new knights, a sonne[a] of Sir John Fortescues, Rotherham[b] of Bedfordshire, and one Captain Berry.[c] We have an uncertain rumour of treasure come thether out of Spaine, with powder and munition and armes for 4,000 men. Some of the Quenes ships are making redy to looke after the Spaniards that are comming for the Lowe Countries, but I thincke they will do no more to them, though they shold fall in theire mouth. The

---

[a] Sir William Fortescue ; knighted at Drogheda, November 17th, 1600. [Knights made in Ireland, published by Sir Thomas Phillipps.]

[b] Sir John Rotherbam, knighted November 17th, 1600. [Ibid.]

[c] Sir Benjamin Berry, knighted November 19th, 1600. [Ibid.]

Scottish King hath another sonne:[a] we listen still for newes from thence as if there were some tempest abrewing. Sir William Evers hath ben tampering that way whatsoever it is, wherupon he was sent for up and first committed to his owne lodging with a man of Mr. Secretaries[b] to attend him; then was he set over to one Harvy that executes the lieutenancie of the ordinaunce for Sir George Carew, and it is feared he will kisse the Towre in the end. Our East Indian viage goes slowly forward; I doubt they wilbe prevented, and theire market marred by the Hollanders or Frenchmen that are setting foorth fowre ships thether from St. Malos. We heare of divers ships laden with wines cast away comming from Bordeaux. The Court is setled here for all Christmas. Mr. Secretarie entertaines the Quene this day to dinner at his lodging in the Savoy, if the appointment hold, as it hath already failed twise. He hath set his witts and frendes aworke to geve her all contentment, and to receve her with all fine and exquisite curiosity. The Lord Norths funerall is kept this day at Powles.[c] The Countesse of Essex is lately brought to bed of a daughter. Mrs. Pranell[d] is like to make a wide stride from that she was, to be Countesse of Hartford; the world sayes they be assured alredy, if not maried. Sir Henry Killegre[e] maried a daughter[f] the last weeke to one Seymour of Devonshire. There was a great commission at Lambeth the other day about the controversie twixt Alderman Banning[g] and his wife; the Lord Archbishop,[h] the Lord Admirall,[i] the Lord Cham-

[a] Prince Charles, born 19th November, 1600.   [b] Sir Robert Cecil.
[c] Roger second Lord North, K.G. buried at Kirtling, Dec. 22. [Dugdale, ii. 394.]
[d] Daughter of Thomas Howard, third Viscount Bindon, widow of Henry Pranell, vintner, of London; married secondly to Edward Seymour, Earl of Hertford; and lastly to Lodovick Stuart, Duke of Richmond and Lenox. [Dugdale, ii. 274.]
[e] Sir Henry Killegrew of Lathbury, Cornwall.
[f] Dorothy, married to Edward Seymour, who was knighted May 22, 1603, and died October 5, 1659. [Brydges's Collins, j. 193.]
[g] Paul Bayning, father of Paul created Baron and Viscount Bayning by Charles the First. He was Sheriff of London in 1593.
[h] John Whitgift.
[i] The Earl of Nottingham.

berlain,[a] and divers other of the Counsail were of it. The world expected great matters of such an autenticall hearing, but in conclusion the woman scaped better cheape then was looked for, having only sentence of separation *a mensâ et thoro*. Sir Robert Drury is committed to the custodie of Alderman Saltingstall for speaking and hearing certain buggswords at his being in Fraunce, as is pretended, but this is rather thought to be colour then true cloth. Litle Brittain remembers you with all kindnes. I am going to morrow, God willing, to Knebworth, where I know you wish us a mery Christmas, and we *pour la pareille* will wish you many goode yeares.

From London this 22th of December 1600.

      Yours most assuredly,
        JOHN CHAMBERLAIN.

[*Addressed,*]
 To my assured goode frend
  Mr. Dudley Carleton
   give these
    at the Haghe.

## LETTER XXXVII.

[Domestic Correspondence, State Paper Office, Feb. 3, 1600-1.]

GOODE MR. CARLETON,

Till your letter[b] came that brought your Christmas commendations I looked dayly for you, for so did the housekeper of Puddle wharfe informe my man when he went to learne how I might send to you, and found the letter I wrote before my going to Knebworth[c] not sent away at my returne from thence two or three dayes within

[a] George Lord Hunsdon.
[b] The letter referred to is in Holland Correspondence, Jan. 14, 1600-1.
[c] Letter XXXVI.

the terme, which did quite discourage me, and made me presume that, if I shold write, you would kepe your old wont, and meet it or misse it by the way; and I was the rather perswaded because in yours (otherwise stored with much good matter) you made no mention at all whether you meant to abide at the Haghe, or remove further, or return; but now, upon pause of seven or eight dayes after the receit of your letter, seing I heare no more, will defer no longer, but shoote one arrow after another, and let them take theire fortune. Sir Gerrard Harvy, with his lady, mother, and sisters, kept theire Christmas at Knebworth, where I had much goode companie of his brother John, and ran over many old stories of you and Ostend. Your cousen Lytton is in towne, and tarries all or most part of the terme. Your brother Carleton came yesterday, and your cousen Acton is looked for within two or three dayes to come and sojourn in Litle Brittain. For matter of newes I know not where to begin, unles I shold continue a pettie chronicle from my last, which, though it be somwhat laborious, and perhaps wilbe unwelcom to send you *cramben bis coctam*, yet to punish myself for flattering my idlenes, and seeking to excuse it, I will make it my penaunce. Upon twelft day the Quene feasted the Moscovie ambassador,[a] who hath ben since invited to divers other places, and taken his pleasure abrode in hunting. During the holydayes here was the Duke of Bracciano (cheife of the familie of the Orsini by Rome) that came into Fraunce with the new quene[b] his cousen germane. The Quene entertained him very graciously; and, to shew that she is not so old as some wold have her, daunced both measures and galliards in his presence. He was feasted by the Lord Burleigh for some favor shewed to Will Cecill or his other sonnes at theire being in Italie, and shold have ben by the Lord Treasurer,[c] and by Grayes Inne, that made preparation of shewes to entertain him, but he made such haste away that they were disappointed. The Quene, at his parting, sent him a cup of gold of sixescore pound, and a jewell, for the

[a] Gregory Ivanowich Meklin.    [b] Marie de Medicis.    [c] Lord Buckhurst.

which he gave the bringer, Michaell Stanhope, a chaine of fowrescore pound. He went hence to visite the Archduke [a] and Infanta,[b] leaving behind him the generall report of a very courtlike and compleat gentleman. Somewhat more then three weekes since the Lord Gray and Erle of Southampton had a little bickering in the Strand on horsebacke, for the which the Lord Gray was committed to the Fleet, and hath lien there till yesterday that he was relesed, notwithstanding all the frends he could make. During his restraint the old Countesse of Bedford [c] died, and left him not above 300*l.* The greatest part of her wealth she bequeathed to younge Norris,[d] and yet the world sayes, by that he hath discharged her funeralles and other legacies, there will not be 3,000*l.* left for his share. The Erle of Pembroke [e] died a fortnight since, leaving his lady [f] as bare as he could, and bestowing all on the young lord,[g] even to her jewells. Michaell Heneage died in Christmas, and his office of keping the records in the Towre was promised to Dr. James of the Court, but he followed him within a fortnight after, and now Lambert [h] of Lincolnes Inne hath the executing of it, but not the graunt. In the absence of the Lord Chamberlain,[i] Sir John Stanhope was appointed to serve as Vice-Chamberlain, which most men interpret to be a goode step to the place. One Radney [k] of Somersetshire, nephew to Sir Edward Dyar, was lately knighted; but, whether he were overjoyed with that dignitie, or overawed with the love of Mrs. Pranell (whom he woed and could not obtaine), or, as some say, so doated upon a greater mistris that his braines were not able to beare the burthen, but have plaide banckrout, and left him raving.

[a] Albert of Austria.   [b] Isabella of Spain.
[c] Bridget, daughter of John Lord Hussey, widow of—1. Sir Richard Moryson; 2. Henry Earl of Rutland; and 3. Francis second Earl of Bedford, who died 1585.
[d] Francis, afterwards second Lord Norris of Rycot.
[e] Henry Herbert, second Earl, K.G.; died Jan. 19, 1600-1. [Dugdale, ii. 260.]
[f] Mary, daughter of Sir Henry Sidney. [Ibid.]
[g] William Herbert, third Earl, K.G ; died April 10, 1630. [Ibid.]
[h] Died Oct. 1601. See Letter XLIII.   [i] Lord Hunsdon.
[k] Sir George Rodney. He afterwards committed suicide. See Letter XL. p. 112.

We have great speach of building twelve gallies—fowre by the Quene, two by this Citie, two by Essex, Suffolke, Norfolke, and Lincolnshire, two by Kent, Surry, Sussex, and Hampshire, the rest by Somerset, Devonshire, and Cornwall; for the speach is that the Spaniards are to bring more gallies along with them into the Lowe Countries, and we must learne to fight with them after theire owne fence. It was reported awhile that they were severed by tempest, and twelve or fifteen saile of them cast away on the coast of Ireland, but there is no great credit geven to it. But we heare for certain that two Spanish frigates arrived at Sligo with powder, munition, and mony, to furnish the rebells. The Lord Deputie hath don some pretty exploits of late upon some petty rebells about Dublin, and surprised the castle of one Fellom MacFeof, and taken his children, but himself and his wife escaped very narowly. He hath likewise defeated and slaine the greatest part of the followers of Fellom MacToole, another notable rascall, and taken him prisoner. Sir Richard Wingfeld,[a] the Marshall of Ireland, is lately dead there. We are here coining base money for Ireland, hoping thereby to hinder the rebells from providing theire wants from abrode; but I pray God it worke no worse effect; and some men begin to feare it is but a preparative to purge our owne mony of the best juice. The new fort at Plimmouth was lately defaced and blowne up with powder. The Dunkirkers are very busie all alonge that coast, and take prises even in the very harbour. They stay thereabout to convoy the Spaniards that are comming for the Lowe Countries. Here be Privie Seales for 20,000l. come among the straungers, which mony is to be repaide by the States. We have much speach of a new Master of the Rolles, and it is thought Sergeant Heale bids best for it, but Justice Gawdie,[b] Secretarie Harbert, Dr. Cæsar, the Atturney

[a] Of Northamptonshire; knighted in Ireland by the Lord Deputy Russell Nov. 9, 1595. [Knights made in Ireland, published by Sir Thomas Phillipps.]

[b] Francis Gawdy of Norfolk, puisne judge of the King's Bench; knighted July 23, 1603; Chief Justice of the Common Pleas Aug. 26, 1605.

of the Wardes, the Atturnie of the Duchie, and Thomas Spencer, are in some consideration for it. The matter troubles the Lord Keper very much, for he hath lately had some schooling about it; but it seemes he cares not greatly who gets it so Heale may misse it. The Quene hath made choise of our Doctor[a] for her phisition, but he is not yet sworne. I doubt our colledge wilbe dissolved, and some of us sent to seeke our fortune. Dr. Dove,[b] Deane of Norwich, is made Bishop of Peterborough. The Erle of Rutland and the Erle of Hartford stand in election whether shalbe sent into Fraunce to congratulate with the new quene. Yesterday a sonne[c] of Harry Butlers of Hartfordshire stabd one Russell (a kinsman of my Lord of Bedfords that maried Mrs. Skidmores sister) in my Lordes yard, and he died presently. Butler escaped through the Covent Garden, and is not yet heard of.[d] Your cousen Alford hath maried one Momparson, late husband to the old Lady Dudley.[e] Our Lady Wallop[f] is with child, to the no small joy of all the beholders. I remember nothing els but that the crosse in Cheape is going up, for all your Vice-Chauncellor of Oxford[g] and some other odd divines there have set downe theire censure against it. We have daily here many new experiments made, as the last weeke one came hopping from Charing Crosse into Powles bounde in a sacke, and this morning another caried up a horse and rode upon him on the top of Powles steeple, with divers other such wagers; and, among the rest, Green, that was lately your cousen Lyttons man, hath set up a printed paper, and doth challenge all commers at wrastling. When I was now bidding you farewell yonr brother Carleton

[a] Dr. Gilbert.
[b] Thomas Dove; consecrated Bishop of Peterborough April 26, 1601; died Aug. 30, 1630. [Courthope's Nicolas.]        [c] Henry Butler.
[d] He was taken at Carlisle about Oct. 1602.
[e] Mary, daughter of William Lord Howard of Effingham, K.G. was married first to Edward Lord Dudley, afterwards to Richard Montpesson, esq. [Dugdale, ii. 279.]
[f] Wife of Sir Henry Wallop.
[g] George Abbot, D.D. Master of University college, afterwards archbishop of Canterbury.

comes in and prayes me to put in his commendations, and to tell you that your place in Oxford will tarry for you one yeare more. *Vive vale.*
From London, this third of February, 1600.[a]
Yours most assuredly,
[*Addressed,*] JOHN CHAMBERLAIN.
To my very goode frend
Mr. Dudley Carleton
geve these, at the Haghe,
or elsewhere.

## LETTER XXXVIII.

[Domestic Correspondence, State Paper Office, Feb. 24, 1600-1.]

GOODE MR. CARLETON,
Yours of the 14th [b] of this present found so redy passage that I marvaile how ours at other times stay so longe by the way. This is my fourth [c] letter since the middle of January that I came from Knebworth, besides one I sent at my going thether, and it is straunge to me that our ill newes shold flie so fast as to overtake you in five dayes when our ordinarie letters can not find the way in five weekes. I was out of the way when your letter came, and when the messenger gave warning of his sodain departure, for the covie is now dispersed, and we are driven to seeke our feeding further of, our Doctor [d] being alredy setled in Court, e and I redy to go to Askot, and there and in such like places to lead a country life; so that you must take

[a] In 1601 Chamberlain and Carleton dated their letters according to the civil year— in the previous year they used the historical date.
[b] The Letter referred to is in Holland Correspondence, State Paper Office, Feb. 14, 1601.
[c] Carleton appears to have received only the letter of the 3rd of February. See Holland Correspondence, March 16, 1601.
[d] Gilbert. [e] As physician to the Queen.

a short pittaunce, sith I am so shortened in time. I wrote you in my last as well as I then could the beginning and progresse of our troubles and as many particulars as I could bethincke me of in such huddling haste. No doubt you have many relations there by this time of all that happened, and you must excuse me if I do not ingulfe my selfe into a longe narration without a constant setled winde to carry me through. I do not well remember whether I sent you word of Tom Leas [a] traiterous enterprise to possesse himselfe of the privie chamber, which he communicated to Sir Henry Nevill that maried my Lord Treasurers daughter,[b] and to Sir Robt. Crosse, who revealed him both at once, and he being apprehended confest his meaning was but to have gotten the Quene to have signed a warrant for the noblemens deliverie, wherin if he had found difficultie, he knew not what wold have followed, and those shold have ben guiltie of any harme might come to her, that had hindred his attempt; but at his arraignment, though he were confronted by Sir Robt. Crosse and the rest, yet he stoode to the deniall, affirming his intent to be only to have angred her for one half howre, that she might have lived the merrier all her life after; and in this tune he died the 17th of this present at Tiborne very resolutely, and, to seeming, religiously. The 19th hereof the Erles of Essex and Southampton were arraigned at Westminster before the Lord Treasurer, Lord High Steward of England for that day, and 25 of theire peeres, wherof were 9 erles and 16 barons. The only matter objected were his practise to surprise the Court, his comming in armes into London to raise rebellion, and the defending his house against the Quenes forces. To the two later he aunswered that he was driven for safety of his life, to the former that it was a matter only in consultation, and not resolved upon, and, if it had taken effecte, it was only to prostrate himselfe at her Majesties feet, and

---

[a] Examinations of Captain Thomas Lea are in Domestic Correspondence, State Paper Office, Feb. 13. He was executed Feb. 17, 1600-1.

[b] Mary, daughter of Thomas Sackville, Lord Buckhurst, was married to Sir Henry Neville, son of Edward Lord Abergavenny, and who succeeded to that title in 1622.

there manifest such matters against his ennemies as sholo make
them odious, and remove them from about her person, and recall
him to her former favour. This was the summe of his aunswer, but
delivered with such bravery and so many wordes that a man might
easilie perceve that, as he had ever lived popularly, so his cheife
care was to leave a goode opinion in the peoples mindes now at
parting. But the worst of all was his many and lowde protestations
of his faith and loyaltie to the Quene and State, which no doubt
caught and carried away a great part of the hearers; but I cannot be
so easilie led to beleve protestations (though never so deep) against
manifest proofe, yet I must needes say that one thing stickes much
in many mens mindes that, whereas divers preachers were commaunded the Sonday before to deliver to the people, among his
other treasons, that he had complotted with Tirone, and was reconciled to the Pope; and wheras Mr. Atturney,[a] at Tom Leas[b] arraignment, averred the same combining with Tirone, and that he had prac-
tised by the meanes of seminarie preists with the Pope and the King
of Spaine to be King of England, there was no such matter once
mentioned at his arraignment, and yet there was time enough for it
from nine aclocke in the morning till almost seven at night. At
his comming to the bar his countenance was somwhat unsetled;
but, after he was once in, I assure you I never saw any go through
with such boldnes and shew of resolution and contempt of death;
but whether this courage were borrowed and put on for the time,
or naturall, it were hard to judge. But I heare he begins to relent,
and, among other faults, to acknowledge and be sory for his arro-
gant (or rather, as Mr. Secretarie well termed it to his face), his
impudent behavior at his arraignment, and, which is more, to lay
open the whole plot, and to appeach divers not yet called in question. His execution was expected on Satterday, then yesterday,
now to-morrow,[c] or on Thursday. Most of the counsaile have ben

[a] Sir Edward Coke.  [b] Capt. Thomas Lea.
[c] Wednesday, Feb. 25th.

with him these three or fowre dayes together. The Erle of Southampton spake very well (but we thought somwhat too much as well as the other); and as a man that wold faine live, pleaded hard to acquite himself, but all in vaine, for it could not be, wherupon he descended to intreatie, and moved great commisseration; and, though he were generally well liked, yet methought he was somwhat too low and submisse, and semed too loth to die before a prowde ennemie. Here have yet no more ben brought to triall save nine the next day to the Kinges Bench bar, but six of them were carried back again without triall, and only Sir Edmund Bainham, John Littleton [a] of Worcestershire, and one Capt. Orwell, were condemned but not yet executed, for it is thought my Lord himself shall first lead the way, and then they shall follow thicke and threfold. Yet the generall opinion is, there wilbe no great executions, for the Quene is very gracious, and inclines much to mercy. Since I wrote last, Savill of Eaton, Deane Woode, Dr. Fletcher, Dr. Hawkins, and divers others, are committed to private custodie, and Sir Harry Bronksy [Brounker] to the Towre: it is feared Sir John Scot may follow him. Sheriffe Smith and his wife [b] are likewise in durance, and is thought are in daunger of misprison, once he is set beside his offices and another alderman and another sheriffe chosen in his roome. It may be there be divers other things I shold impart to you if either I had leysure, or that they came redilie to hand, but they can be of no moment, and I have gon beyond that I thought I could have don when I began. Your cousen Lytton is here with his trained band of 300, and other captaines with some 2,000 men of the neighbour shires here about, and we have continuall watch and ward day and night in armes through the citie, and these straungers at court, and places adjoining. I thancke you for your large and liberall letter, but yet I heare not what course you meane to take with yourself;

---

[a] Of Frankley, Worcestershire; condemned for being concerned in the Essex insurrection; died in the King's Bench, 1601. See Letter XLI.

[b] The examinations of Thomas Smith and Sarah his wife are in Domestic Correspondence, State Paper Office, March, 1601.

whether you come backe or go for Italie; which way soever you take I will wish you all prosperitie, and so I end.

From London, this Shrove Tewsday, the 24th of February, 1600.

Yours most assuredly,

JOHN CHAMBERLAIN.

[*Addressed as before.*]

LETTER XXXIX.

[Domestic Correspondence, State Paper Office, May 27, 1601.]

GOODE MR. CARLETON,

I am driven to such straights that I know not what to say but *quid scribam, aut quid non scribam?* The uncertaintie of your stay, my long absence from this towne, the unluckines of my letters to be lost or overlooked, and the difficultie of finding fit messengers, have almost quite discouraged me, and made me a truant *en vostre endroit*, for so will I acknowledge it to you, howsoever to others I could salve and make all whole with passable and pregnant excuses; but with so goode a frend I will never disguise, but tell the plaine troth and (which is worst) without hope of amendes, for I know not how to redeeme that is past with future diligence, being (since the dissolution of our societie [a]) become altogether a countriman, and not appearing here but as a termer. I could dilate longe upon this theme; but, having very short warning of my Lord of Northumberlands departure, I am forced to knit up all I have to say in a narrowe roome and time, and rather acquaint you with particular affaires then any publicke busines, which you may better learne of

[a] The College, which was broken up on Dr. Gilbert's being appointed physician to the Queen.

this bringer,<sup>a</sup> who, as your sisters tell me, is to go this night, and now it is even supper-time, so that you must accept in goode part whatsoever comes next to hand in this hudling haste. Your frends have not ben unmindfull of you, for, upon the first bruit that Mr. Cecill shold go ambassador ligger into Fraunce, your consen Lytton was with him to make your way; but both he, Mr. Bodley, Sir Robert Sidney, Sir Edward Wotton, Sir Thomas Parry, Sir Antony Mildmay, and some others that were named to that place, having flatly refused or avoided it, as yet *sub judice lis est*, which of them, or whether any at all, is to be sent. In the meane time Mr. Winwod supplies the place, and hath the Quenes letters to the French King for his credence. Sir Harry Nevill<sup>b</sup> is in the Towre, which at first made many men thincke he shold come to his aunswer, but, this whole terme having past without any arraigument, makes me thincke there shalbe no more bloud drawne in that cause. The rather for that there is a commission to certain of the counsaile to raunsome and fine the lords and gentlemen that were in the action, and have alredy rated Rutland at 30,000*l*. Bedford at 20,000*l*. Sands at 10,000*l*. Mounteagle at 8,000*l*. and Cromwell at 6,000*l*. Catesby at 4,000 marks, Tresham at 3,000 marks, Percies and Mannors at 500*l*. and 500 marks; the rest at other summes, *et sic de cæteris*. Only my countryman Massam is not yet dispatcht, nor knowes not his paines. Our two new Knights of the Garter, the Erle of Darbie and the Lord Burghley, were installed yesterday at Windsore. The Erle of Marre<sup>c</sup> went away the last weeke, and left behind him the report of a courtly and well-advised gentleman. The Lord Zouch is come out of Gernesey, being sent for, as is thought, to go ambassador into Scotland. The Moscovie ambassador<sup>d</sup> tooke his leave at court on Sonday<sup>e</sup> was sevenight like a daunsing beare, and

---

<sup>a</sup> Mr. Burgoin, a cousin of Carleton's, who went over in the suite of the Earl of Northumberland.
<sup>b</sup> See p. 104.
<sup>c</sup> Ambassador from James VI. of Scotland   <sup>d</sup> Gregory Ivanowich Meklin.
<sup>e</sup> May 13th.

is gon homeward. The Spaniards have taken a rich ship worth 40,000*l*. of our Turkie marchants, comming out of the Levant. There is a commission for a new sale of the Quenes lands. The Lord Cobham hath married the Lady of Kildare, but I heare of no great agreement. Here were latelie 15 or 16 youths of goode houses taken as they were going over to the seminaries. Antony Bacon died not long since; but so far in debt, that I thincke his brother[a] is litle the better by him. I heare that Sir Edward Norris shold be daungerously sicke. He was noted of late to make mony by all meanes possible, as though he had some great enterprise or purchase in his head. The younge Lady Compton is brought a-bed of a sonne, and yet the hardhead, her father,[b] relents nere a whit. I send you here these shreds as patterns, that, by these gentlemens meanes that come over with my Lord of Northumberland, you may match them out of the whole cloth. I go to-morrow to Knebworth, though I came lately thence about the middle of this last terme, being sent for from Askot some three weekes before to meet your cousen and Mrs. Lytton at Farley[c] about a match for my wife,[d] which is since dispatcht with younge Gifford,[e] a kinseman of her owne. She asked me kindly for you, and willed me to remember her to you. Your cousen Lytton, with her two daughters, the Lady Wallop[f] and Mrs. Cary, are all with child, and my cousin Stukeleys wife comes in to make up the messe. Kate Cheyney is toward a husband; and Mr. Edmunds, your good frend, hath married a sole daughter of one Woode, Clerke of the Signet. You see this is a great yeare of wiving and childing; if you were here you were like inough to be in daunger of one of them, and the other not impossible, as Mr. Winwod wrote me lately of a priest at Paris that

---

[a] Sir Francis Bacon.
[b] Sir John Spencer, alderman of London.
[c] In Hampshire, the seat of Sir Henry Wallop, Treasurer of Ireland.
[d] Winifred Wallop, sister to Sir Henry: see before, p. 70.
[e] Sir Richard Gifford of Sombourne, Hampshire.
[f] Elizabeth daughter of Mrs. Lytton by her first husband, Robert Corbet, esq.

is with child at this instant. I know I have forgot many thinges, and put that last that I meant first, but you must *æqui bonique consulere* whatsoever cannot now be amended; and so, wishing you all health and goode hap, and to know how you will settle, and how I may send, I bid you farewell this 27th of May, 1601.

From my lodging at Wingfeld House in more then post haste.

Yours most assuredly,

[*Addressed,*]   JOHN CHAMBERLAIN.

To my assured goode frend
Mr. Dudley Carleton
geve these
at the Haghe,
or elswhere in Holland.

---

LETTER XL.

[Domestic Correspondence, State Paper Office, July 8, 1601.]

GOODE MR. CARLETON,

I am glad you are so well lodged and setled at Paris,[a] where I hope my letters shall have better lucke and meanes to finde you out, for, though you complaine not, yet I must accuse my extraordinarie ill-fortune since your last going over, that though by reason of my absence I wrote not so often, nor, as it were, weekely (as I was wont to do), yet of those I did write I cannot perceve that halfe are come to your handes; and I take the losse of the last[b] more impatiently then the rest which (by your sisters meanes) was committed to Mr. Burgoin that went over with the Erle of Northumberland; for therein I certified you of Sir Edward Norris sicknes, and some other

[a] See Carleton's Letter in the French Correspondence, State Paper Office, July 1, 1601.
[b] Letter XXXIX.

things I was willing you shold know. I wrote not since that time by reason of the uncertainty of your abode, and your brother Carleton (who was here in the terme) made full account you wold be here without faile, which I could have wished had so fallen out, for I perceve by him that Sir Edward is not so thoroughly recovered but that he is in daunger of a relapse, which it were goode you listened after, for, though he had dealt very kindly and bountifully with you if he had gon in his last sicknes, yet I am perswaded your presence had doubled his kindenes, for I presume he had as much confidence in you as in Captain Wainman and Captain Whiddon, whom he had made his executors. I know nothing more in this matter then I had from your brother, who no doubt hath certified you of all to the full if he have written since that time, or els Mr. Bolton,[a] if he be so kinde to deale plainly with you; wherfore in my opinion it were not amisse (if you understand Sir Edward to continue still crasie) to take the first opportunitie or least invitement to come over and be about him; but you are best able to geve yourself counsaile in this case; and I. at my going to Askot within these three or fowre dayes, will learne what I can and geve you advertisement and cause your brother to do the like. Your sister Williams and her crew went to Aldersbrooke[b] in Whitson weeke, so that I saw them not since I delivered my last letter to you to be sent, which (as I say) I am very sory it miscaried, because it conteyned the whole abridgement of my progresse into Hampshire, my wifes marriage,[c] and a great rabblement of such other like matter. It were *post festum* to write you any newes now that Mr. Edmunds hath stored you to the full, and fed you with dainties; yet because sometimes *gratæ divitibus vices*, it may be you will not scorne coarser lutes, but find some taste in sleighter dishes of lesse curiositie and cost. Mr. Bodley sets up his shop against this act at Oxford, and opens his

---

[a] In Domestic Correspondence, State Paper Office, July 11, is a letter from William Boulton to Dudley Carleton, telling him that his master, Sir Edward Norris, had made his will, and left Carleton a lease of 60 pounds a-year and some money.

[b] Near Wanstead.   [c] See Note to Letter XXXIX.

librarie to the number of three or fowre thowsand volumes. Mr. Howson [a] is become vicar of Milton and canon of Christchurch in Mr. Porfiries roome.[b] Dr. Andrewes was installed Deane of Westminster on Satterday [c] last; and, on Sonday night, Mr. Beeston and I supped with him in the hall among the Electors. The Lord Cheife Justice [d] and Mr. Secretarie have taken great paines to compound the quarrell twixt Martin and Davies, which they have effected to the satisfaction of both parts. One Sir [George] Radney,[e] of Somersetshire, (nephew to Sir Edward Dyar) that went out of his witts about Christmas for Mrs. Pranell (lately maried to the Erle of Hartford) comming by the place where she dwells, cut his owne throat as an earnest of his love. Oliver Cromwell,[f] a widower (sonne to Sir Harry [g]), hath maried the Lady Palaviciue. Secretarie Harbert [h] is become a double or treble secretarie, having gotten that of Yorke *in commendam*. The Chauncellorship of the Duchie is like to fall on Sir Edward Stafford. The Lord Mordant,[i] the Lord Norris,[k] and the Lord Willoughby [l] made great haste to overtake one another, and died in few dayes. We had lately a new call of counsaillors, the Erle of Shrewsbury (who is likewise named to be President of Wales), the Erle of Worcester, Master of the Horse, and Sir John Stanhope, Vice-Chamberlain. We understand litle what the campes do at Berke and at Ostend, only it is said Sir Francis Vere shold have put himselfe into Ostend, which I do not easilie beleve, no more then I did a flienge report was current here awhile that at a banquet in the Lowe Countries the Erle of Northumberland had stroken him,

---

[a] John Howson; elected to the bishoprie of Oxford Sept. 12, 1618, translated to Durham Sept. 17, 1628, died Feb. 6, 1631-2. [Courthope's Nicolas.]
[b] John Purefoy, Canon of Christchurch 1588, died May 13, 1601.
[c] July 4th.   [d] Sir John Popham.   [e] See p. 100, note [f].
[f] Of Hinchinbroke; knighted 1598, died Aug. 28, 1655. [Brydges's Collins, ix. 477.]
[g] Knighted 1563; died 1604. Ibid.   [h] John Herbert.
[i] Louis Mordaunt, third Baron; died June 16, 1601.
[k] It will be seen by this, that Dugdale's date of the death of Lord Norris is incorrect.
[l] Peregrine Bertie, Lord Willoughby (of Eresby); died 1601. [Courthope's Nicolas.]

whereas it is most certain they have not met there since theire last going over. You wold litle thincke that Mr. Warcop is still in question to be sent ambassador lidger into Fraunce,[a] which if it so fall out, *quid non speremus amentes?* Sir Henry Nevill was called before the Lords at the Lord Kepers[b] this day, but what fine[c] or other penaltie was imposed upon him I cannot learne. So with all hearty goode wishes, I bid you farewell.

From London, this 8th of July. 1601.

Yours most assuredly,<br>JOHN CHAMBERLAIN.

Mr. Gent, at his going out of towne yesterday, willed me to commend him to you. We shall meet very shortly. God willing, at Askot. If you direct your letters either to my lodging,[d] or to Mr. John Nortons,[e] they will finde me out.

[*Addressed*,]

To my assured goode frend<br>Mr. Dudley Carleton<br>geve these<br>at Paris.

---

## LETTER XLI.

[Domestic Correspondence, State Paper Office, August 13, 1601.]

GOODE MR. CARLETON,

There is sure some adverse planet or malignant constellation that haunts and hangs over my letters now adayes, for, though I be never so provident or carefull for theire conveyaunce, yet it succeeds not, as

---

[a] Sir Thomas Parry was sent thither in 1602.   [b] Sir Thomas Egerton.
[c] The commuted fine amounted to 5,000*l*. [Nichols's Prog. of James I. i. 455.]
[d] At Wingfield House.   [e] A bookseller in London.

(besides others) I perceve now by my last which I wrote at my comming from London, and see no reason but they shold finde as spedy passage as Mr. Gents that were written at the same time. I receved yours of the 24[a] of the last here at Askot, full of varietie and pretty observations; having nothing to requite you and *rendre la pareille*, unles I shold tell you how forward we be in harvest, and what a drie season we have had till now of late, or what a dearth and scarsitie we have here of all manner fruit, but specially of plummes. But, least you shold condemne mine idlenes, or thincke mine affection or invention more drie and barren then the weather, I will force out some fruitles advertisements from this privat abode. Sir Edward Norris and his lady tooke this house in theire way as they came from Englefeild towardes the funeralles[b] at Ricot; they were very well receved here, and had kinde usage. Some sixe or eight dayes after Mr. Dormer and I visited them at Beckley Park, and had goode welcome and ordinarie entertainment; we coursed, and killed, and caried nothing away. At the funerall I heare there was some chopping and lowde speach twixt him and Mr. Controller[c] about the stewardship or some other such place in Sunning, which some thincke had ben better forborne in respect the other came so far to honor the solemnitie. He is still at Beckley, but wold faine remove and borrow Mr. Dormers house at Hampton Poile, either for his pleasure of hawking and hunting, or for that there is some sicknes and light infection amonge his people at the lodge. To tell you my opinion freely in this (as I use in all thinges els), if I had once more visited him[d] at Englefeild, I thincke I shold take my farewell, for I am nothing fond of his favours, *car il tient sa gravité comme un, etc.* His ladies belly is well taken downe, but whether it be with hard travaile or diet I know not. We were all the last weeke with Sir Henry Lea at Woodstocke, where we had great sport, and skirmished as fast with our bowes as they do at

[a] I have been unsuccessful in a search for this letter.
[b] Of Lord Norris, on the 5th of August.   [c] Sir William Knollys.
[d] Sir Edward Norris.

Ostend with theire peeces. In Ireland, the Lord Deputie hath fortified upon Lough Sidney, thereby to bringe vittualles more easily to the fort of Blackwater, which he tooke without fight, being abandoned by the rebells, but spoiled and naked of all things; and some say we be gon further, and have taken Dongannon. Dr. Latware [a] had ill lucke to be slaine there with a shot in an obscure scarmouch. John Littleton [b] is lately dead in the Kinges Bench, wherby the Lord Thomas Howard hath lost a goode raunsome. The Quene is come to Windsore, and is expected shortly at Mr. Comptrollers [c] at Causham, and so the progresse shold hold on as far as Litlecot, a house of the Lord Cheife Justice [d] in Wiltshire, but there be so many incounters to hinder it, that I will lay no great wager of the proceding. I am going to-morrow toward Hampshire, to gossip with my Lady Wallop, lately brought to bed of a sonne, and so forward to my wifes [e] to see how she is accommodated of all manner implements; and then am I bound for Harfordshire till toward the terme for ought I know. Thus I set you downe my gistes, for want of matter of more moment. Mr. Dormer, his lady, and Mr. Gent commend them to you in the kindest manner; and, if you will do as much for me to Mr. Winwood, I have no more to say at this time, but God save you.

Askot, this 13th of August, 1601.

Yours most assuredly,<br>
JOHN CHAMBERLAIN.

[*Addressed as before.*]

[a] Chaplain to the Lord Deputy Mountjoy.
[b] He was condemned for being involved in the Essex conspiracy: see p. 106.
[c] Sir William Knollys.   [d] Sir John Popham.
[e] Winifred wife of Sir Richard Gifford: see pp. 70, 109.

## LETTER XLII.

[Domestic Correspondence, State Paper Office, Sept. 19, 1601.]

Mr. Carleton,

I aunswered your letter of the 24th of July from Askot, where I since receved another of yours of the fift of August,[a] at my returne from my Hampshire progres, the progresse wherof is not worth the writing, save only that I came to the churching of my Lady Wallop, who is not a litle prowde of her litle boy, and visited mine old wife [b] at her new home, where she playes the huswife out of crie, but will have much ado to bringe that riotous and disordred house into any order, yet her vertue will shine the more if she can bring light out of darkenes, or alter the frame of that confusion into any reasonable government. Once the place and state of that living is worthie of her travaile, and I do not greatly dispaire of the successe, having so kinde and tractable a husband [c] towards her, and one that makes very much of her, wherof I take no small comfort, and the more for that it is thought she is prettily forward with child, though I need not bragge nor boast of it. I visited likewise my niece St. John, newly brought a bed, and my niece Siukeley, that lookes very shortly, and now I am come hither to Knebworth, where your cousen Lytton [d] is redy to ly downe, and lookes howerly; so that this hath ben a gossipping journey, and full of increase. The Quene is now in progres as far as Basing, a house of the Lord Marques,[e] where she entertained your Frenchmen [f] with all favour and gracious usage. I cannot tell you the particulars, for I was nothing neere. Our frend the Sheriffe of Barkshire [g] was almost out of hart at the first newes of the Quenes comming into the country, because

---

[a] The letter referred to is in the French Correspondence, State Paper Office.
[b] See note, p. 70.
[c] Sir Richard Gifford.
[d] Mrs. Rowland Lytton.
[e] Of Winchester.
[f] Maréchal de Biron and his suite.
[g] Samuel Backhouse. [Nichols's Prog. iii. 567.]

he was altogether unacquainted with courting,[a] but yet he performed it very well and sufficiently, being exceedingly well horsed and attended, which wan him great commendation on all sides. The Quenes first remove from Windsor was to Mr. Wardes, then to Reding. During her abode there she went one day to dinner to Mr. Controllers [b] at Causham. Mr. Green, Sheriffe of Oxfordshire, met her at the bridge very well accompanied. Mr. Controller made great chere, and entertained her with many devises of singing, dauncing, and playing wenches, and such like. At her going thence she made three knights, your cousen Sir Francis Goodwin,[c] Sir Edmund Fettiplace [d] and Sir Richard Warde; but what need I trouble you with these thinges when your brother was there in person, who can relate all at large, *et quorum pars parva fuit*, for I imagine his small troupe was halfe drowned in the sea of such shewes as the Oxfordshire men made when Sir Antony Cope, Sir Richard Wainman, and the rest set up all theire sailes, and Mr. Dormer, for his part, came with ten or twelve men well mounted. Two or three dayes after the Quene dined with Sir Edward Norris at Englefeld, where I heard of no wonders, but that she knighted Sir Rhead Stafford and his ladies father. Some do much marvaile that he wold be the meanes to make such a Sir John Norris From thence the Quene removed to Sir Humfry Fosters,[e] and so meant to have gon on to the Lord Chiefe Justices [f] and the Erle of Hartfords [g] if these Frenchmen had not staide her, but now I thincke she be at the farthest for this yeare, and they say is drawing back to Windsore, where at her last being I forgot to tell you that

---

[a] *i.e.* with the duties and services of a court.
[b] Sir William Knollys.
[c] Of Buckinghamshire; M.P. for that county, 1604; High Sheriff, 1624 [Nichols's Prog. iii. 567.]
[d] Of Bedfordshire. [Ibid. 568.]
[e] Sheriff of Berkshire 1594. [Ibid.]
[f] Littlecote, the seat of Sir John Popham : see p. 115.
[g] At Elvetham, Hampshire. [Ibid. 568.]

she made a step to Mr. Atturneys [a] at Stoke, where she was most sumptuously entertained and presented with jewells and other gifts to the value of a thousand or twelve hundred pound. This weeke he maried his daughter [b] at London to Sir Thomas Sadlers sonne,[c] of this country, with whom he gave 3,000*l.*, and furnished the feast with all magnificence. The plate geven by frends to the bride came to above 800*l.* We shall have a parliament towards the end of October. I heare that Doctor Parkins is made secretarie for the Latin tongue, and is like to come embassador [d] into Fraunce. We have nothing of late out of Ireland: only Ostend findes us talke, where we have lost many men, among whom Captain Holcroft and Mr. Lucas are of most marke. I did not thincke he had ben there, but it seemes he came too soone. I wold you could have kept him still with you, for he was like to prove a very sufficient man, and is much lamented. Mrs. Bodley [e] hath likewise lost one of her younger sonnes there, and so hath Mr. Poulter. I saw not your brother [f] many a day, nor have we heard how the world goes at London, so that you must take this country pittaunce in goode part, and supplie all the wants with harty goode wishes, and many commendations from your cousen Lytton and my self.

From Knebworth, this 19th of September, 1601.

Yours most assuredly,    JOHN CHAMBERLAIN.

[The following postscript is in the hand of Rowland Lytton:]

I have not fraught for a cole lading, and therefore I will imbarke my commendations in this vessell, adding onely for nues, that since the beginning of this letter my state is mended by the worth of one daughter more which my wife hath brought; and so, with the best wishes of an assured frend and loving kinsman, I committ you to God.    Yours ever soe,

[*Addressed as before.*]    R. LYTTON.

[a] Sir Edward Coke.   [b] Anne.   [c] Ralph Sadler, Esq.
[d] Sir Thomas Parry went thither in 1602.
[e] Anne daughter of Mr. Carew of Bristol, widow of Mr Ball, and wife of Thomas Bodley. [Chalmers's Biog. Dict. v. 469.]   [f] George Carleton.

## LETTER XLIII.

[Domestic Correspondence, State Paper Office, Oct. 31, 1601].

Mr. Carleton,

The last I wrote you was from Knebworth, whence I came eight dayes since, and I brought nothing with me but rheumes and toothaches; and, to mend the matter, find nothing here but subsidies and payments to Ostend, and such other odde reckenings. Our parliament began on Tewsday,[a] whether the Quene went with ordinarie solemnitie. The Recorder of London[b] is Speaker; Dr. Sutcliffe[c] prolocutor of the Convocation; and Dr. Barlow[d] made the *concio ad clerum*. I make no doubt but your eares ringe with the report of the Spaniards landing in Ireland—they are betwene three and fowre thousand under the conduct of Don Juan D'Aguilar (that was in Britain). They fortefie at Kinsale, a haven within ten or twelve miles of Corke. The Lord Deputie[e] is not far from them with 6,000 men, and here be 4,000 foote and 300 horse going with all possible haste to renforce him, besides sixe of the Quenes ships, and as many marchants to kepe them in at sea. In the meane time, Tirone, with 4,000 foot and 700 horse, gallops the pale, and burnes and spoiles where he list. Many of our discoursers geve the Spaniards for lost, and make it a matter of case to defeat them by sicknes, famine, or the sword; for mine owne part, I see not that Spaine is so overladen with people, nor thincke not so meanly of theire wit that they wold wilfully cast them away, or not provide for so open and ordinarie inconveniences. Sir Robert Mansfeld and Sir Amias Preston have brought in sixe Easterlings into the river that came out of Spaine laden with spices and some bullion, which we pretend shold belong to certain Portugalles.

[a] Oct. 27th.  
[b] John Croke of the Inner Temple.  
[c] Matthew Sutcliffe, D.D. the eminent controversialist.  
[d] William Barlow, D.D. Dean of Chester; elected to the bishoprie of Rochester, May 23, 1605; translated to Lincoln, May 21, 1608; died Sept. 7, 1613. [Courthope's Nicolas, 572.]  
[e] Lord Mountjoy.

It comes well to passe if it fall out so in the end; but many doubt they will scant prove goode prise. The Quene sells land still, and the house of St. Johns is at sale.[a] This is all I can tell you of publicke matters, unles the death of Dr. Grant,[b] of Dr. Balgay[c] of the Temple, of old Powle and Lambert of the Chauncerie, of Crompton of the Fine Office, of the Lady Ramsey,[d] of Sir John Davies lady, of divers rich marchants in the citie, and such like, may be referred to a common losse.

My niece Stukeley was lately brought a bed of a sonne; but the joy lasted not longe, for they both vanished soone after. Hugh Beeston had some mishap of late in Cheshire, first, in burieng of his old father, and then in having a quarrell with one Sutton, a desperate cutter of that country, who, in assaulting him, miscarried (by what hand is not certainly knowne), but without all daunger to Mr. Beeston, being in his owne defence. Here is much justling and suing for places in the Privie Chamber, by reason that most of them being growne old, and wearie of waiting, wold faine bring in a successor; as Mr. Killegrew his sonne, Sir Thomas Gorge his cousen Ned, Sir Edward Carie his sonne Phillip; but most voices run with your cousen Mountperson and Wat Cope. Sir Edward Norris lies here in towne, but is not of the parliament. Capt. Whiddon and I meet sometime in Powles, and he wold faine draw me to Puddle wharfe, but I have no inclination to it, for methincks I have *satis superque* of his and such like great acquaintaunce. I looked for your brother[e] yesternight, and I thincke he be a burgesse. We were together last weeke in Knebworth, whether he came accompanied with his case of pistoll boyes. Tobie Mathew is newly come to towne with his lord father,[f] and

---

[a] The house in the priory of St. John's at Clerkenwell, which had been the town residence of her sister Mary before she came to the throne.

[b] Edward Grant, D.D. formerly Master of Westminster School, which post he resigned in 1592; and a prebendary of Westminster.

[c] Nicholas Balgay, D.D. Master of the Temple.

[d] Relict of Sir Thomas Ramsey. She was a munificent benefactress to Christ's hospital, where her picture is preserved. Her funeral is noticed hereafter, p. 122.

[e] George Carleton.   [f] Dr. Toby Mathew, Archbishop of York.

mother. Your cousen Lytton will not be here till next week. They be all well in Litle Britain. If here·be anything worth Mr. Winwods knowledge I pray you impart it to him with my kindest salutations. I wold have written to him if I had more ease or more matter, for I assure you I write now in paine, and therefore without further ceremonies commit you to God.

From London, this last of October, 1601.

Yours most assuredly,

JOHN CHAMBERLAIN.

[*Addressed as before.*]

## LETTER XLIV.

[Domestic Correspondence, State Paper Office, Nov. 14, 1601.]

MR. CARLETON,

I wrote to Mr. Winwod the last weeke, and sent him such poore occurrents as the time affords. I meant to have saluted you likewise, and geven you thancks for yours of the 24th [a] of the last, which came to my hands that weeke, but I could neither find time nor place, unles I shold have crept into some scriveners shop, for Mr. Lytton, whiles he is here, hath so much companie, and so much to do, that he possesseth every corner, so that I am driven to a narrow shift to write now. He hath brought up his sonne William, and placed him at Westminster, and himself stayes the longer in towne about a troublesome busines to get his horse (that he sent for Ireland, and is returned from Bristow as unsufficient) to be seene and allowed. There were certain commissioners appointed to receve and ship them, who were so curious and daintie, that of 50 horse sent by the clergie they returned 28, and of 10 sent out of Hartfordshire refused 6, and so of other countries, with very uncivill and untrue certificats; wherupon the clergie have so followed the cause (that for all the

[a] This letter is in the French Correspondence, State Paper Office.

difficultie of discountenancing commissioners) they have theire horses reviewed here, and sent backe upon theire charges that refused them; and Mr. Lytton hopes for the like conquest, for he stands much upon his reputation in these points. We have not a word out of Ireland, the wind stands so full in theire teeth, which I hope hath carried our ships thether by this time unles they loyter too much at Plimmouth. The Duke of Lenox, after twise or thrise putting off, was at Court on Wensday. The Parliament huddles in high matters, only they have had a cast at Osbornes office, to correct and amend it at least, but there is no great hope of successe. The Alpha and Omega is concluded alredy—I meane the graunt of fowre subsidies and eight fifteens. Dr. Bond[a] hath heard of his old ruddockes again, and recovered all saving fourty pound. A fellow of his owne house, Dr. Humfries[b] youngest sonne, and a townesman were the actors. The younge Erle of Desmond died here the last weeke. The Lady Ramsey[c] was buried on Thursday at Christchurch; and, at her sixepeny dole kept at Leaden Hall, the number of beggers was so excessive and unreasonable that seventeen of them were thronged and trampled to death in the place, and divers sore hurt and bruised. Sir Samuel Bagnoll hath his government of the Newrie taken from him by the Lord Depntie of Ireland, and Sir Gerrard Harvy hath lost his companie with too longe absence from thence. Sir Calisthenes Brooke is made Colonell of sixe companies of English at the seige of Bolduke by his Excellencie. Massam lies still in the Marshallsea because he will not pay the fine imposed upon him for the Erle of Essex action. He pretends that he had compounded for 200 with Mon[sr] Crequires mistris to have his *quietus est*, and had paid the mony, wherupon he presented his complaint to the counsaile table against her and somebody els; but all the remedie he hath is, that his mony is restored as but borrowed, and hath driven her to make an apologie that goes up and downe in writing. I had almost

[a] Probably Nicholas Bond, D.D. President of Magdalen College, Oxford, and Vice-Chancellor of the University 1590; died 1607-8. [Birch MSS. No. 4,173.]
[b] Lawrence Humphrey, D.D. who died 1 Feb. 1589.   [c] See p. 120.

forgot to aske you what those Poukes or Pouges waters are, for I never heard more or lesse of them then by your former letter. Here hath ben much speach, and among the great ones, that the Mareshall Biron shold have committed a fowle outrage, and slaine a president; but, because neither you nor Mr. Winwod make any mention of the matter, I thincke it a mcere fable, though methinckes so great a smoke shold not rise without some fire. I shold geve you many thanckes for your pamflets, which are very welcome, and stand me in goode stead, but I will reserve them till our meeting; and in the meane time wish you all health and goode hap.

London, this 14th of November, 1601.

Yours most assuredly,

JOHN CHAMBERLAIN.

[*Addressed as before.*]

## LETTER XLV.

[Domestic Correspondence, State Paper Office, Jan. 10, 1601-2.]

GOODE MR. CARLETON,

I shold have geven you thanckes before this time for your first letter,[a] but that I was still in hope of your comming, which your cousen Lytton and I expected with great devotion, both for your goode companie, and to have heard the particulars of these late services, wherof your last of the 5th of this present[b] hath fully satisfied us. We had heard a noise and uncertain bruit of something don,[c] which made us the more impatient till we might learne the truth, for, with much disputing and discoursing at all adventures, we so hammered out the matter and the manner that we had almost

---

[a] After Carleton returned to England. [See Domestic Correspondence, Dec. 29, 1601.]

[b] See Domestic Correspondence, State Paper Office.

[c] A victory gained over the Spanish and Irish before Kinsale. [See Irish Correspondence, State Paper Office, Jan. 1.]

wearied our wits, so that your relation came in goode time to relieve us and settle the controversie. Besides, you deale so liberally with us every way, that I know not how to requite it either in deede or worde, for (as one saide in another case) *leves gratiæ loquuntur, ingentes stupent;* but yet, to incourage your well doing, I will only tell you that your letters are exceeding welcome to your cousen Lytton; and that with one labour you deserve double thanckes, and serve two pigeons with one beane. This place affoords no novelties. We passed the Christmas with the ordinarie courses, only one thing was very straunge and extraordinarie in this countrie, that was a nest of younge ravens, which may be added to the wonders of this season. Of all this house only Mr. Lytton and a maide or two perceved the earthquake [a] on Christmas eve, myself and the rest found no alteration. I have nothing now to write to Mr. Gent, but only thanckes for his bookes, and to pray him to commend me to Askot, where I wold gladly know how they do. I send this by the little pursuivant Will Lytton,[b] who returnes to his taske. Commend me to your good self, and all our frends; and so I commit you to God.

From Knebworth, this 10th of January, 1601.

Yours most assuredly,

JOHN CHAMBERLAIN.

[*The address is wanting.*]

## LETTER XLVI.

[Domestic Correspondence, State Paper Office, April 26, 1602.]

SIR,

Your packet [c] was the first frend I met with at my comming to towne on St. Georges day; and it was the more welcome for that I

---

[a] Carleton mentions the shock in his letter of Dec. 23.
[b] Son of Rowland Lytton and pupil at Westminster School.
See French Correspondence, April 7, 1602.

had ben so longe fasting, and found therin such plentie and varietie. I am glad you had so short and safe a passage,[a] which I made account you could not want, cariong so many goode wishes alonge with you. I met your brother[b] here the next day after my comming, who told me Sir Edward Norris is in towne. Mr. Gent is not yet come, but wilbe here shortly. Many other frends are missing that we looke for daily. I went to Knebworth some fowre or five dayes after your departure, where we found a sad and sorrowfull house,[c] and I led a mournefull life; but, by the helpe of the bookes you left with me, I made shift to convert a goode part of my melancholie into devotion. Your cousen Lytton did all he could to bend himself, and to put on sometimes a philosophicall sometimes a Christian resolution, yet his patience was not of proofe to beare out such a triall, but that many times it failed him when he had most neede. We found him very much dejected, and altogether out of taste with any comfort that could be affoorded him; yet many wholesome cordialls went downe without relish at unawares that have since had goode operation, and I doubt not but the approved medicine of time will worke as well with him as with others. The funerall was performed very orderly, and with goode solemnitie, and the more by Mr. Clarencieux[d] frendly presence, who came from the buriall of the Lady Barrington unlooked for and unrequested, but went not empty away as he pretended, and wold needes have done. Your frend Christians brother hath buried his faire younge wife; and the Lord Delaware[e] is lately dead, and some say the Lord Stafford.[f] Many die here almost sodainly, as Cawoode the printer,[g] and two or three more of my knowledge. Here were three seminarie priests hangd and quartered the last weeke, but what is that among so many? Captaine Heine (Mrs. Fowlers mignon) was hangd lately

[a] To France.  
[b] George Carleton.  
[c] Mrs. Lytton died Feb. 23, 1601-2.  
[d] William Camden.  
[e] Thomas West, Lord De la Warr.  
[f] Edward Lord Stafford died in 1603, according to Nicolas.  
[g] Gabriel Cawood, son of John the Queen's printer, and master of the Stationers' Company in 1592 and 1599. [Nichols, Lit. Anecd. iii. 587.]

in Smithfeld for killing his fellow prisoner in the Fleet, and they say blazoned her armes at the gallowes very brodely; but, as one shrewd turne seldome comes alone, much about the same time her brother Boughton, that served the Archbishop of Cannterbury, was stabd and kild in a brabble at bowles by his Lords page (a sonne of Sir Thomas Willfords) with the bishops owne knife. The youth is escaped, but the archbishop takes it so greviously that the Quene herself was faine to come and comfort him at Lambeth. Will Cope was maried in Easter weeke to his mother-in-lawes daughter,[a] and the Lord St. Johns heire [b] to a daughter of the Lady Fines.

Your French gallants were gon before I came to towne; these have somewhat mended the matter, and redeemed the rascall report that Biron and his traine left behinde them, for I heare theire cariage well commended, especially the Duke of Nevers, saving that the Quenes musicians and other inferior officers complaine that he was very drie-handed. The Quene graced him very much, and did him the favor to daunce with him. We heare he is gon into Holland, and so to the Duke of Cleve, his kinsman. Sir Fra. Vere is here solliciting for men. He sent his forerunners before him, who came downe into the country with the counsailes letters to take up voluntaries; but, in most places, with drumming and all they could do, they scant got two men in three dayes, so that, seing it will not fadge that way, it is said we shall have a presse, and send him away with 3,000 men. I heard but yesternight that my Lord of Northumberland had put him a question, and that he aunswered it

---

[a] William eldest son of Sir Anthony Cope (and afterwards the second baronet 1615) married Elizabeth daughter and sole heir of Sir George Chaworth of Wiverton, Notts. His father Sir Anthony's second wife was Anne daughter of Sir William Paston, and had been previously married, first to Sir George Chaworth, and secondly to Sir Nicholas L'Estrange of Hunstanton. [English Baronetage, 1741, i. 118.]

[b] Oliver afterwards fourth Baron St. John 1618, created Earl of Bolingbroke 1624, died 1646. His wife was Elizabeth, daughter and heir of William Paulet of Ewaldon, co. Bedford, by Elizabeth daughter and coheir of Henry Codenham, a Londoner, and widow of Richard Fiennes, Lord Saye and Sele (?). [Dugdale's MS. additions to his Baronage, in Collectanea Topogr. et Geneal. ii. 205.]

home. If I can learne what it was you shall have it in my next.
We talke of 3,000 men likewise to goe presently for Ireland. The
last newes we heard thence was that the Lord Deputie came very
sicke of a colde and a fluxe to Dublin, and that he prepared upon
his amendment to go against Tiron. 500 of the Mounster rebells
have gotten into Beere Haven, where they have all provisions and
five peeces of ordinaunce. They brag that they will kepe the place
till they heare out of Spaine, whether they have sent for succours.
Sir George Carew and the Erle of Tomond are gon to see if they
can ferret them out. I heare much talke of three prises taken by a
ship of Sir John Gilberts (with two or three more in consort) as
they were comming out of the mouth of the river of Lisborne; two
of them were laden with corne, munition, and monie, for the pay
and provision of a garrison towne on the coast of Africke. The
other was a ship of 500 tunne, very rich of pepper, sugars, and other
rich commodities, besides 300 weight of perle. The Italians lay a
coulorable claime to the best part of this lading, which, if it prove
prize, is assuredly thought will amount to almost an hundred thousand pound. I can write you nothing of your Lord Ambassador,[a]
for I have not ben abrode since I came, further then Powles, or Sir
Henry Wallops, where your cousen Lytton lies all this terme with
his three litle daughters, and where you were very kindly remembred yesternight from all sides. If here be anything worth Mr.
Winwods knowledge, I pray you impart it, and excuse me to him
till the next weeke, when he shall heare of me if I can light upon
anything worth the sending. I have had but one day since my
comming to towne to do my necessarie busines and visite frends.
Touching your Catholique sister,[b] I know not what to write nor
what to thincke, she is so irresolute and inconstant, and yet peevish
and wilfull *au bout*. She doth exercise herself and her frends

[a] Sir Thomas Parry.
[b] I have been unable to discover which sister this was, but Carleton in one of his letters calls her the proselyte widow. She did not become a convert to the Church of Rome, though there was much talk of her intention of doing so.

very much, and hath raised many tragedies since you went. The
worst is, she vexes Mr. Williams so that he growes weary of her;
and she is become so cunning, and hath profited so well in that
schoole of dissimulation, that she sayes, if it had not ben for that she
told you and me of Valentine all had ben well, which, seing they
know not, there is no reason they shold watch or restrain her. Your
paltrie niece is the instrument and the bellowes that hath kindled
this unnaturall heat among them; but she escapes not scot-free, for
the poxe have so peppered her that they have almost put out her
eyes, and mard her bad holyday face. The day that you went we
had a great bickering about the continuall passage and entercourse
of messages and letters which your brother and sister complained of,
wherin she set us, you, and all at nought, whereupon I told her my
minde in the best termes I could, and meant to absent myself; but
the day before I went she sent for me, having reconciled herself to
her brother and sister, and of her owne accord shewed me divers
of theire letters, wherein I am canvassed and tossed like a tennis
ball, and withall told me she was fully minded to forsake those
courses, and to cut of all occasions; but I was no sooner gon but the
devill hath put in his foote again, and now at my comming I finde
Totnam turnd French, and your niece is removed to a new lodging,
where now is the rendezvous and all the revell of the men you wot
of; and there she is whole dayes and nights, and will not be spoken
to by brother nor sister, and more foolishly obstinate in her aunswers
then ever I knew her. I verely thincke she seekes occasion of some
unkindnes from your brother and sister, whereby she may have some
colour to cast herself away. I am almost weary of writing, so that
*neque mens neque manus suum officium facit,* and I am more weary of
those domesticall brabbles among them, so that I meane to strive no
more against the currant, but let them brew as they bake, and have
theire owne swinge, for I see it is but *laterem lavare* to deale any
more in it; yet if you can bethincke or devise any better course
wherin I can do any goode, in goode faith I will adventure that for
your sake that I will not do for hers, and yet I protest there is no

breach nor unkind word hath past between us, but only that I see she is not the woman I tooke her for. One thing I had almost forgotten (which I wold not willingly, that you may have a taste of her judgement,) that she told those parties she had acquainted us with theire estate and condition. I have an inckling (but you must take no notice of it in any wise,) that your wisest and best esteemed sister is taken in the same trap; so that I see, if wenches have not theire will, and that husbands come not at call, we shall have them all discontented and turne Turke. Well, I have wearied you and myself; but pardon this once, for it may be I shall not do it often, and yet I assure you I will not faile, God willing, to trouble you as often as I can send, though I write but commendations. God kepe you.

London, this 26th of Aprill, 1602.

Yours most assuredly,     JOHN CHAMBERLAIN.[a]

[*The address is wanting ; Carleton was then in Paris.*]

## LETTER XLVII.

[Domestic Correspondence, State Paper Office, May 8, 1602.]

SIR.

By my last of the 26th of Aprill, I informed you of all that then came to minde. Since, I receved yours of the 6th [b] of this present, so well stored in itself, and so well accompanied, that I may justly say of it, as the Spaniards do of some of theire phrases and proverbes, that they be *hinchados*, that is, with child, and that not with single and simple babies, but with twinnes, wherein I assure you I know not

---

[a] There is a long and interesting letter from Carleton, dated at Paris, June 18th, N.S. in which he says, " Our poore mother will witnes harty sorow when she shall see her self paid with the sk[emes of?] her fantasticall daughters for her religious care in bringing them up." After thanking Chamberlain for his love to them all, and begging him not to desist in his friendly endeavours in advising his sisters against listening to false friends, he continues, " but I dare not urge you to it, lest with your labor you draw on an inconvenience disagreable to your quiet and settled course." [French Correspondence.]

[b] See French Correspondence, State Paper Office.

whether I shold more commend your bountie or your judgement in foreseing I shold meet with beggars, and therefore had need be double stored. Well, you must devise how I may have my revenge of you, els my dull head will never finde out the meanes. I can send you no newes of your lingering Lord Ambassador,[a] but that he is not yet come to town. Some say his instructions are not yet finished, and that is the cause of his stay; but I rather impute it to his owne loitering. He hath many forerunners and attendants here that wold faine be going. One Hay, of Balioll Colledge, comes as his preacher. It shold seeme his Lordship lookes for great imployments that he brings a leash of Secretaries with him. Packer told Mr. Clarencieulx[b] of Davison,[c] and one Gosnall that was secretary to the Erle of Essex in Ireland; and Mr. Allen tells me of one Fitzherbert[d] of New Colledge. I know not what construction to make of it, but that he is of so facile a nature that he cannot say nay to his frends; but when he is there will cassheere them one after another, and I make no question but with a litle patience you will hunt all these beagles out of breath. I heard a soveraine peece of newes yesterday that wold mend all if it prove true, that, when this Lord Deputie[e] comes out of Ireland, Sir Edward Norris shold go in his place: at all adventures, I wold it were no worse, but to-morrow comes not yet. Sir Robert Gardiner, the Cheife Justice, and Sir Oliver St. John are newly come thence to inform her Majestie of the state of that country, which were likely to come to good termes were it not for the untimely revolt of O Suillviant in Mounster, and the taking of Beere Haven by the rebells, where they have store of vitaile and fowre or five peeces of ordinaunce, which drawes the Lord Deputie again into those parts, now that he was going northward to strike at the head of the rebellion. Sir Henry Docwray hath lately taken Balishannon, a place of goode strength and import-

[a] Sir Thomas Parry.      [b] William Camden.
[c] Francis Davison, whose father had been Secretary of State. [Birch MS. No. 4173.] Parry dismissed him from his service before he went to France. [See Letter XLIX.]
[d] Richard Fitzherbert, afterwards Archdeacon of Dorset. [Birch MS. No. 4173.]
[e] Lord Mountjoy.

aunce twixt Tiron and Odonell, which, together with Lough Foile and the Fort of Blackwater (if they be well garrisoned and maintained) do so pen and coape up Tiron, that he shold soone be brought *aux derniers abbois*. Divers of his followers began to fall from him, and one Terlogh O Neale, a bloudy rascall that had much annoyed Sir Henry Docwray, was slaine, and his head sent in by a lady of his owne faction. We are sending 3,000 men thether out of hand, which are levieng in the west and north country. Sir Francis Veres voluntaries come not in so fast but that we are faine to come to a presse of 1,000 men out of the neighbour shires, and 2,000 out of this towne, which is so disorderly performed by taking, and, as it were, sweeping away, serving men, country folkes, and termers of all sorts, and carieng them violently to the ships, that it is a generall grevaunce and scandall at home, and a great dishonor to be heard of abroad. The Lord Gray prepares to go into the Lowe Countries, and to have the command of a troupe of three or fowre hundreth horse; but whether he provide them here or there I heare not. He stoode at first upon some punctillos, not to be commanded by Sir Francis Vere, but since they be agreed, and become goode frends. The Erle of Northumberland sent Capt. Whitlocke with a letter to Sir Francis Vere, that if all were true he had heard, he had wronged him in such and such points, and therefore desired to be satisfied, wishing him to take his horse and bring one with him, as he of his honor wold do the like, and meet him where he shold apoint, willing him to send his determination, yea or no, by word of mouth, and not by writing. Sir Francis Vere wrote an aunswer, and sent it by Captain Ogle, which the Erle refused to receve. The contents were, that though he assured himself he could satisfie him, yet he would not go about to satisfie any man that had his sword in his hand; but if they might meet in peaceable manner before any persons of state whom his Lordship wold choose, he wold give him reasonable satisfaction, otherwise let him take what course he thought best. In this interim, Monsr. Charon, *en ayant senty le vent*, went and informed the Quene of it, who sent expresse charge to the Erle upon his alleageaunce not to molest Sir Francis any way, for that she had speciall service to imploy him in. The Erle obeyed, but sent her Majestie word she shold find Sir Francis a knave, a coward, and a buffon, which comming to Sir Francis eare, he geves out that the Erle is a liar, and a base-minded man. This is the substance of that I have heard. Sir Thomas Sherley,[a] with his fleet of fowre ships and two pinnesses going from Southampton, had not ben ten dayes at sea, but was faine to put in at Falmouth for lacke of vitaile, where he hath casheered his army, and brought his voyage into a compendious abridgement, selling fowre of his ships to furnish two, and so begins upon a new reckening. This weeke two pretty ships went out of the river very well furnished and vitailed by our marchants for almost two yeares, under the conduct of one Captain Waymouth, to seeke the north-west passage to the Indies, which, if it hit right, will be a matter of great importaunce. He carieth letters in divers languages from the Quene to any princes of name he shall light on. We heare nothing of Sir Richard Lewson since he went; but here be sixe or eight more of the Quenes ships making redy. The weather growes here so warme that divers of our aldermen disrobe themselves, and geve over theire cloakes, some for one cause and some for another, as Sir Nic. Mosley[b] for that he retires himself altogether into the country; Sir Richard Martin, as some thincke, for that he is *non solvendo*; one Clarke,[c] for that he is weak and impotent; and Alderman Banning for spite, that he wold not have his wife Lady Mayores.[d] One Pelham,[e] a lawyer, was made sergeant to be sent Cheife Baron into Ireland; but now he hath got the coife he makes no haste, but had rather tarry by it here. We heare that Dr. Overall,[f] divinity reader at

[a] Son of Sir Thomas Shirley, of Wiston, Sussex; born 1564; died July 13, 1628.
[b] Lord Mayor 1599. [c] Sir Roger Clarke, Sheriff 1600.
[d] The wife of alderman Bayning (see p. 97) was Anne, dau. of Sir Henry Glemham.
[e] Sir Edward Pelham, younger brother to Sir William sometime Lord Justice in Ireland. He died 1606. [Collins's Peerage, 1741, i. 410.]
[f] John Overall, D.D. Dean of St. Paul's 1602, Bishop of Lichfield and Coventry 1614, of Norwich 1618, died 1619.

Cambridge, shalbe Deane of Powles, and Dr. Barlow [a] Deane of Chester. Two dayes since Frauncis Mannors [b] maried the Lady Bevill.[c] Your frend Tobie Mathew is newly recovered of a longe and shrewd fit of his old infirmitie. Sir Henry Bromley is at libertie, and Sir Henry Nevill lookes every day to come out of the Towre, having agreed for the payment of his fine of 5,000*l.* by 1,000 a-yeare, and the first payment in present. Massam was indited, and the bill found at the last sessions, which (whether it were in good earnest, or *in terrorem,*) wrought so with him, that I heare he hath made his peace, but on what conditions I cannot learne. On May-day the Queen went a mayenge to Sir Richard Buckleys [d] at Lewsham, some three or fowre miles of Greenwich; and this weeke she came to St. James Park, where she was feasted by Mr. Controller. And, now you have all, it is time to bid you God [*sic*] night, wishing you all health and goode hap.

From London, this 8th of May, 1602..

Yours most assuredly,
JOHN CHAMBERLAIN.

[*No address; Carleton was then in Paris.*]

## LETTER XLVIII.

[Domestic Correspondence, State Paper Office, May 17, 1602.]

SIR,

Since my last of the eighth of this present I have neither written nor heard from you; now, being *in procinctu* to leave this towne, and within fowre or five howres to go with Mr. Lytton and his litle

---

[a] William Barlow, D.D. Dean of Chester 1602, Bishop of Rochester 1605, of Lincoln 1608, died 1613.

[b] Afterwards sixth Earl of Rutland, K.G.; died 1632. [Courthope's Nicolas, 409.]

[c] Frances, daughter of Sir Henry Knevet of Charlton, Wilts; widow of Sir William Bevill of Kilhampton, Cornwall. [Dugdale, ii, 208.]

[d] Of Beaumaris, knighted 1576. [Nichols's Prog. Eliz. iii. 577.]

ones to Sir Henry Wallops to kepe Whitsontide, I cannot depart without taking my leave and saluting you. Your Lord Ambassador [a] is not yet come to towne, or at leastwise was not on Satterday night. It is much spoken of at Court that, having had his entertainment so longe time advanced, he shold be no more forward. No doubt his irresolution is his cheife impediment. I heare his lady comes along with him, and such a troupe of other attendants that it seemes, as one said (not improperly), he will go over with a great power. Your brother Carleton is in towne, and is very carefull in your behalfe, and hath conferred with divers your goode frends about this flush of secretaries, but nothing can be thoroughly thought on or concluded till you see how his Lordship will marshall his matters; only I would wish you not to take the alarme too soone, but to worke out your goode fortune *labore et constantia*. Sir Francis Vere hath taken his leave at court, though perhaps he will not be gon these three or fowre dayes, for his numbers are not yet full, for all the violent pressing, which was so generally misliked that the counsail were faine to take other order, and blame the citie for that disorderly course. I have no great opinion of this sommers service, for, of every hundred that come out of the country, the fourth part run away before they come to this towne, which makes me misdoubt they wilbe as unwilling to fight as they are unwilling to come. Yet divers younge captains raise voluntarie companies, as Sir Rob. Wroths younger sonne hath one of 200, and Dr. Doylies [b] sonne wold faine make up another; but, one and other, it is thought there be better then 1500 voluntaries. The Lord Gray caries over neither men nor horse, but relies wholy upon the States for his intertainment; only he hath made over goode summes of monie, which is like enough to prove but a poore bargain *spem pretio emere*. The Erle of Clanrickard, Sir Rob. Gardiner, and Sir Oliver St. John, are come out of Ireland, and bring nothing extraordinarie, but

[a] Sir Thomas Parry.
[b] Dr. D'Oylie, who had been probationary fellow at Magdalen College, Oxford, took the degree of doctor of physic at Basle. [Birch MS. No. 4173.]

only that the Lord President of Munster[a] besieges Beere Haven, and that the Lord Deputie[b] will shortly make toward the North. He hath lately[c] made two new knights, Sir Miles Fleetwod, sonne to the recever of the Court of Wardes, and one Sir [Henry] Slingsbie of Yorkeshire. Some eight or ten dayes since one Patricke Duffe, an Irishman, was arraigned and condemned at the Kings Bench for traiterous speaches against her Majestie spoken at Roan, but he is not yet executed. This last weeke, one Pie, an utter barrister of the Inner Temple, stoode on the pillorie before the Temple gate and lost both his eares for contriving and plotting the death of one of his fellow lawyers by the way of justice. Sir Thomas Throgmorton, a knight of Glocestershire, was likewise fined in the Starre Chamber at 2000 marks, imprisonment during pleasure, and disabled from bearing any office in the commonwealth, for divers fowle matters and extorsions committed in his country. The gowte hath lately arrested the Lord Keper, and kepes him within doore, which comes ill to passe for those that have causes in Chauncery, that begin now to wish and looke after a Master of the Rolles.[d] On Ascension day younge Sir Thomas Savage[e] was exalted and maried to his faire mistris Darcie. The poore Count Egmond, that flourisht here a while with his coaches and liveries, lies now at gage in so poore state that divers noblemen are faine to make a purse to relieve him. Here is a Sicilian jugler that workes wonders at cardes, and gets very much otherwise of our curious and credulous women. The Dunkirkers are very busie abrode, and have taken divers ships, and now last one richly laden going to Meluin[f] in Prusse or Poland. There be likewise sixe or eight Spanish ships of warre that lie in the Sleeve

[a] Sir George Carew.  [b] Lord Mountjoy.
[c] April 2J, 1602. [Knights made in Ireland, published by Sir Thomas Phillipps.]
[d] The Lord Keeper, Sir Thomas Egerton, held the post of Master of the Rolls until James gave it in 1603 to Edward Bruce of Kinloss.
[e] Created Viscount Savage of Rocksavage, co. Chester, in 1626, and ancestor of the Earls Rivers. His father-in-law Thomas third Lord Darcy of Chiche was created Viscount Colchester 1621, and Earl Rivers 1626, with remainder to Viscount Savage, who died before him in 1635.
[f] Meluing is a town in Norway.

twixt Fraunce and England; three of them lighted on two of our marchant ships comming from Barberie, who put them of well enough, and bringe word that Sir Richard Lewson, having but sixe of the Quenes ships in his companie, met with the West Indian fleet, which came so strongly guarded with sixeteen gallions that he could do no goode on them, but only chaunged some few shot with the admirall. The Lord Norths[a] licence to travaile was signed the last weeke, and yet some thincke he will make no great haste, for that his lady[b] is with child. The Deane of Windsor[c] is like to carry the bishoprick of Hereford, and yet some say the Almener[d] layes in for it, and Dr. Edes[e] for his place at Chichester. He was very well liked in Court for his sermon this Lent, which, they say, was all needle worke. I remember nothing els now, but that the gentlewoman[f] you wot of followes still the old haunt, and will not be beaten from it by faire meanes nor fowle. It hath vext your frends where she is, more then needes; but all will not serve, for she must have the bucklers, and that she standes upon. I come litle there, but even for fashion, and meddle neither one way nor other, for I see it were to no purpose but to minister matter that she might carry to and fro, wherein she is become very cunning, and makes a kinde of profession to run with the hare and hold with the hound. The other gentlewoman[g] of Farringdon is fallen away, as I understand by Mr. Gent; but my more certain intelligence is, that she is but falling, and hath geven her promise to stand out no longer if she can be resolved of one point, which you must thincke shall not be longe a doing, for Valentine is the man and mediator between them. You may take as litle knowledge of these matters as you list, for I

---

[a] Dudley, third Baron; died 1666. [Courthope's Nicolas, 355.]
[b] Frances, daughter and co-heir of Sir John Brocket of Brocket Hall, Herts.
[c] Robert Bennet, D.D. before noticed in p. 58.
[d] Dr. Anthony Watson, Bishop of Chichester 1596, died 1605.
[e] Richard Eedes, D.D. Dean of Worcester 1596; died 1604 (not a Bishop).
[f] One of Carleton's sisters. See p. 127.
[g] Another sister, who also talked of becoming a convert to the Church of Rome. Carleton had four sisters, Elizabeth, Bridget, Anne, and Alice.

only write them that you might know how the world goes; and yet I leave all to your choise and discretion. And so, wishing you all happines, I commit you to God.

From London, this 17th of May, 1602.[a]

Yours most assuredly, JOHN CHAMBERLAIN.

You must not forget all kinde compliments in my behalf to Mr. Winwod.

[*Addressed,*]
  To my assured goode frend
   Mr. Dudley Carleton
    geve these,
     at Paris.

## LETTER XLIX.

[Domestic Correspondence, State Paper Office, June 17, 1602.]

SIR,

It is now so longe since I heard from you, that I had a great longing to come to towne, in hope to find letters, the rather for that I have had no aunswer to any of those three I sent you the last terme, which makes me suspect that either mine be miscaried, or that some of yours of later date have met with false measure, for the last I had from you is of the sixt of May, *stilo novo*;[b] and I will not beleve that your minde or your messengers be so slowe as to lie idle eight whole weekes. I wrote you in my last that I was going into Hamshire, but that jorny altered upon an howers warning by reason that one fell sick of the small pockes in Sir Harry Wallops house, wherupon Mr. Lytton caried away his litle ones in all haste to Knebworth, and I tooke the next way to Askot, where I continued till the 14th of this present, a great deale longer then I

[a] The answer to this letter is in the French Correspondence, State Paper Office, June 24, 1602, N.S.
[b] The letter here alluded to is also in the French Correspondence.

meant or was willing, but that I could by no meanes leave Mrs. Dormer[a] in extremitie, which I assure you was such that I did not thincke she wold have scene this day, and had she not had all the help that nature and arte could affoord it had ben impossible she shold have held out, whatsoever she do yet, for I will lay no great wager of her life, though she were somwhat amended at our comming away. Mr. Gent was sent for in post haste to take his last farewell, and he taried there some ten dayes; and on Monday last we came away together, but he goes backe again to-morrow. If God do call her, I shall thincke this a dismall unluckie yeare to loose my women frends so fast. Your boy was with me yesterday, which was the first time I saw him since you went; he told me the Lord Ambassador[b] goes not yet these eight or ten dayes, and that his lady goes not at all. I perceve he begins to see his error, and shakes of his followers as fast as he tooke them. He hath alredy dismist Davison, and some say Gosnall; but all is one, for his vanitie and overweening will shortly dismisse itself, for I heare he geves it out and is plotting alredy to be left agent when his Lord comes away. I doubt we are not like to have Mr. Winwod so soone as he and we wold, for there is no such great opinion of his[b] sufficiencie that is to succeed, but that he must stay longer to tutle and direct him till he be thoroughly acquainted with those courses. I wold have written so much to him, but that I know it will not be welcome, and I am loth to discourage my frends, and therefore I pray you impart it when you see fit time, as likewise that it is for the goode conceit of him and his service, which Mr. Secretary[c] is not sparing to publish upon any occasion or mention of him, as I have often heard and understoode by goode meanes. Our frend Capt. Whiddon was so wearie with tarieng for winde at Chester and Holyhead that he is come backe to this towne,[d] with intent to go for the Lowe Countries; but Sir Edward Norris will not suffer it, but that he must needes hold on his course for Ireland, whence we have no manner of newes, which I marvaile at, that Tiron being now

[a] Wife of Michael Dormer.　[b] Sir Thomas Parry.　[c] Sir Robert Cecil.　[d] London.

brought lowe, we do not prosecute to make a finall end of that unluckie warre. Your cousen Saunders[a] tells me that he and the Lord North begin theire travaile about a weeke hence, and meane to take theire way by the Lowe Countries and see this sommers service. Sir John Gray is stolen thither alredy, and divers other gentlemen. We have great expectation of the States army and provisions; God send the successe aunswerable to the lowde noise! We have as great a crie of your garboiles in Fraunce, and we have beheadded Mareshall Biron and the Count d'Auvergne[b] alredy; for my part, I cannot yet beleve all that is reported, though I make no doubt but he is in great daunger; but I cannot perswade myself that so fowle a canker could breed in an open souldierlike breast. We have likewise much talke of one Dethicke (sometimes factor for Hickes[c] in Cheapeside at Florence), that shold come thence into Scotland with intent to kill the Kinge; but not being able to beare the burden of such an enterprise, fell distract and beside himself and light upon another, yet, comming to himself, confessed his devilish purpose, and upon better advisement denies it againe. We shall know the circumstances more at large hereafter. We heare the States have put in 1,200 men into Emden during the jarres twixt the Count and the towne. Home newes we have none at all, but that the Lord Zouch was made President of Wales on Monday[d] last, and Sir Edward Stafford[e] is like to be Chauncellor of the Duchie, but with some restraint. Gray Bridges[f] hath hurt Ambrose Willoughby in the heade and body for abusing his father and himself at a conference of arbiterment twixt them and Mrs. Bridges. Old Mrs. Davers, Mr. Doylies mother,[g] is dead; and I was at her

[a] Related to Carleton on the maternal side; Mrs. Anthony Carleton having been previously married to Robert Saunders, of Flore, Northamptonshire.
[b] He was not put to death.
[c] Sir Baptist Hickes, afterwards Viscount Campden.   [d] June 14th.
[e] He had been many years ambassador in France.
[f] Afterwards fifth Lord Chandos, K.B.; died 1621. [Courthope's Nicolas, 99.]
[g] Frances sister to Sir Christopher Edmonds, widow of John D'Oyly, esq. ob. 1569, and of Richard Danvers, esq. [History of the House of D'Oyly, by W. D'Oyly Bailey, 1845, p. 24.]

funerall, where there was no mourning. The old Lady Fitzwilliams hath left the world likewise, with many other old women, among whom there is come a kinde of mortalitie. I send you here all the proceedings twixt the Erle of Northumberland and Sir F. Vere at large.[a] The case stands doubtfull, as it did at first, for the fautors on both sides lay the imputation according to theire owne partialitie; for my part, I am very indifferent, and respect neither of them greatly, yet that litle inclination I have differs I doubt from yours; but let them brabble and fight it out if they will, so we continue frends. Your brother Carleton is in towne, and your cousen Lytton, who commends him to you very kindly. If you will do as much for me to Mr. Winwod, I will commend you to the protection of the Almighty.

From London, this 17th of June, 1602.

                                 Yours most assuredly,

[*Addressed as the last.*]             JOHN CHAMBERLAIN.

## LETTER L.

[Domestic Correspondence, State Paper Office, June 27, 1602.]

SIR,

I will not take upon me to vie and revie thanckes with so goode a gamester, specially the odds of play and otherwise being so much on your side; but, seeing you put me to silence, make the best I can of a poore game. Yours of the 26th of this present arrived here before that of the 18th;[b] but, the last geving notice of the first, I made all meanes to finde out Mr. Savile;[c] and, by younge George Beestons addresse, met with my letters two or three dayes after.

---

[a] The papers inclosed by Chamberlain are probably those giving an account of these proceedings, now found in the State Paper Office, Domestic, April 28, 1602. The same subject is also treated of in Collins's Peerage, vol. v. p. 428, ed. 1768, and in Whitelocke's Liber Famelicus (Camd. Soc.), p. 10.

[b] June 18 and 24, N.S. [See French Correspondence, State Paper Office.]

[c] The person to whom Carleton intrusted a packet for Chamberlain.

Hugh Beeston is not a litle proude of his sonnes French, and caries him about to all his frends to be posed; indeed, he speakes it prettelie, with all the appurtenances, graces, faces, shrugg, and all. Mr. Secretarie[a] and his other frends wold have him sent again; but the father will in no wise heare of it, because he is such a jewell, and the staffe of theire house. Your letters were the more welcome for that I perceved by them there was nothing miscaried, which I was in great doubt of, as I wrote you by my last of the 17th of this present. The Lord North and your cousen Saunders went toward the Lowe Countries three or fowre dayes since, and Capt. Whiddon, with much grumbling, towardes Ireland on Satterday, for Sir Edward Norris wold by no meanes agree he shold chaunge his course, and he durst not dispute it here; but, when he hath shewed his obedience, and is come into Ireland, he sayes he will tickle him with a letter, and so lay the law to him that he shall see there is nothing to be learned nor gotten there. At all adventures, I wold there were litle worke for him, and such as he is, but we heare of 6,000 Italians redy in Spaine to come thether, and stay for nothing but shipping, which I doubt they shall too easilie compasse nowe our fleet comes away to convoy home the carraque they have taken within the mouth of the river of Lisbone. If our people had not plaide the men every way, she had escaped theire fingers, by reason she was got so far within the river among flats and shallowes and had receved a supplie of three or fowre hundred fresh men besides a guard of ten gallies to tow her up and defend her; but our ships so plied the gallies that I thincke they will have no list to incounter them any more. Sir Richard Leveson and Sir William Mounson have gotten great commendation, both for courage and advice. What her value may be we cannot yet guesse, but sure she was a rich ship. Marry, there goes a report all the short ends were conveyed away before our men could come at her; but most men thincke that but a colour for them that have, and mean to make, theire market. Once here is order taken that no goldsmiths or

[a] Sir Robert Cecil.

jewellers shall go into the West countrie; and Fulke Grivell is gon downe post to Plimmouth, and so to the sea, to meet her and kepe her from comming into that pilfering towne (as they terme it), but to bringe her alonge to Portesmouth. Sir Thomas Gorge, Sir Henry Broncker, Sir Thomas Knevet,[a] and a counsailor not yet named, are appointed commissioners; and, if she come to Portesmouth, it is thought greater personages will go to see and dive into her. Two Zealanders comming from the East Indies found a carraque at S^ta Helenas that began to brabble with them for not vailing or striking saile. From wordes they fell to blowes; and in the end, after two or three dayes fight, the Dutchmen tooke her, but are thought will have much ado to bring her home for want of men. There be three ships sent from Middleburg to see if they can meet and garde them home. The Lord Gray hath not that commaund nor entertainment in the Lowe Countries that he propounded to himself, the envie whereof his frends (and some say the States themselves) are content shold light on Sir Francis Vere, and yet I know he dealt very plainly and directly with him both here and there, and told him what he was to looke for. I am much of your opinion touching the States course in this sommers action, and thincke they play too great game to cast at all. God send them well to do, and not to playe banckerout; for I begin to have an extraordinarie care of them, and methinckes heare a great venture with them now we are so far ingaged in honor, and have eight thousand English in theire camp, which is the greatest number of disciplined men of our nation that hath bin seen together in our age. Here is speach that the plague shold be in Ostend, which, if it cease not the sooner, will soone make an end of that siege. The counsaile have lately spied a great inconvenience of the increase of housing within and without London, by building over stables, in gardens, and other od corners, wherupon they have taken order to have them puld downe, and this weeke they have begun almost in every parish to light on the unluckiest, here and there one, which God knowes is far from removing the mischeife. The

[a] Created Baron Knevet of Escrick in 1607, died 1622. [Courthope's Nicolas, 275.

old Lady Walsingham [a] died the last weeke almost sodainly, or within an howres warning, and is buried secretly in Powles by her husband. Dr. Overall, the divinitie reader at Cambridge, is installed Deane of Powles. Your cousen Goodwin,[b] Howson,[c] Kinge,[d] and Spenser[e] proceed doctors this act at Oxford, at which time the librarie shalbe opened with great applause. Here is talke of a match toward twixt the Lord Kepers sonne [f] and the Lady Fraunces second daughter of Darbie, and twixt Sir Henry Cary [g] and Mr. Tanfeilds daughter with 2,000*l.* presently, 2,000*l.* at two yeares, and 3,000*l.* at his death, if he chaunce to have more children, otherwise to be his heire *ex asse*. Mr. Phillips sonne,[h] the lawyer, shall mary a daughter of Sir Thomas Gorges, and one Poultney, a younge gentleman of Northamptonshire, M[rs] Padge Fortescue; and, on Wensday next, (twixt June and July, when he shold kepe his mouth wet and somewhat els drie) our Mr. Trot shall marry one Mr. Perins daughter of Hartfordshire, a lusty tall wench able to beat two of him. Newes came this morning that Fulke Grivell is returned, and that the carraque is arrived at Plimmouth; yet it is thought she must come about to Portesmouth. Younge Coppinger, that was comming into Fraunce, turned his course and went to sea with Sir Richard Lewson; and, being at the taking of the carraque, was sent with the first newes, and hath waited hard at Court since in hope to be knighted; but he speedes no better then his fellowes, of whom fowreteene have attended all this terme with great devotion to make

[a] Ursula (St. Barhe), widow of the great Sir Francis Walsingham.

[b] William Goodwin, sub-almoner to Elizabeth; Dean of Christ Church 1611, afterwards Archdeacon of Middlesex; died June 11, 1620. [Birch MSS. No. 4173.]

[c] John Howson: see p 112.

[d] John King, Bishop of London, Dec. 8, 1611; died March 30, 1621.

[e] John Spenser, afterwards President of Corpus Christi College. [Birch MSS. 4173.]

[f] Sir John Egerton; this marriage is also noticed at p. 94.

[g] Afterwards Viscount Falkland. His wife was Elizabeth daughter of Sir Laurence Tanfield, who died Lord Chief Baron of the Exchequer, April, 1625.

[h] Sir Robert Phillips, son of Sir Edward Phillips, Master of the Rolls, married Bridget, dau. of Sir Thomas Gorges and Helena dowager Marchioness of Northampton. [Hoaro's Wiltshire, Hundred of Cawden, p. 30.]

theire wifes ladies; but hitherto they have lost *oleum et operam* ; and some of them, for expedition, having paide theire mony before hande, are in great daunger to loose theire ernest. Sir Thomas Sherly is returned with his navie royall; and yesterday with his lieutenant generall Colonell Sims posted to the Court as though they had brought tidings of the taking of Sivil, or some such towne, whereas, God knowes, they have but sackt two poore hamlets of two dozen houses in Portugal, the pillage wherof he gave to his army, reserving to himself only two or three pesaunts to raunsome, of whom when he saw he could raise nothing, he wold not bring them away for shame. The Quenes ships have taken two or three Lubeckers comming out of Spaine with great store of coine (we say) to the Archduke. The last day of the terme, at the Starre Chamber, Atkinson, Wilkinson, Elson, and Cawley, the accusers of the Lord Treasurer,[a] were, after a longe and tedious hearing, condemned in a fine to be whipt, to stand on the pilloric and lose theire eares, and to the gallies, or perpetuall imprisonment. The first and the third found some litle favour, and were dispensed withall for whipping and theire eares, in consideration the one was very penitent, and had revealed the whole plot and drift; the other for that he was a souldier, and so more subject to discontentment. Now, if I had told you that your Lord Ambassador [b] had newly shipt his stuffe, that he had taken his leave at Court, that he meanes to set forward next weeke, and that he geves you very goode wordes, I had drawne myself drie, and saide all I have to say, saving that, if here be anything more then in Mr. Winwods letter, you wold geve him his part; and so I commit you to God.

From London, this 27th of June, 1602.

    Yours most assured,               JOHN CHAMBERLAIN.

Your posts be such couscuing companions, that, many times when they make us beleve they wilbe gon this day or to morrow, they tarry eight or ten dayes after.

[*Addressed as before.*]

[a] Lord Buckhurst.               [b] Sir Thomas Parry.

## LETTER LI.

[Domestic Correspondence, State Paper Office, July 8, 1602.]

Sir,

If I were not now taking my leave of this towne for the best part of this vacation I shold have put of this letter somewhat longer to see if any thing wold have risen worth the tlienge at; for, since my last of the 27th of June, we have had so small store of game, that all I could catch or come by wold scant stretch to make a poore present to Mr. Winwod, wherein though I know you are like to have your part, yet, that you may reserve your appetite, and make choice according to your stomacke, I will set you downe the bare dishes. On Wensday last Atkinson and his fellowes had theire payment in Cheapside according to the sentence in the Star Chamber.[a] We were very forward here a while in setting foorth our fowre gallies in hope to have met the States army at Dunkirke; but our heat is much abated since we heare no more of a great blow they shold have geven to the Archduke,[b] but rather of great triumphes and *feux de joye* in his camp, the reason whereof we cannot attain to, unles it be cogging and outfacing one another. Our carraque is come to Plimmouth, where it is thought she shall unlode; for, being of so great burthen, they are loth to hasard her any further; and those that command in her have the same reasons to keep her aloofe that others have to bring her neerer. The Dutch carraque is in the Downes, and stayes but for a winde to carrie her into Zeland. The two ships that tooke her arrived at Middleburgh on Sonday was sevenight with the creame and choise of portable and pocket commodities. The Lord Deputie of Ireland hath so straightened Tiron by planting a garrison at Dongannon, that he hath made him forsake his countrie, and retire to Macguire, where he lives in a lake amonge islands. Matters succeed not so well in Mounster with Sir

[a] See p. 144.      [b] Albert of Austria.

George Cary,[a] who writes that Beere Haven cannot be taken by force, but by famine; but the world hath no great opinion that he will compasse it by either. Sir Walter Raleigh is upon the way to his government in Gersey, and Sir Robert Sidney must follow to Flushing. Sir Richard Knightly hath buried his lady. On Friday last the Erle of Shrewsburie and Mr. Secretarie were gossips to Mr. Edmunds, and christened his younge sonne in Holbourne. The Lady Hatton was godmother, and the childes name Talbot.

Sir Thomas Parry makes many pauses, and I cannot learne of any body when he means to set forth.[b] He caries no great reputation with him if all be true I have heard, that eight or ten younge gentlemen come alonge with him that give him an hundred crownes a yeare a peece for theire boord, which were all one as to kepe an ordinarie. Once I heare he caries an extraordinarie opinion of you, which I make no doubt but will do you both goode; for I impute his oversights altogether to importunitie of frends, to his owne facilitie of nature that cannot say nay, and specially to want of advise, and one to stand by him and hold him up when he is in the right. It seemes younge Davison[c] meanes to take another course, and turne poet, for he hath lately set out certain sonnets and epigrams.[d] The thunder and tempestuous weather you write of hath found the way over sea and playde his part here all the last weeke more continuall then ever I knew it. We were not so forward at first to cut off Birons head as we are now to pardon him, and say that matters are not so heinous nor proofes so pregnant as they were taken. We have speach of a progresse to begin toward the latter end of this moneth: first to Sir John Fortescues in Buckinghamshire, then to the Erle of Hartfords and the Lord Chiefe Justice,[e] where there were jewells and presents provided the last yeare, that wold not be

[a] Carew.
[b] He arrived in Paris Aug. 23, N.S. [French Correspondence, State Paper Office.]
[c] See p. 130.
[d] A Poetical Rhapsody of Sonnets, Odes, Elegies, &c. by Francis Davison. Republished by Sir Harris Nicolas in 1826.    [e] Sir John Popham.

lost; and so to Bath and Bristow to visit the Lord Chamberlaine [a] that lies there for help. I know not which way my progresse will hold further then Askot, unles it be to Sir Henry Wallops, whether your cousen Lytton hath caried his litle ones for the most part of this sommer. If you write, direct your letters to Nortons,[b] and I will leave order to have them sent after me. Mrs. Dormer mends apace, and I hope this hath clarified her from all old grevances. I wold this enclosed medicine, sent you from your sister Alice, could do as much for you: once it is a very easie receit, *et de facile parabilibus*, so that it can be no great hurt to trie. Litle Britain [c] is translated to a house without Criplegate, where they have more elbow roome, but scant better aire. Your faire neice is gon into the countrie, but hath *animum revertendi* at Michaelmas. In the meane time meetings are not so frequent, but postillions and messengers walke as fast twixt the parties you wot of. Marry, matters are caried more close, and I must not be acquainted with theire proceedings, which doth nothing displease me, for I see she must have her swinge, and delights *nager entre deux eaux*, so that it were lost labour to seeke to divert her from them that feed her curiosity with idling and vaine secrets. But now domesticall quarrells are somwhat qualified by the incounter of a forrain ennemie, I meane your brother Carleton, against whom of late she declaimes with open mouth, and he for his part is nothing behinde hande with her, so that it seemes they take pleasure to spit theire venome and vent theire ill nature one upon another. Mrs. Farringdon [d] came not to towne as she appointed. I thincke I did covertly breake the neck of that jorny, and presume it was a goode peece of service, for, had she come, no doubt there had growne such an alliance that the knot wold never have ben untied without cutting, whereas now your letter (which I sent her) may prevent the mischeife, and do great goode, for she is yet but sliding, and stands to be satisfied in some points wherein she

[a] Lord Hunsdon.     [b] A bookseller in St. Paul's Churchyard.
[c] This refers to the removal of Mr. Alexander Williams and his family.
[d] See p. 136.

wold faine have had a conference before her at Oxford by a great
man in that place, and some of the other side. I liked your letter [a]
exceedingly; it was so well and cunningly convayed to beate the
whelp before the lion, and reade her her lesson in her fellowes booke.
Your boy was with me this afternoone, and will needes make me
beleve his lord [b] goes on Monday. I am in a mammering whether
I were better commit this letter to him or commend it to the next
messenger at all adventures, or els take a middle course, and send
Mr. Winwods by the next post, and yours by your owne postillion,
with charge to see it sent away if he go not the sooner himselfe.
Well, I will do as God shall put in my minde, to whose holy protection I commit you now and ever.

From London, this 8th of June,[c] 1602.

Yours most assured,

JOHN CHAMBERLAIN.

[*No address; Carleton was then in Paris.*]


## LETTER LII.

[Domestic Correspondence, State Paper Office, Oct. 2, 1602.]

SIR,

I know you thincke it longe till you heare from me, and I am in
your debt for two letters at least, which I received whiles I was at
Knebworth, wherein you served two pigeons with one beane, and
they could not come where they shold finde better welcome; for we
were all alone, and the first [d] brought with it much goode companie

---

[a] Carleton inclosed a letter for his sister, unsealed, to Chamberlain, and desired him to read it.      [b] Sir Thomas Parry.

[c] Evidently a mistake for July.

[d] The letter referred to is in the French Correspondence, State Paper Office, Sept. 10, N.S.

of pictures and discourses that intertained a goode part of the time
that otherwise wold have ben very tedious, for I cannot well disgest
the solitarines of that house[a] that was wont to be so stirring and
cherefull. I came thence yesterday thincking to mend myself here
in our old garrison, but I see I am fallen out of the frieng pan into
the fire, for here is *solitudo ante ostium, solus sannio servat domum*.
Old Tom and Timme stand sentinell without doore, and one poore
maide mans the whole house within. Mr. Bodley nor Mr. Gent
are neither of them come to towne, so that I have nobody nor
nowhere to learne any thing on the sodain; and yet, hearing of a
post that goes away soone, I wold not omit to write, though I have
nothing but countrie occurrents, which you shall have as redelie
as I can remember them in this haste, even *ab ovo*. The commencement at Oxford was very famous, for plentie of doctors, that
were fifteen, twelve divines, and three lawyers; for store of venison,
whereof Dr. Kinge had 27 buckes for his part; for royall chere, and
an excellent *concio ad clerum*, wherein your cousen Dr. Goodwin[b]
bare the bell; for the exceeding assemblie of gentles, but specially
for the great confluence of cutpurses, whereof ensued many losses and
shrewde turnes, as first Mr. Bodley lost his clocke, Sir Richard Lea
two jewells of 200 markes, which Sir Harry Lea and he meant to
have bestowed on the bride,[c] Mr. Tanfelds daughter; and divers
other lost goode summes of five, eight, and fourteen pounds, besides
petty detriments of scarfes, fans, gloves; and one mad knave, whether
of malice or merriment, tooke the advantage to pull of a gentle-
womans shooe, and made the goose go home barefoote. I was not
there myself; but, understanding what a high tide there was like to
be, wold not commit myself to the streame, but lay quiet at Mr.
Dormers, where we had your brothers companie now and then, who
is become a great man at Ricot with the younge Lord;[d] and so great,
that I doubt it will diminish his greatness at Englefeld in time, for

---

[a] In consequence of Mrs. Lytton's death.
[b] See note at p. 143.
[c] Lady Cary, wife of Sir Henry: see p. 143.
[d] Francis second Lord Norris.

it is odds that between two stooles somewhat will go to the ground; but the matter is not great if he go alone and carrie but his owne waight. From Askot I met Mr. Lytton at Sir Harry Wallops, where I found my wife[a] brought a bed of a boy, wherein I tooke no great comfort (as I told her) having so little part in him. Thence we came to Knebworth, and so into Bedfordshire to the Lady Pelhams, into Huntingdonshire to the Lord St. Johns and Sir Gervais Cliftons, and into Cambridge to Sir William Russells. I neede not relate our sports of hawking and hunting, wherein I was not extraordinarily affected, saving at the chase of a huge stag at the Lord St. Johns, which we hunted a force, and kild him in Bedfordshire, and brought away the head to set up for a trophee in Knebworth Hall. This is all the successe of this sommers progres, unles I shold tell you that I never knew a later, nor withall a better or more plentifull harvest. The Quenes progres went not far—first to Cheswicke to Sir William Russells, then to Ambrose Coppingers,[b] who, because he had ben a Master of Art, intertained her himselfe with a Latin oration. Then to Harvill [Harefield] to the Lord Kepers,[c] so to Sir William Clarkes at Burnham, who so behaved himselfe that he pleased no body, but gave occasion to have his miserie and vanitie spread far and wide; then to Otelands, where she continues till the seventh of this moneth that she comes to Richmond. The causes that withheld her from the Erle of Hartfords and the Lord Cheife Justices[d] were the fowle weather and a generall infection of the small pockes spred over all the countrie. The Lord Hume[e] came this way home, and had audience at Court on Sunday. The Quene was very pleasant with him, and well disposed. I doubt not but you have heard of our commissioners that are gon to treat with the King of Denmarke and the Hans Townes at Breame, the Lord Evers, Sir

[a] Lady Gifford, wife of Sir Richard. [See pp. 70, 109, and 115.]
[b] At Harlington in Middlesex. He was son of Henry Copinger of Allhallows, Kent; knighted July 23, 1603; died March 17, 1603-4. [Nichols's Prog. Eliz. iii. 579.]
[c] Sir Thomas Egerton.   [d] Sir John Popham.
[e] Sir George Hume; created Baron Hume of Berwick July 7, 1604; Earl of Dunbar July 3, 1605; K G.; died 1611. [Courthope's Nicolas, 260.]

John Harbert newly knighted, Doctor Dun made Master of the Requests for this voyage, and Le Sieur; where they be lodged safe and sure till the springe, if not longer. We heare out of Moscovie that the King of Denmarkes brother is lately arrived there to marrie the Emperors daughter. Mr. Gilpin[a] is dead at the Haghe; I cannot imagine who shold succeed him, except one Wheeler, secretarie to the marchants at Middleburgh. Sir Francis Vere is saide to be well recovered of his hurt, but is thought shall have an impediment in his tongue, which some thincke to be no great harme. We heare that Grave Maurice hath ben daungerously sicke of the plague, and that the sore is burst out in his necke. This sommers worke with such an armie and such a noise hath lost them a great part of mine opinion of their souldiership, to make such a perambulation to no purpose, and not to dare to follow any part of theire first project. Sir Robt. Mansfeild and the Vice Admirall of Flushing met with sixe of Spinolas gallies, and have stemd or overrun two of them, and, they say, spoiled the rest, so that they be unprofitable, wherof one is run on ground at Callis. The reports of the manner of the fight are so uncertain and contrarious that I know not how to set it downe, but will leave it to time to discover. Out of Ireland we heare nothing but that Tiron runs up and downe distressed, and offers to come in upon any conditions with life. The Erle of Clanrikard followes the Court, and aspires to high favor. I have heard he was offered a great match to marrie the Lady Straunge, but it seemes he more regardes courtly hopes then present profit. Sir Ed. Michelborn and Sir Edward Baynam were lately in the field together, and both sore hurt, but I know not the quarrell. Willes[b] is quite discarded out of Mr. Secretaries service; I cannot yet learne the cause,[c] but when I see Mr. Cope or Hugh Beeston I will sound

[a] George Gilpin, resident at the Hague; died Sept. 1602. [Holland Correspondence, State Paper Office.]

[b] Simon Wyllis, secretary to Sir Robert Cecil.

[c] It was for fear that Willis should discover Cecil's correspondence with the King of Scots. [See the Sidney State Papers, ii. 326.]

what I can. The Lady of Northumberland is newly brought to bed of a sonne. The Lord Chamberlain[a] is come home from the Bath, but neither much better nor worse then when he went out. Sergeant Heale was made the Quenes sergeant this sommer, and rode circuit with Judge Gawdie in Sussex, Surrey, Kent, Essex, and Hartfordshire, wherein he plaide such pranckes, and so demeaned himselfe, that he is become both odious and ridiculous. I see not your frends without Criplegate; but I heare your sister Williams hath had a sonne. You must excuse my hudling haste, and commend me in all kindues to Mr. Winwod, to whom I wold have written if either I had more matter or leisure; but you may supplie that default with acquainting him with what you thincke worth the imparting; and so I commit you to Gods holy protection.

From London, this second of October, 1602.

Yours most assuredly,
JOHN CHAMBERLAIN.

[*No address; Carleton was then in Paris.*]

## LETTER LIII.

[Domestic Correspondence, State Paper Office, October 2, 1602.]

GOODE MR. CARLETON,

Now I have dispatcht the ordinarie occurrents, it will not be amisse to informe you of some privat matters apart, which course you may hold with me (if you please) in whatsoever you wold have kept close or reserved; for both you and I have so many goode frends here in common, that, if they heare of any post or packet, they thincke themselves wronged if they see not the originall, whereof I assure you I am not so liberall, but that they see it comes *incita Minerva*, and not at first call. Upon my first comming to towne, Mr. Cope

[a] Lord Hunsdon.

inquired when I heard from you, and told me of two papers he had
delivered you of the genealogies and matches of the great houses of
France, which he desired you to continue and draw out till this
time. I gave no great care to him then; but, upon a second and
third summons, I told him what other imployments and busines
withheld you, that you could not attend such trinckets; his aunswer
was that you might get some expert Frenchman to do it for you
according to those copies, or at leastwise send him backe his owne
papers which he had out of his old lords [a] memorialls. Though I
hold him neither apt nor greatly able to do any frend he hath goode,
yet must we sometimes hold a candle before the devill, and do as
the people of Calicut, that worship him, not so much for any help they
looke for at his hands, as because he shold do them no harme. I
use him somwhat after that kinde; and, though for some inward
respects I maligne him as much as any old frend he hath, yet I com-
plie thus far with him as to serve his humor now and then when it
comes upon me. As this other day, expostulating with me why I
did not present Mr. Secretarie [b] with some toyes to kepe me in his
remembraunce, I delivered him some of those pictures and verses
you sent me in your hand which I presume Mr. Secretarie knowes,
at leastwise I told Wat Cope I had them from you, and he sayes Mr.
Secretarie chose the last picture and the last verses you sent, so that,
if it do me no goode, it can do you no harme. If you did not know
me so well as you do, me thinckes you might guesse I aime at somwhat, but I vowe and sweare unto you by our love and frendship
(which is a sound oth) that I am past all ambition, and wish nor
seeke nothing but how to live *suaviter* and in plentie. To which
end and to your owne goode, if you sometimes furnish me with such
toyes as you thincke fit, it will not be amisse; and withall any
pamphlets of the Jesuites, or such like, specially " La Verité De-
fendue," so often alleaged by Arnault [c] in his " Franc Discours," [d]

[a] Lord Burghley.     [b] Sir Robert Cecil.     [c] Antoine Arnauld.
[d] Le franc et veritable Discours du Roi, sur le rétablissement qui lui est demandé
par les jesuites. [Biographie Universelle, ii. 498.]

wherof Dr. Andrewes is very desirous, and I have promised it him if it be to be had. You see how bold a beggar I am; but it is upon confidence you will alwayes use me as boldly if ever it come to my turne to stand you in stead. Your cousen Lytton and I have conferred upon your letter, and are not very hastie to follow that course you speake of; for though Willes [a] be removed (only upon his insolent and harsh behavior towards his master,[b] as both Wat Cope and Hugh Beeston have told me in confession), yet the places are full and supplied by Bruerton and Levinus;[c] and, if you were once in his service, what usage soever you found there is no starting, but that you are lodged, whereas now it is *integrum* to you to take what way you list, and that may serve for *ultimum refugium*, and I hope for better at your hands then a bare service; the place you are in will make you knowne, and there wilbe awayes meanes to further you to his favor. If there be not extreme cause to the contrarie I wold wish you to continue awhile as you are, for I assure you both Court and countrie take notice of you and geve you your due; therefore you must not *succumbere oneri*, but go on cherefully to the journies end. Touching the little gentlewoman [d] without Criplegate, she continues still wavering and redy to slide upon every occasion, yet it may be but a naturall inconstancie, and that she will not fall downeright, but loves to hold her frends in suspence, unles the comming of your faire niece and your sister Faringdon (who are shortly looked for) alter the case. M[rs] Faringdon sent her your monitorie letter, with advise not to neglect the counsaile of so carefull and loving a brother; marry for her part she wold not intermeddle in such matters, but wisht her to follow her conscience, with divers other clauses that puld downe as fast as she set up, which shew that she herself is far gon; and, indeed, I heare she is fully perverted. The little gentlewoman tore the letter in the middlest, and sent her backe halfe, with this aunswere, that, seeing it most concerned her, she thought it reason to kepe her part, wherewith the other was not

[a] Simon Willis.    [b] Sir Robert Cecil.
[c] Levinus Monk.    [d] One of Carleton's sisters: see pp. 127, 129, 136.

so well satisfied but that it made a little pique. All that I have gotten by medling in these matters is (which I alwayes suspected and looked for) to be traduced and tossed like a tennis ball among the faction; so far foorth that Valentine sought out Mr. Gent at Oxford, and told him how far he had prevailed, and that she was fully resolved,[a] had not I reclaimed her, and withall told him many lieng and ridiculous reasons that I had used to that purpose, whereas I never spake with him past once in my life, and then had not many words neither; but I perceve cogging and grosse lienge is a great part of their profession. Your sister Williams hath had pretty doings in her new house for so small time; first, in burieng out of it one Mr. Gifford, whom they tooke in of kinde hart when he was past all recoverie, to season it and die there; then in a christening of her sonne; and now shortly in a mariage of one of her maides. You see I am willing you shold know all, and more peradventure then I shall have thancks for. *Vive, vale.*

Yours,<br>J. C.

[*Addressed,*]
    To your owne goode selfe,
        Mr. Carleton.


## LETTER LIV.

[Domestic Correspondence, State Paper Office, Oct. 15, 1602.]

SIR,

Since my last (or rather my first after so long a pause) of the second of this moneth, I have not heard from you, nor heard anything els of worth that might hasten my writing; but that I had a

---

[a] To become a Roman Catholic.

desire to salute Mr. Winwod, and tell him what is spoken of his succeeding Mr. Gilpin,[a] wherin no doubt his presence wold carry it from all the concurrents if he were here, Mr. Bodley having refused it faire and flat (as being of a higher forme and past it), and your frend Mr. Edmunds and John Wroth having theire particular impediments. The Lord Gray is come newly out of the Lowe Countries, and railes freely on Sir Francis Vere, whose hurtes are not yet so secure but that there is daunger. Sir Robert Sidney is lately arrived, and most of our captaines are shortly expected, now they may have time to play and refresh themselves after so much induring in the siege of Ostend and this sommers service. We heare that the horsemen of Berghen and Breda have lately surprised certain bands of ordinaunce that lay loose, and have brought away better then 500 horse and 50 prisoners of note, besides much plate and other boote. I cannot learn what is become of your cousen Saunders or the Lord North. His lady, with the Lady of Effingham and younge Mrs. St. John (the Lady Fines daughter), are all saide to be breeding and with child. Younge Paget[b] hath lately married Mrs. Knolles,[c] daughter and heyre to Mr. Controllers eldest brother, an old love of your cousin Will Copes, whom he longe aimed and shot at. I heare of another match brewing twixt Mrs. Bridges of the Court and her cousin Gray Bridges,[d] whereby all suites and quarrells shold be ended and concluded. Gommershall, the mercer of Temple Barre with the faire wife, hath laide the key under the doore and is become banckrupt. His wife was prettely well furnished when among her inventarie thirty of her smockes were prised at threescore pound. Here is speach that a Dunkirker shold be cast away on the coast of Norway, as he lay waiting for some straglers of our Moscovie fleet. We have nothing out of Ireland more then I wrote you, save that some say the Lord Mountjoyes commission is re-

[a] As Resident at the Hague.
[b] William Paget, son of Thomas fourth Baron Paget, who was attainted in 1587. William was restored to his father's lands and honours 1 James I. Died 1629.
[c] Lettice, daughter and co-heir of Henry Knolles.
[d] Grey Bridges did not marry Mrs. Bridges.

newed for three yeares longer. The Lord Zouch playes *rex* in Wales,[a] and takes upon him *comme un Millord d'Angleterre*, both with the counsaile and justices, as also with the poor Welchmen, whom they say he punishes extreemly for pewtry (*sic*). Dr. Redman, Bishop of Norwich, accounted one of the wisest of his coate, is lately dead.[b] The Court came to Richmond the eighth of this present, where the Queen findes herself so well that she will not easilie remove. Our discoverers that went to seeke out the north-west passage are returned *re infecta*, but yet make shew they will proceed afresh the next yeare. Here was one Mowbray, a Scottish man, accused by one Daniell,[c] a little pigmee Italian fencer, that he wold have suborned him to have slaine the King of Scots. The other denies it constantly; wherupon he was demaunded by the Lord Hume to be sent and tried there; the counsaile condescended so far as to send him away with him, but to be staide at Berwicke, and the dwarfe Daniell must follow, or is alredy gon to trie it out to the utterance, if the Scottish king thincke fit, and will give them *campo libero*. I heare that king is printing a little peece of worke christened with a Greeke name, in nature of his last will or remembrance to his sonne,[d] when himself was sicke, and because it hath gon abrode subject to many constructions and much depraved by many copies, he will now set it out under his owne hand. Yesterday was the Erle of Northumberlands sonne christened at Essex house, the Queen, by the Lady Marquise[e] her deputie, being godmother, and the Lord Treasurer[f] and Lord Admirall[g] godfathers; the child is called Algernon,[h] after one of his first auncestors that came of the house of Brabant; it is thought somwhat a straunge and disused name,

[a] As Lord President.  [b] William Redman, Bishop of Norwich 1594, died Sept. 25, 1602.
[c] Daniel Archdeacon, or Archideaquila. See Scotch Correspondence, State Paper Office, Feb. 1603, for an account of Mowbray's death and the grant by the King of Scots of a pension to Daniel of 90 marks per annum.  [d] His Basilicon Doron.
[e] Of Northampton.  [f] Lord Buckhurst.  [g] Earl of Nottingham.
[h] The Earl had already had his two sons named Henry after himself, and they had died infants. This son succeeded as Earl in 1632, and was Lord Admiral in the reign of Charles I.

but it is better to have a straunge name then none, as your Dolphin [a] hath not that I can heare of; I pray you send us the misterie why he stayes so longe out of the faith. When I had ended Mr. Winwods letter, and was thus forward on yours, comes my Lord Norths man with your pacquet of the 10th,[b] and, ere I had fully read it, a post with a letter from Mr. Winwod, of the 8th of this present; and now withall, ere I had read his, Mr. Gent sends for my letters, because Peter Browne is presently going; so that I must defer thancks and all other ceremonies till better leysure. Yet for all the haste forget me not to Mr. Saunders, and so I commit you to God.

From London, this 15th of October, 1602.

Yours most assuredly,

[Addressed,]                JOHN CHAMBERLAIN.

To my assured goode freud
Mr. Dudley Carleton
   geve these at Paris.

## LETTER LV.

[Domestic Correspondence, State Paper Office, Nov. 4, 1602.]

SIR,

I have had leysure enough to bethincke myself how and in what sort to thancke you for your packet I receved at the closing up of my last that went by Peter Browne, but the more I thincke the lesse I am satisfied to see that wordes are but a windie requitall for so many pretty discourses and presents, and that I have none other meanes to acknowledge your kindnes, so that you must even put me in the number of your doubtfull or rather desperate debtors, except some extrordinarie goode fortune come to cleere me out of your booke; and now was I leaving this theme, and falling to other matters, when your cousen Lytton calles me foorth to receve a

---

[a] The Dauphin being still unchristened.

[b] See French Correspondence, in which there is a long account of the execution of Maréchall de Biron.

pacquet sent from Mussi your post, three or fowre dayes after his
arrivall, for the which I can adde nothing to that I saide before,
but rather, if it had come sooner, might chaunce have said lesse, for
*leves gratiæ loquuntur, ingentes stupent.* Now comming so fresh from
reading your letters and discourses of Biron, I cannot go on without
touching a point or two *en passant.* Let the French twaddle what
they list of his dieng *en soldat,* I cannot perceve by ought I have seen
or heard but that he died very timerously and childishly, which shewes
that his valour was rather a French furie, then true fortitude. Another
observation came to my remembraunce in reading his proces, of three
straunge disasters befallen three great men,[a] in three neighbour countries in three yeares successively (this, you see, passes *tres sequuntur
tria*), and all theire cases so intricate, specially the two straungers, and
theire persons and services so magnified that a great part of the world
rests unsatisfied in their deaths, and will not be perswaded against
their deserts by any undeservings; but *mundus vult decipi,* and so let
it go. I can finde neither rime nor reason in such extraordinarie
usage and entertainment of your Suisse,[b] being more then they were
fit to receve, and more then beseemed the King to geve to such
muffes; so that we censure it here either for indiscretion or abjectnes;
and for the 800,000 crownes yearly (but that you write it) I shold
hardly beleve the King wold buy them so deare. The third part of
that pension being much and more then they are worth. Your
brother and sister Carleton are both in towne about the funerall of
Mr. Marsh, his goode hoste and frend, who died apoplecticall. No
doubte but he will informe you of whatsoever he can come by.
You writ to him of the comming of your boy, of whom as yet
we have no tidings. We heare out of Spaine that ODonell,[c] riding
toward the Court at Valladolid, died sodainly by the way, and
being opened there was found in him a serpent (as some call it),

[a] Earl of Essex, Maréchal de Biron, and the Earl of Gowrie.

[b] There is an account in Carleton's handwriting, entitled "The manner of the Switch sweareing the League with the French King," in the French Correspondence, State Paper Office, Oct. 1602.

[c] See the Spanish Correspondence, State Paper Office, Oct. 3 and 10.

or rather a worme, with two heades, of eight foote longe. Matters begin again untowardly in Mounster, where one Cormach Mac Teaghe (or, as some terme him, Mac Dermond), a great man, being apprehended by the Lord President for suspicion of intelligence with Spaine, made an escape, and is out in action, together with the Lord Roche, and divers other of his frends and followers. He had a sonne, a proper youth, at Oxford, who was lately sent for, and committed to the keper of the Court of Wardes. They speake of an embargo in Spaine of all Scottish and Irish, so that they must seeke traffieke elswhere. We have much talke of an apparition in Wales, not far from Chester, of great troupes of horse and foote in battell array, seene upon a mountaine by sixteen or eighteen persons of credit, but when they came to discover what they were sodainly vanisht. We have here foure youthes come from Moscovie to learne our language and Latin, and are to be dispersed to divers schooles at Winchester, Eaton, Cambridge, and Oxford. One Perkins,[a] a prime man at Cambridge, and of great esteme with the precise faction, is lately dead; and another eclipse is befaln that Universitie, for Dr. Plaifer, the Divinitie reader, is lately crackt in the headpeece for the love of a wench, as some say. Sir Walter Lewson is dead in the Fleet, and so his creditors paide in theire care. Mrs. Bodley hath lately lost her eldest sonne, Captaine Ball,[b] in the Lowe Countries by sicknes. The young Lady North is brought to bed of a sonne; and the common report is that Dr. Dee hath delivered the Lady Sandes of a devill, or of some other straunge possession. Your Lady Thomas Norris is become a great Catholique, and takes great care and paines to convert her sisters. I have nothing els, but to pray you commend me to Mr. Winwod if he be still there, and tell him the voice runs still with him for Mr. Gilpins place; and yet I am told there be above twenty suters, besides Wheeler[c] and blacke Milles. Since before dinner I have

[a] William Perkins, minister of St. Andrew's parish, Cambridge. [Birch MS. No. 4173.]
[b] By Mrs. Bodley's first husband: see before, p. 118.
[c] Secretary to the Merchants of Middleborough. [See p. 151.]

heard further that Sir Francis Vere hath ben robd in his chamber of 2,000*l.* in gold, and some say he is dead of his hurt. Besides Captaine Ball, there be many other Captaines lately dead in the Lowe Countries, as Lile, Clifford, Keyes, Richards, Vanifor, Deacons, Crofts, Drake, and above fowre thousand of the sixe that went last over. Harry Butler,* that killed Russell, is taken at Carlile, going for Spaine, with letters for the Duke of Feria. This is all, unles I shold tell you that a prentise, pursued by his master to be beaten, lept out of a garret by Holbourne Bridge, and fell upon a porters necke and got away without harme. Mr. Backhouse and Mr. Borlas have them kindly commended to you; and the drie-handed Knight must not be forgotten, for he remembered it to me by a letter out of the countrie. And so I leave you to Gods holy protection.

From London this 4th of November, 1602.

Yours most assuredly, JOHN CHAMBERLAIN.

The Dutch men had set out a relation of the fight with the gallies, which we allow not, neither indeed do theire owne tales agree; whereupon I thought goode to send you this report of Sir Robert Mansell, in aunswer of those drunken companions.

[*Addressed,*]
To my assured goode frende
 Mr. Dudley Carleton
  geve these.

## LETTER LVI.

[Domestic Correspondence, State Paper Office, November 19, 1602.]

SIR,

Your posts take so uncertain a course, and are so longe in goinge, that I have commonly more trouble in huntinge them out then in writinge. Mr. Winwods reckening drawes so neere, that it were

* See p. 102.

but lost labour to adventure a letter; for, as I remember, he made account to be here about the 20th of this moneth. My last to you was of the fourth or fift of this present, since which time here hath ben a very dull and dead terme, or els I am quite out of the trade, which may well be, by reason of a new devised order to shut the upper doores in Powles in service time, wherby the old entercourse is cleane chaunged, and the trafficke of newes much decayed. Some ten or twelve dayes since we were halfe afraide of Mr. Secretarie,[a] upon a soduin accident that came by a cold, with a swelling in his throat or squinancie, which hindered him that he could neither swallow nor scant breath; but the daunger lasted not longe, for, upon letting bloude, and some other applications, he presently mended. The Lord President of Yorke [b] is come hither to his old winter garrison; belike he findes his government too far from the sun. We had lately a proclamation against Jesuites and priests theire adherents, that they are to avoide the realme within thirty dayes upon theire perill, and the secular priests before the beginning of February at farthest, unles they will submit themselves to the Quenes mercy, and make profession of theire loyaltie, in which case further order shalbe taken with them; and what a vaine thinge it was in them or any other to dreame of a toleration, whereas her Majestie had never any such meaninge, nor any of her counsaile durst ever make such a motion. This was the effect of it; now what effect it will worke, or how they are affected with it, we shall see hereafter. I feare it comes very late, yet better late then never. The Kinge of Scotland led us the way, and went somwhat beyond us, in taking an othe of all his nobilitie, gentrie, and men of qualitie, not to harboure nor receve any of them hereafter. The Quene came to Whitehall on Monday [c] by water, though the Lord Mayor [d] with his troupes of 500 velvet coates and chaines of gold was alredy mounted, and marching to receve her at Charing Crosse. The sodain alteration grew upon inckling or suspicion of some daungerous attempt. Her

[a] Sir Robert Cecil.  [b] Lord Burghley.  [c] November 15th.
[d] Sir Thomas Bennett.

day[a] passed with the ordinarie solemnitie of preaching, singing, shooting, ringing, and running. The Bishop of Limmericke, Dr. Thornborough,[b] made a dull sermon at Paules Crosse. At the tilt were many younge runners, as you may perceve by the paper of theire names. Your foole Garret made as faire a shew as the prowdest of them, and was as well disguised, mary not altogether so well mounted, for his horse was no bigger then a goode ban-dogge; but he delivered his scutchion with his *impresa* himself, and had goode audience of her Majestie, and made her very merry. And, now we are in mirth, I must not forget to tell you of a cousening prancke of one Venner, of Lincolns Inne, that gave out bills of a famous play on Satterday was sevenight on the Banckeside, to be acted only by certain gentlemen and gentlewomen of account. The price at comming in was two shillings or eighteen pence at least; and, when he had gotten most part of the mony into his hands, he wold have shewed them a faire paire of heeles, but he was not so nimble to get up on horsebacke, but that he was faine to forsake that course, and betake himselfe to the water, where he was pursued and taken, and brought before the Lord Cheife Justice,[c] who wold make nothing of it but a jest and a merriment, and bounde him over in five pound to appeare at the sessions. In the meane time the common people, when they saw themselves deluded, revenged themselves upon the hangings, curtains, chaires, stooles, walles, and whatsoever came in theire way, very outragiously, and made great spoile; there was great store of goode companie, and many noblemen. Our Commissioners and the the Danes are met at Breme:[d] the Quenes ship that caried them, comming backe with other in her companie, met with a huge number of whales on the coast of Holland that indured many shot, and plaide many gambolls. The like number hath not ben scene together, specially in these parts, for they say they saw above two hundreth. Here is much descanting what they should portend

[a] November 17th, the day of Elizabeth's accession.
[b] John Thornborough, afterwards Bishop of Bristol and of Worcester.
[c] Sir John Popham. [d] See p. 150.

more then the tempest that followed. The Lord Deputie of Ireland [a] kepes his residence at Connagh, as fittest for intelligence, and for opportunitie, by the neernes, to annoy the ennemie. Tirrell had made a head of 800 foote and 100 horse; but he was almost surprised in the middest of his forces, being faine with his wife to flie away naked, with the losse of 200 men and his baggage. Mowbray the Scot and Daniell the Italian have performed the combat in Scotland, or on the borders, wherein they are both slaine;[b] yet the little dandelot had the honor to leave his ennemie dead in the feild, though himself lived but two dayes after. On the Quenes day [c] ten were taken at a masse in Newgate. It is not like but you have heard that Junius, the divine, is dead of the plague at Leiden. This morning Robert Knolles had a great mischaunce in riding a horse of Mr. Controllers [d] in the tilt yard, that came over with him, and hath sore brused or, as some say, broken two of his ribbes, others his bulke, [sic] but all generally agree that he is in great daunger, and will hardly scape. Your sister Bridget [e] is come to towne with her lady; and your brother Carleton is likewise here plodding about his father Harrisons [f] office; but, with all his cunning, he cannot worke him to any certain conclusion. I send you here the Quenes entertainment at the Lord Kepers;[g] if you have seen or heard it alredy, it is but so much labour lost. If Mr. Winwod be still with you, I know you will make him partaker of this, and whatsoever els of any worth comes from me to your hands. Commend me, I pray you, to Mr. Saunders; and so I commit you to God.

From London, this 19th of November, 1602.

Yours most assuredly,         JOHN CHAMBERLAIN.

[a] Lord Mountjoy.

[b] This is incorrect; Mowbray afterwards killed himself in endeavouring to escape from Edinburgh Castle, and Daniel lived to enjoy a pension which was granted him by the King of Scots. See pp. 157, 165, 177.

[c] November 17th.       [d] Sir William Knolles.

[e] Bridget Carleton, subsequently married to Sir Hercules Underhill, knight.

[f] Mrs. George Carleton's father held a post in the Queen's stable.

[g] At Harefield house, Middlesex, in August, 1602. The interlude and poems are printed in Queen Elizabeth's Progresses, iii. 586-595.

Yesterday here was a running report that the Frenche Kinge was slaine by a friar. It was very current, and tooke fire like a traine or a squib: I never knew any newes spread so sodainly; for in lesse then three howres it was all over the towne; but this day it cooles again, and we cannot learne how it shold rise. Though, at the hottest, I did not thoroughly beleve it, yet did it more appall me then any publicke newes I heard these seven yeares.

[*Addressed,*]
 To my assured goode frend
  Mr. Dudley Carleton,
   geve these,
    in Paris.

## LETTER LVII.

[Domestic Correspondence, State Paper Office, December 4, 1602.]

SIR,
 This is more of custome, and to convey these inclosed, that I write now, than for any materiall busines or novelties I have to send you. The last I had from you was of the 29th of October,[a] and the last I sent of the 19th of November, wherin I must recall the combat in Scotland, for there was no such matter, but they are (or were very lately) both alive, and in the Castle of Edemburgh. We had had so longe a dearth of newes that some goode fellowes thought it a fitt time to set the mill a worke, and found utterance at will. We are now as busie about the Duke of Buillon, and coine many messages, aunswers, and replies, besides large discourses what course he

[a] The letter referred to is in the French Correspondence, State Paper Office.

will or shold take. We heare the Dolphin hath a younge sister,[a] wherewith we say the Kinge is as little pleased as his ambassador here that his wife hath brought a daughter. Sir Henry Davers is come out of Ireland, and bringes nothing more then I wrote you. The Lord Chaundos[b] is lately dead; and the controversies twixt M[rs] Bridges and the younge lord,[c] are compounded, or upon the point, without mariage. The Quenes shippes are come from the coast of Spaine, and have met with no adventures. They arrived at Plimmouth in poore and weake case; nine more are making redy to second and supplie them. Three Dunkirkers set upon the Crane, a ship of the Quenes that convoyed a marchant, and put her to her shifts, having slaine the captaine, one Jones, and divers of her men. At the end of the terme here was a speach of a call of sergeants; but many lawyers complaine, and say they had more neede of a call of clients. We had no new sheriffes till Sunday[d] last; and then not all neither, but some on Thursday,[e] and some are yet to set downe. Mr. Manwoode is for Kent, Sir Ed. Fettiplace for Berkshire, Mr. Farmer for Oxford, one Chester for Buckingham, Sir Edward Denny for Hartfordshire, Mr. Wendie for Cambridge, *et sic de cæteris*. The Quene shold have come to the warming of Mr. Secretaries[f] new house on Monday, but then the cold hindred it, and on Wensday the fowle weather, and whether it hold appointment this day is a question. On Monday or Tewsday next the Lord Admirall[g] is to feast her at Arundell House; and then the Lord Thomas Howard and the Lord Chamberlain,[h] and all is to entertain the time, and win her to stay here if it may be. Your brother Carleton is in towne; we are like to have his companie often, now he is sworne, and executes his father Harrisons place,[i] where I

[a] Born 12 Nov. 1602. The Queen, being disappointed in the sex, was answered by the King that God first made man and then woman. [See Parry's letter, French Correspondence, State Paper Office, Nov. 24.]   [b] William fourth Lord Chandos.
[c] Grey, fifth Lord Chandos (son of William), and his cousin the heiress of Giles the the third Lord, who died s. p. m. in 1593 : see before, p. 156.   [d] November 28th.
[e] December 2nd.   [f] Sir Robert Cecil.   [g] The Earl of Nottingham.
[h] Lord Hunsdon.   [i] In the Queen's stable : see p. 164.

doubt he shall reape no great profit nor reputation, specially during the old mans life, who will not resigne. Mr. Cope is very hot and earnest for his papers; I wold you could tell how to stop his mouth. This packet to Mr. Cressy from the Lady Taisborough was commended to me by Mr. Gent, who went this morning toward Askot to fetch Mr. Dormer and his lady to sojourne here this Christmas, and longer, as they like it. I have looked so longe for Mr. Winwod that I have almost given him over. I have not written to him because I have nothing more to say, but only that his frend Hatton Farmer [a] is toward a match with a daughter [b] of the Lord Andersons; and so I commit you both to Gods holy protection.

From London, this 4th of December, 1602.

Yours most assuredly,

JOHN CHAMBERLAIN.

Upon the posts lingering, I have kept this letter open a day or two longer, in which space I have learned that the bullet is lately cut out from under the bone of Sir Francis Veres eye, and that he is perfectly cured. The Quenes letters have wronge from him a captaines place in the Brill for Warberton the pencioner. I forgot to write you that Clarke, the gentleman usher, died before Mighelmas. Your old frend Captaine Calfhill was employed in the Quenes ships, and came home sicke to Plimmouth before the rest of the fleet, where he was brought very low and leane; but, upon his recoverie, and his stomacke comming to him againe, he so laid about him that they say he burst with eating. The Lord Keper [c] is gon into the countrie upon pretence that the small poxe be in his house; but some will needs suspect that to be *non causa pro causa*. The Quene dined this day at Mr. Secretaries,[d] where they say there is great varietie of entertainment prepared for her, and many rich

---

[a] Son of Sir George Fermor of Easton Neston, co. Northampton ; he was knighted in 1603, and died 1620.
[b] Elizabeth daughter of Sir Edmund Anderson.
[c] Sir Thomas Egerton.   [d] Sir Robert Cecil.

jewells and presents. It is somwhat spoken of about the Court that they heare no oftener out of Fraunce, and you are counted but slacke there amonge you; but this is to your self, and so kepe it. *Iterum atque iterum vale.* This 6th of December, 1602.

[*No address.*]

LETTER LVIII.

[Domestic Correspondence, State Paper Office, December 23, 1602.]

GOODE MR. CARLETON,

I am litle beholding to the post that brought Mr. Winwods letters and yours of the 23th [a] of the last and 7th [b] of this present, for he kept them a whole weeke in his hand after his arrivall, so that I had scant leisure to run over the inclosed discourse, for that your brother was to go that day homeward, and Sir Edward Norris went away not past two dayes before. A third of the 12th [c] of this present I receved three dayes since; in aunswer to all which I can say litle for the present, being full fraught with splene and indignation of such unworthie usage; and he were a wise man could tell what were best to be don in the case; but at all adventures I wold you had sett all at sixe and seven in the instant, and left him [d] in the lurch, whereas now *lupum auribus tenes*, and it is alike difficult and daungerous to hold or let go. I understand Mr. Winwod is to come shortly away, but I doubt his absence will not remove the mischeife, for there is some further matter of degenerate jealousie that will not endure your sun shold dimme his torch; howsoever it

[a] French Correspondence, State Paper Office, November 23rd.
[b] Ibid. December 7th.   [c] Ibid. December 12th.
[d] Sir Thomas Parry. See Domestic Correspondence, State Paper Office, December 7, 1602, for a letter to George Carleton, in which Dudley gives a long account of the ill usage he received from the ambassador. The document covers 17 pages.

be, I looke for no goode ende of so bad beginnings, but wish you to resolve some other way, and what course soever you take shall have my voice, for I know it wilbe grounded upon reason and judgement, and no man can give you better advise then your self, because all circumstances and your owne inclination (which is not the least point to be considered) are better knowne to your self then to any looker on; but, if you rest unsatisfied in your self, and relie more upon other mens opinion, I dare not alone undertake such a taske that requires the heads and hands of all your best frends. I am going to-morrow to kepe Christmas at Knebworth,[a] whether I am so vehemently urged that it were no goode manners to forsake them now in their solitarines,[b] havinge always had so great part of theire pleasure and plentie. I mean not to stay there long, and whatsoever we can hammer out there together you shall heare by my next. I make full account that when your honorable frend [c] shall understand the whole matter he will not be quiet till he see you better provided, and that this disgrace will double his care and kindnes towards you. I have pacified Wat Cope in shewing him what you write touching his papers. Mr. Secretarie did him a very extraordinarie favor to admit him a partner in his entertainment to the Quene, and to permit him to present her with some toyes in his house, for the which he had many faire wordes, but as yet cannot get into the privie chamber, though he expect it daily. You like the Lord Kepers devises so ill, that I cared not to get Mr. Secretaries that were not much better, saving a pretty dialogue of John Davies,[d] twixt a maide, a widow, and a wife, which I do not thincke but Mr. Saunders hath seen, and no doubt will come out one of these dayes in print with the rest of his works. The Lord Admiralls[e] feasting the Quene had nothing extraordinarie, neither were his presents so precious as was expected; being

[a] At Mr. Lytton's.  [b] By reason of Mr. Lytton's death.
[c] Sir Edward Norris, to whom Chamberlain was requested to mention Sir Thomas Parry's treatment of Carleton. [See French Correspondence, Dec. 12.]
[d] Davies of Hereford.  [e] The Earl of Nottingham.

only a whole suit of apparell, whereas it was thought he wold have bestowed his rich hangings of all the fights with the Spanish Armada in eightie-eight.[a] These feastings have had theire effect to stay the Court here this Christmas, though most of the cariages were well onward on theire waye to Richmond. The Quene christned the French ambasadors daughter, by her deputie the lady Marquise, the Countesse of Worcester and the Lord Admiralle being the other assistants. There is some fertile planet abrode that layes downe our ladies so fast, for the Lord Thomas Howards, Sir Robert Sidneys, and young M$^{rs}$ Hatton, are all in the straw; and the Lady Wallop, with our M$^{rs}$ Anne, or Smith, are prettelie forward. You may tell Mr. Saunders that the Bishop of London,[b] Sir John Scot, and the Lady Hatton were gossippes to Mr. Fanshawes sister, and have made another grand Christopher.[c] Here is a buzze alredy that the Lord of Northumberland shall go to the christening of your *fille de France;* if it so fall out you may bethincke your selfe what use might be made of it. Dr. Mount,[d] master of the Savoy, is lately dead, and Dr. Neale,[e] Mr. Secretaries chaplain, hath his roome. We heare that Ostend had almost ben betrayed by the Sergeant Major, who is apprehended and sent to the Haghe. Tirrell was almost taken again in a straight, but for the unluckie going of of a peece, whereat he tooke the alarme, and got away, but some of his companie paide the reckening. Our commissioners at Breme they say are comming home overland, and cannot agree with the Danes. Alderman Skinners eldest sonne, having spent the most of that he had,

---

[a] Which corresponded no doubt with those which remained within memory in the House of Lords. They were designed by Henry Cornelius Vroom, at Haerlem, and woven by Francis Spiring.

[b] Richard Bancroft.

[c] Alice, daughter of Thomas Fanshawe, esq. and wife of Christopher Hatton, of Kirby, co. Northampton, esq. created K.B. at the coronation of James I. The "grand Christopher" now christened was made K.B. at the coronation of Charles I. and created Baron Hatton of Kirby in 1643.

[d] William Mount, of whom see Athenæ Cantabrigienses, ii. 271.

[e] Richard Neale, ultimately Archbishop of York.

and bought a place in Barwicke, hath ben tampering with somewhat that he is called in question for, and clapt up close prisoner in the Gatehouse. The small pockes drave the Lord Keper[a] into the countrie; but, his house continueng still infected, he and his lady are returned, and lodge at the Rolles. There is no shew of any great doings at Court this Christmas. Sir Walter Raleigh hath caried away the Lord Cobham, the Lord Compton, and others, to Sherbourn; and Sir John Harrington meanes to kepe a royall Christmas in Rutlandshire, having the Erles of Rutland and Bedford, Sir John Gray and Sir Harry Carie,[b] with theire ladies, the Erle of Pembroke, Sir Robert Sidney, and many more gallants. Yesterday, when nobody lookt for it, Sir Edward Wotton was made Controller, and Sir William Knolles translated Treasurer. The little gentlewoman[c] without Criplegate sends you word that her mother[d] marvailes she cannot heare of you. I have sent you here an almanack, that you may see how our yeare passeth away, which I wish as happy to you as I wish to my self; and so, being redy to horsebacke, I commit you to God.

From London this 23th day of 10ber, 1602.

       Yours most assuredly,

[*Addressed*,]       JOHN CHAMBERLAIN.

 To my very assurede frend
  Mr. Dudley Carleton
   geve these,
    at the Lord Ambassadors
     in Paris.

---

[a] Sir Thomas Egerton.
[b] Cary.        [c] One of Carleton's sisters.
[d] Joyce, daughter of John Goodwin, of Winchendon, Bucks, widow of Robert Saunders, of Flore, Notts, and wife of Anthony Carleton, of Baldwin Brightwell, Oxon.

## LETTER LIX.

[Domestic Correspondence, State Paper Office, January 17, 1602-3.]

JOHN CHAMBERLAIN TO RALPH WINWOOD.[a]

SIR,

The post that brought your last of the twelfth of December,[b] hath taken me napping the next day after my returne from Knebworth, and calles for an aunswer; and, though I am not yet fully setled, nor have not sufficiently informed my self how the world hath gon here in mine absence, yet, least he shold go empty, and so make an ill impression, I have thought goode to send you what I have got at the first sight The world hath not ben altogether so dull and dead this Christmas as was suspected, but rather the Court hath flourisht more then ordinarie, whether it be that the new Controller[c] hath put new life into it by his example (being allwayes freshly attired, and for the most part all in white *cap a pied*), or that the humors of themselves grow more gallant; for, besides much dauncing, beare baiting, and many playes, there hath ben great golden play, wherin Mr. Secretarie[d] lost better then 800*l.* in one night, and as much more at other times, the greatest part wherof came to Edward Stanleys and Sir John Lees share. Here is young Hawkins come lately out of Spaine (whether by exchaunge or raunsome I know not), and bringes word of great preparations, and of divers of our marchants ships and venturers taken about the straights, among the rest one Capt. Middleton, whom the Spaniards, with a hatefull and ridiculous fallace (to kepe theire word that they wold do him no harme), forced his owne men to strangle. The Quenes ships have staide foure Lubeckers in the narrow seas, laden with armes and munition for Spaine, who report that fouretene more with the like fraught are gon about by the north of Scotland. The rebells come in daily in Ireland; and it is thought that Tirone himself shalbe shortly admitted to parlee. Our Commissioners stay

---

[a] This letter is inserted here, because it was begun with the intention of its being sent to Carleton. [b] See French Correspondence, State Paper Office.
[c] Sir Edward Wotton. [d] Sir Robert Cecil.

still at Breme, though it were geven out that the treatie was broken of; indeed the Danes were departed, but are to return again out of hand. Sir Edward Conway is newly come from the Brill,[a] and Sir Robert Siduey as lately gon to Flushing. Dr. Bennet [b] Deane of Windsore is preferred to the bishopricke of Hereford; there is much canvassing for his deanry and mastership of St. Crosse,[c] which George Brooke [d] wold faine ingrosse. The bishopricke of Norwich is conferred upon one Dr. Griggon [e] of Cambridge. Sir Thomas Taisborough is lately dead, as it were almost sodainly. There was a quarrell growing at Court twixt Younge Wharton [f] and Ashley about a mistris, or some such waighty matter, and the lie past; but the counsaile in theire wisdomes vouchsafed to compound it.

Sir, the truth is, that when I began this letter I meant it to Mr. Carleton, but Mr. Gent comming in the nicke, and shewing me yours of the fourth of this present, brought by Peter Browne, I altered my mind. not knowing what termes he standes in, nor with what safetie letters come to his handes; desiring you to acquaint him with it if you please, and to tell him that his turne is next. I am sory we shall not see you so soone, for I and some other of his frendes relie altogether upon your relation and advise what course he and you shall thincke to be best for him; and so, with my best wishes to you both, I commit you to God.

From London, this 17th of January, 1602.

Yours most assuredly,

*Addressed*,]   JOHN CHAMBERLAIN.

To my assured goode freud
  Mr. Raphe Winwod,
      geve these
        at Paris.

---

[a] Of which he was governor.   [b] See before, pp. 58 and 136.
[c] James I. bestowed the Mastership of St. Cross on Dr. Lake, brother of Sir Thomas Lake.   [d] Brother of Lord Cobham.
[e] John Jegon; elected Bishop of Norwich, Jan. 18, 1602-3; died March 13, 1617-8.
[f] Son of Lord Wharton.

## LETTER LX.

[Domestic Correspondence, State Paper Office, Jan. 27, 1602-3.]

Sir,

I have neither written nor heard from you this yeare. I hopte at my comming from Knebworth to have founde somwhat; but, seing nothing came either then or since, it makes me suspect that you may not remember your frendes as you were wont, or els your messengers play the truants by the way. I had begon a letter to you the second day of my comming to towne; but ere it was fully ended, it chaunged copie and turned to Mr. Winwod.[a] The contents were indifferent to you both, only ordinarie occurrents, and such as might easilie be parted between you. I heare he hath his crosses and traverses there [b] as well as other folkes, which no doubt will make the letters that are gon to call him home the more welcome. The Court removed hence to Richmond the 21th of this moneth in very fowle and wet weather; but the wind sodainly chaunging to the north-east hath made here ever since the sharpest season that I have lightly knowne. The Monday before her going the Quene was entertained and feasted by the Lord Thomas [c] at the Charterhouse. Two dayes after, the Lady of Effingham was brought to bed of a daughter, altogether unlooked for, and almost before she or any body els suspected she was with childe. The deanry of Windsore is (or like to be) bestowed on Dr. Tomson [d] that was of All Soules. The Quene seekes to discharge herself of her great charge in Ireland, and hath lately cashiered 4,000 men there. Here be likewise projects to ease her of the burthen of keping the narrow seas; for, seing her ships serve to so litle purpose against the Dunkirkers, it is propounded that the Citie shold maintain two ships and a pinnesse, the Northern coast as many, or more, and the West country in like proportion; and so to make triall what goode

[a] See Letter LIX. p. 173.   [b] See Winwood's Memorials, i. 453 and 460.
[c] Lord Thomas Howard, afterwards Earl of Suffolk.
[d] Giles Tomson; installed Dean of Windsor March 2, 1602-3; died Bishop of Gloucester, June 14, 1612. [Courthope's Nicolas, p. 551.]

may be don upon them. In the mean time the Quenes ships shall serve for the coast of Spaine, and Sir Richard Lewson is preparing thitherward with eight of her navy, and some other assistants. The combat [a] is not yet performed in Scotland, whatsoever is the hinderaunce, for the lists and scaffoldes were prepared and redy three weekes or a moneth agon. Sir Edward Norris is in towne, much visited by the cavaliers. I heare he kept a great Christmas, and that Capt. Whiddon is alredie wearie of Ireland and returned, but appeares not yet in Powles. I know not whether it be newes to you, as it was tother day to me, that the Lady Pawlet died of a consumption five or sixe monethes ago; but I am sure it will be newes to heare that Mr. Evers hath got him a younge wife in Lincolnshire, where he was hammering about her all the last terme, and hath not yet shewed his face here among his frends. Mr. Edmunds wifes sister hath likewise got her a husband, one Clarke of Hamshire, that shalbe a man of faire living. Your brother Carleton is not yet come to towne, nor none of our old frends. The Lady Umpton went into the country on Friday last. I can assure you now that neither Mrs. Faringdon nor her sister [b] are so far gon [c] as theire Valentine wisht and reported, only I perceve they tooke a light tincture, but no deepe dye, which I hope in time will weare out well inough. I know not if here be ought may please Mr. Winwods taste, howsoever I pray you make him partaker of my best wishes and commendations; and so I commit you to God.

From London, this 27th of January, 1602.

                Yours most assuredly,

[*Addressed,*]                       JOHN CHAMBERLAIN.
To my assured goode frend
    Mr. Dudley Carleton
        geve these,
           at the Lord Ambassadors
                in Paris.

---

[a] Between Mowbray and Daniel. See pp. 157, 164, and 177.
[b] Two of Carleton's sisters.     [c] Towards Roman Catholicism.

## LETTER LXI.

[Domestic Correspondence, State Paper Office, Feb. 11, 1602-3.]

SIR,

Mr. Winwod was the more welcome for bringing your letters,[a] which were so long wanting that I began to suspect all was not well on our side, and did sometimes call myself to account to see wherein I had failed; but, finding nothing, I easilie concluded that either your leisure or the place you hold wold not permit often writing, or els that some whispering and schooling monitor (either here or there) had counsailled you to the contrarie. It was never my desire nor meaning to incroach upon newes or secrets, specially as long as Powles is so furnisht that it affords whatsoever is stirring in Fraunce, and I can gather there at first hand to serve my turne sufficiently (saving for certain particulars), so that I shall not neede to put you to trouble or paines, but only to understand your estate. *ut vales, ut memor es nostri,* and such other complements of kindnes and frendship. Mr. Winwod hath ben but once with Mr. Secretarie,[b] but makes acccount to go with him to Court to-morrow. I have brought your cousin Lytton, your brother Carleton, Mr. Edmonds and him together, and have had some speach of your busines;[c] but, to tell you truly, me thinckes we are like phisitions that consult of a patient without feeling any part of his paine, and, finding the disease somwhat difficult, applie no other remedie but goode wordes and goode wishes, and make him beleve that time and goode diet will cure it alone. Indeed patience and time must be your best medicine till we see what Mr. Winwods absence from thence and his presence here will effect. You still forget Mr. Cope, whom I could wish you had at this time remembered. Captain Whiddon is come newly out of Ireland very weary of those warres. Tiron, Tirrell, and most of the other rebels are now retired into the North;

[a] See French Correspondence, Feb. 10, 1603, N.S.
[b] Sir Robert Cecil.
[c] A difference between Sir Thomas Parry and Carleton.

and in theire passage thether slue one Capt. Malbie, a proper gentleman, with most of his companie. A Spanish ship laden with wolles, wine, and oiles wrackt at Dover in a mist on Sonday last. A Hollander comming from the East Indies was driven to that extremitie for want of vitaile that they eate one another, and were growne so feeble that in a small storme they were seene by an English ship to sinke not far from our coast. Mowbray[a] the Scot, seeking to breake prison, and escape out of the Castle of Edenborough (as I take it), his sheetes, ropes, and other provisions were so short that he fell downe and bruised himself so sore that he lived not past two howres after. On Monday last here was a great prise and challenge performed at the Swan betwene two fencers Dun and Turner, wherin Dun had so ill lucke that the other ran him into the eye with a foile, and so far into the head that he fell downe starke dead, and never spake word nor once moved. The case is and wilbe much argued by lawyers whether it will prove chaunce medley, manslaughter, or murder, by reason of malice, and many challenges past betweene them before. One Starkie a preacher, well learned and languaged, not longe since chaplain to the old Countesse of Shrewsburie or the Lady Arbella, honge himselfe here in towne the last weeke, which ministers much matter of talk and many surmises.[b] The Quene before her going hence named eleven new sergeants at law,[c] that is to say, Altham of Grayes Inne; Hubert,[d] Hawten,[e] and Harris of Lincolnes Inne; Phillips and Nichols of the Middle Temple; and of the Inner house, Crooke the recorder, Coventrie, Tanfield, Foster, and Barker, for whose preferment the world findes no other reason but that he is Mr. Atturneys brother in law,[f] or els (as one saide) that amonge so many biters there shold

---

[a] See Scotch Correspondence, State Paper Office, for further particulars about Mowbray

[b] M. de Beaumont in a letter to Henry IV. enters upon this subject. [French Correspondence, State Paper Office, Feb. 22, 1603, N.S.]

[c] Some only of these serjeants were called immediately, the rest early in the following reign: see Dugdale's Chronica Series.

[d] Henry Hobart.      [e] Robert Houghton.

[f] Robert Barker, serjeant-at-law, married Margaret sister to Sir Thomas Coke.

be one barker. Doctor Howson,[a] Vice-Chauncellor of Oxford, made a sermon there on the Queens day[b] that is accused of false doctrine, and hath bred much brabling, and raised such a dust there that I thincke will put out some of theire eyes. Dr. Ayrie[c] and divers others are sent for up and imprisoned here, and some there. I send you here the sermon,[d] and a defence[e] of Mr. Hooker against a Puritane pamflet[f] that came out above a yeare ago. I heard not of Peter Brownes dispatch till he was gon, so that I must seeke out or tary for some other messenger. Yesternight Mr. Edmunds, Mr. Winwod, your brother, Mr. Gent, and myself supt at the Mermaide,[g] where your health was often remembred, and better provided for *inter pocula* then our owne, for I have ben distempered ever since. The Venetian ambassador or agent had audience on Sonday last the sixt of this moneth; and so with my best wishes I commit you to God.

From London, this 11th of February, 1602.

Yours most assuredly,

[*Addressed*,]               JOHN CHAMBERLAIN.

To my assured goode frend
   Mr. Dudley Carleton
      give these
    at the Lord Ambassadors
        in Paris.

[a] John Howson, afterwards Bishop of Oxford (1618). Wood, (Ath. Oxon. edit. Bliss, ii 517,) gives some account of the attacks made by the Puritans on his doctrines.

[b] November 17.

[c] Henry Airay, D.D. Provost of Queen's college, Oxford, a zealous Calvinist.

[d] "In defence of the Festivities of the Church, and namely that of her Majesties Coronation," by John Howson, D.D. [Birch MS. No. 4173.]

[e] "A just and temperate Defence of the Five Books of Ecclesiastical Polity, and against an uncharitable Letter of certain English Protestants." London, 1603. 4to. By William Covel, D.D. [Ibid.]

[f] "A Christian Letter of certain English Protestants, unfeigned lovers of the present state of religion authorised and professed in England, unto that learned man Mr. Hooker, requiring resolution in certain matters of doctrine expressly contained in his five books of Ecclesiastical Polity." Printed in 1599 in 4to. [Ibid.]

[g] The famous tavern in Bread Street.

## LETTER LXII.

[Domestic Correspondence, State Paper Office, Feb. 23, 1602-3.]

Sir,

I shall not neede to write you what favorable accesse and audience Mr. Wiuwod found at her Majesties hands, nor any thing els concerning him, sith he is best able to relate it himself, and is now dispatching letters by a messenger of Mr. Saviles towardes you. Mine only errand is to thancke you for yours of the 23th of this present, with the jesuiticall Apologie, wherin (for so much as I have read) I find litle but that I have seen in other theire pamflets before, so that it seemes they are faine to feed us with crambe, for want of better provision. You make mention of another little discourse to be interpreted to the litle gentlewoman,[a] but either it is shroncke in the carriage or you forgot to send it. The twelfth of this present one Richardson, a preist, was taken in Clements Inne, and executed at Tiborn the sixteenth. The last Starchamber day one Darling, a youth of Merton Colledge (that pretended heretofore to be dispossessed of a devill by Darrell), was censured to be whipt and loose his eares, for libelling against the Vice-Chauncellor of Oxford,[b] and divers of the counsaile. He had part of his puuishment the last weeke in Cheapeside, the rest is or shalbe performed at Oxford. Doctor Bennet[c] and Dr. Griggons[d] were consecrated at Lambeth on Sonday[e] was sevenight, the one Bishop of Hereford, the other of Norwich. The Countesse of Nottingham is lately dead, which the Lord Admirall[f] takes exceding grevously. Sir John Payton hath likewise buried his lady; and Smith, brother to the Lady Fortescue and the Lady Anderson, hath left behind him two or three goode offices, for which there is much labour and suit. Your good frend Sir Calistenes Brooke is saide to have maried a widow in the Lowe Countries, of no great goode report for wealth or otherwise. Because I could heare no tidings of his comming, nor Mr. Rodwayes, I left your letters at his fathers to be conveyed. The Coun-

[a] One of Carleton's sisters. [b] See p. 177. [c] See pp. 58, 136, & 173.
[d] Dr. Jegon: see p. 173. [e] The 20th. [f] The Earl of Nottingham.

saile have ben much busied of late about Irish matters, and whether Tiron be to be receved with the conditions offered him by the Erle of Essex; upon which pointes he staundes, and is thought shall obtain, for he gathers head again, and many of the souldiers that were cashiered and lacke worke increase his numbers. New troubles arise daily in Scotland, but the worst of all is the domesticall daungers and hartbreaking that Kinge findes in his owne house. Mr. Dormer and his wife are gon downe; I feare her disease growes on her again, for the which she is minded to go shortly to the Bathe. I had thought to have spent some part of this springe at Askot, but now for ought I know I shall kepe Lent at London, whence you shall heare of me as often as I shall have commoditie of matter or messenger. And so I commit you to Gods holy protection.

From London, this last of February, 1602.

Yours most assuredly,

JOHN CHAMBERLAIN.

Here is fresh newes come out of Spaine of one Newport, a seaman, that with two shippes hath taken five fregats laden with treasure comming from Cartagena and Nombre de Dios towardes the Havana. If all be true that is reported it will prove the greatest prize that ever I heard of, for they that are most modest talke of two millions at least. The King of Spaine[a] hath sent out eight men of warre to waylay and intercept him if he chaunce to touch at the Terceras or thereabout, and some are comming to the coast of England. One Griffith, a Welch pirate, is lately taken at Corke, in Ireland, and his lands, which some geve out to be 500*l*. a yeare, geven to the Lord Gray, to hold him up a while longer. The last I wrote you was about the tenth or eleventh of this present, and I sent it (with a booke or two) by one Gresham, that kepes a bugle shop in St. Martins.

[*Addressed as before.*]

[a] Philip III.

# INDEX.

Abbeville, 9
Abbot, George, D.D. 102
Abergavenny, claim to the peerage of, 32, 45
Acton, ——, 99
Adelantado, the, 67, 71
Airay, Henry, D.D. 178
Alabaster, William, 7, 64
Albert, the Archduke, 16, 25, 66, 70, 79, 84, 86, 91, 100, 144, 145
Aldegonde's discourse, 19
Aldersbrook, 111
Aldobrandini, bro. to the Pope, 72
Aleppo, 32; the Bassa of, 169
Alford, ——, 102
Allen, Mr. 95, 130
Altham, James, 177
Anderson, Sir Edmund, 53, 167; Catherine, 53; Elizabeth, 167; Lady, 179
Andrews, Dr. 112, 154
Antwerp, 59
Archdeacon, Daniel, 157, 164
Arragon, Ammirante of, 85, 86
Armagh, 17
Arnauld, Antoine, 153
Arundel, Count, 27; Sir Mathew, 41; House, 166
Ascott (co. Oxon.) 1, 13, 77, 95, 103, 109, 111, 113, 114, 115, 116, 124, 137, 147, 150, 167, 180
Ashley, ——, 173
Ashfield, ——, 52; Mr. 76
Atkinson, ——, 144, 146
Audley, George Lord, 38, 49

Babington, Gervase, D.D. 77
Bacon, Anthony, 52, 109; Francis, 29, 62 109

Backhouse, Samuel, 116, 161
Bagnoll, Sir Henry, 17; Sir Sam. 14, 17, 23, 27, 36, 51, 122
Bagshaw, Christopher. M.D. 24
Bainham, Sir Edward, 106, 151
Balgay, Nicholas, D.D. 120
Ball, Capt. 160; Mr. 118
Balyshannon, 57, 131
Bancroft, Richard, 69, 72, 75, 82, 170
Banker, Capt. 182
Bankside, 163
Barbary, 24, 40, 136
——, King of, 91
Barclay, Sir John, 42
Barker, Robert, 50, 177
Barlaimont, Count, 85
Barlow, William, D.D. 119, 133
Barn Elms, 78, 89
Barneveldt, John D'Olden, 12, 84
Barnham, Benedict, 29; Mrs. 29
Barrington, Lady, 125
Basilicon Doron, 157
Basing, 116
Baskerville, Lady, 53
Bath, 147, 152, 180
Bayning, Paul, 66, 97, 132; Mrs. 97, 132
Beale, Robert, 65, 73
Beaumont, Sir Francis, 8
Beckley Park, 114
Bedford, Francis Earl of, 2, 87, 100, 102, 108, 171; Bridget Countess of, 100
Becston, George, 140; Hugh, 4, 35, 112, 120, 140, 151, 154; Mr. 120
Bennet, Robert, D.D. 58, 136, 173, 179; Sir Thomas, 162
Benwood, ——, 85
Bereflect, 81

Berehaven, 127, 135, 146
Berke, 112
Berkshire, 166
Berlotte, La, 85
Berry, Sir Benjamin, 96
Berwick, 52, 157, 171
Bevill, Sir William, 133; Lady, 133
Beza, 96
Billingsley, Sir Henry, 50
Bindon, Henry 2nd Viscount, 92; Thomas 3rd Viscount, 92, 97
Bingham, Sir Richard, 13, 18, 34, 42
Biron, Sir John, 54; Marshall, 116, 123, 126, 139, 159
Blackwater, the fort of, 17, 57, 115, 131
Blackwell, Father, 39
Bletso, 19
Bluet, 14
Blunt, Sir Charles, 10, 14, 39; Christopher, 7, 39, 49
Bodley, Thomas, 9, 24, 51, 108, 111, 149, 156; Mrs. 118, 160
Bolton, William, 111
Bomell, the fort of, 66, 68
Bond, Dr. Nicholas, 122
Booth, Sir George, 53
Bordeaux, 97
Borlas, Mr. 161
Boughton, Henry, 78, 126
Bouillon, Duke of, 165
Boulogne, 73, 75, 81
Bowes, Sir William, 52
Boysicz, Mons. de la, 23,25,37,68
Bracciano, Duke of, 99
Brazil, 56
Bremen, 150, 163, 170, 172
Brest, 62
Bridewell, 78

Bridges, Mrs. 139, 156, 166
Brill, the, 3, 16, 21, 24, 167, 173
Bristol, 49, 121, 147
Brocket, Sir John, 19, 25, 136
Bromley, Sir Henry, 133
Brooke, Sir Calisthenes, 2, 122, 179; George, 41, 173; Sir John, 42
Brounker, Sir Henry, 49, 106, 142
Brown, Peter, 37, 158, 173, 178
Bruce, Edward, 135
Bruerton, 154
Bruges, 81, 86
Brussells, 50, 62, 81
Buckhurst, Thomas Lord, 9, 23, 31, 37, 58, 64, 65, 67, 71, 87, 99, 104, 144, 157
Buckinghamshire, 146, 166
Buckley, Sir Richard, 133
Burghley, William Lord, 6, 15, 16, 23, 64, 153; Thomas Lord, 52, 57, 60, 63, 92, 99, 108, 162
Burgoin, Mr. 108, 110
Burke, Lord, 68
Burnham, 150
Burrough, Thomas Lord, 2, 41; Lady, 24
Busquoy, Count, 85
Butler, Henry, 104, 161

Caen, 6
Cadiz, 7
Cæsar, Dr. Julius, 19, 94, 101
Caietan, Cardinal, 72
Calais, 3, 66, 73
Calfhill, Capt. 167
Camarania, the Bassa of, 69
Cambridge, 54, 56, 150, 160, 166
Camden, William, 125, 130
Canuary, the Grand, 56
Canterbury, 18, 68, 89, 151
Carew, Sir George, 14, 75, 86, 94, 97, 127, 135, 146, 160; George, 14, 35; Mr. 118
Carillo, Don Fernando, 73
Carleton, Anthony, 1, 171; Mrs. 1, 139, 171; Alice, 5, 6, 9, 11, 92, 147; Bridget, 164; Dudley, letters and allusions to, *passim*; George, 1, 11, 15, 18, 29, 42, 49, 53, 64, 74, 77, 99, 102, 111, 118, 120, 125, 134, 140, 147, 149, 159, 164, 166, 176; Mrs. 159; and *see* Farringdon

Carlisle, 161
Caron, Nöel de, 57, 92, 131
Carthagena, 180
Cary, Sir Edward, 120
Cary, George, 46; Sir Henry, 57, 143, 171; Lady, 143, 149; Sir Henry, 63; Philip, 120; Mrs. 109
Catesby, ——, 108
Causham, 115, 117
Cavendish, Sir Charles. 52, 53, 54, 55; Lady, 54; Sir William, 52
Cawley, ——, 141
Cawood, Gabriel, 125
Cecill, Sir Robert, 6, 10, 16, 31, 50, 52, 60, 64, 68, 86, 97, 105, 108, 112, 138, 141, 146, 151, 153, 162, 166, 169, 172, 176; William, 79, 99; Elizabeth, 79
Chambourg, Madame de, 95
Chandos, Giles 3rd Lord, 166; William 4th Lord, 166; Grey 5th Lord, 139, 166
Charter-house, the, 174
Chaworth, Sir George, 126
Cheapside, 78, 179
Cheke, Sir John, 52; Lady, 52
Cheshire, 120
Chester, 49, 160
Chester, Charles, 7
Chester, Sheriff of, 166
Cheyney, Kate, 109
Chiswick. 150
Christian IV. of Denmark, 57, 150
Chute, Capt. 64
Cinque Ports, the, 18
Clanrickard, Earl of, 134, 151
Clarke, Sir Roger, 132; William, 150; Mr. 9; —, 167
Clement VIII. Pope, 71, 72, 91, 96, 105
Clement's Inn, 179
Clerkenwell, 77, 120
Cleves, Duke of, 126
Clifford, Capt. 161; Sir Coniers, 57, 62, 63
Clifton, Sir Gervase, 150
Clink, the, 64
Cobham, Henry Lord, 18, 40, 65, 79, 83, 109, 171
Cocke, Sir Henry, 4
Cockington, 46
Codenham, Henry, 126

Coke, Sir Edward, 29, 63, 105, 118, 177; Anne, 118; Elizabeth, 63
Cole, Dr. William, 27
Colmer, Mr. 27
Compton, William Lord, 3, 43, 50, 171; Lady, (see Spencer, Elizabeth); Thomas, 52
Condon, Patrick, 23, 46
Connaught, 46, 164
Constantinople, 32
Conway, Sir Edward, 173
Cope, Sir Anthony, 41, 117, 126; Lady, 41; Walter, 35, 80, 87, 120, 151, 153, 154, 167, 169, 176; Mrs. 35; William, 74, 126, 156; Mrs. 126
Coppinger, Ambrose, 150; Henry, 150; Young, 143
Corbet, Robert, 5
Cork, 119, 180
Cornwall, 101
Cosbie, Capt. 62
Covel, Dr. William, 178
Coventry, Thomas, 177
Cragius, Nicholas, 34, 38
Crequire, Mons. 122
Cressy, Mr. 167
Cripplegate, 147, 152
Crofts, Capt. 161
Croke, John, 119, 177
Cromwell, Edward Lord, 16, 38, 49, 60, 62, 108; Sir Henry, 45, 112; Sir Oliver, 112
Crosse, Sir Robert, 104
Cumberland. George Earl of, 9, 21, 59; Countess of, 87
Cuniga, Don Baltazar de, 73
Curlews, the, 62

Dacre, Henry Lord, 32; Lady, 32
D'Aguilar, Don Juan, 119
Dale, Dr. Valentine, 4
Daniel, *see* Archdeacon, Daniel
Darcy, Sir Francis, 60; Mrs. 135
Darling, Mr. 179
Darrell, Mr. 179
Danvers, Sir Charles, 18, 39; Sir Henry, 18, 39, 42, 166
Richard, 139; Mrs. 139
D'Aumale, Duke, 86
D'Auvergne, Count, 138
Davies, Sir John, 62; Lady, 120; John, 169; ——, 112

## INDEX.

Davis, Capt. John, 42
Davison, Francis, 130, 138, 146
Deacons. Capt. 161
Dee, Dr. 47, 160
De la Warr, Thomas Lord, 125
Delvin, Lord of, 39, 79
Denbighshire, 2
Denia, Marquis of, 71 ; Marchioness of, 71
Denmark, 14, 33, 72
Denny, Sir Edward, 66, 166
Dentragues, Mdlle. 71, 82
Derby, Ferdinando Earl of, 52, 94;
  Dowager Countess of, 52, 64,
  94 ; William Earl of, 3, 38, 104
Desmond, Earl of, 66, 73, 86, 122;
  Sir James Fitzthomas of, 23
Dethick, Mr. 139
Devonshire, 101
Dieppe, 50
Docwray, Sir Henry, 14, 75, 130, 131
Dongannon, 115, 145
Dormer, Michael, 4, 10, 13, 64, 114, 115, 117, 149, 167, 179, 180; Mrs. 10, 13, 115, 138, 147, 167, 180
Dort, 81
Dove, Dr. Thomas, 102
Dover, 177
Doyley, Dr. 134 ; Mr. 134
D'Oyly, John, 139
Drake, Capt. 161
Drew, Serjeant, 8
Drue, ———, 53
Drury, Charles, 65 ; Sir Drue, 40;
  Sir Robert, 46, 47, 50, 75, 85, 98 ; Lady, 47
Dublin, 34, 37, 57, 79, 81, 101, 127
Dudley, Edward Lord, 102 ; Lady, 102
Duff, Patrick, 135
Duke, Sir Henry, 34
Dun, ———, 177
Dunne, Dr. Daniel, 65, 151
Duns, Old, 4 ; Young, 45
Dunkerk, 82, 145 ; Governor of, 85
Durham House, 89
Duxberry, Capt. 85
Dyar, Sir Edward, 100, 112

East Indies, 40, 88

Eaton, 160
Eedes, Dr. Richard, 10, 136
Edinburgh Castle, 165, 177
Edmondes, Clement, 84; Thomas, 10, 13, 67, 70, 73, 81, 91, 109, 111, 146, 156, 176, 178; Talbot, 146
Edmunds, Sir Christopher, 139
Effingham, Lady, 156
Egerton, Sir John, 94, 143; Lady, 143; Sir Thomas, 14, 39, 42, 69, 76, 77, 79, 87, 94, 102, 113, 135, 150, 164, 167, 169, 171
Egmond, Count, 135
Elizabeth, Queen, *passim*
Elson, ———, 144
Embden, 72, 75, 82, 139
Englefield, 114, 117, 149
Essex, 69, 101, 152
——— House, 18
——— Robert, Earl of, *passim ;* Countess of, 49, 97 ; Walter Earl of, 65
Ethiopia. 40
Evers, Mr. 1, 10, 35 ; Sir Peter, 4 ; Ralph Lord, 10, 150 ; William Lord, 10 ; Sir William, 10, 97
Ewens, ———, 14
Exeter, Thomas Earl of, 29

Falmouth, 132
Fane, Francis, 45
Fanshaw, Thomas, 170
Farley, 88, 109
Farnese, Cardinal, 72
Farringdon, Mrs.(an *alias* for one of the Carleton sisters), 154;
  (another sister was called "the Catholic sister," and "the little gentlewoman ";) *see* pp. 127, 129, 136, 154, 155, 171, 179
Fermor, Sir George, 167; Hatton, 167
Fenton, Sir Geoffrey, 81
Feria, Duke of, 161
Fettiplace, Sir Edmund, 117, 166
Fitzgibbon, Edmund, 23, 75
Fitzherbert, Richard, 130
Fitzwilliams, Sir William, 53; Lady, 140
Flanders, 75, 81, 82, 93
Fleet Prison, 29, 32, 78, 126, 160
Fleetwood, Sir Miles, 135; Mr. 41

Fletcher, Dr. 106
Florence, Duke of, 39, 43, 71
Flores, Island of, 21
Flushing, 7, 44, 146, 173
Fortescue, Sir John, 22, 65, 68, 96, 146 ; Lady, 179; Mrs. Padge, 143 ; Sir William, 96
Foster, Sir Humphrey, 117 ; Thomas, 177
Fowler, Richard, 64, 78; Mrs. 78, 125
France. *passim ;* King of, *passim ;* Inventaire, 32
Fresné, Madame de, 95
Fuentes, Count, 71

Gabrielle, la Belle, 71
Gardiner, Sir Robert, 130, 134
Garret, ———, 163
Gascoin, 78
Gatehouse, the, 37, 58, 171
Gaunt [Ghent], 84
Gawdy, Justice, 101, 152
Gent, Mr. 87, 93, 113, 114, 115, 124, 125, 136, 138, 149, 155, 158, 167, 173, 178
Germany, 90
Germin, Sir Thomas, 39, 42
Gerrard, Sir Thomas, 32, 39, 59
Gertrudenberg, garrison of, 66
Gibson, Dr. John, 8
Gifford, Capt. 34; Mrs. 34 ; Mr. 155 ; Richard, 60; Sir Richard, 70, 109, 115; Lady, (*see* Wallop, Winifred)
Gilbert, Dr. 4, 88, 102, 103 ; Sir John, 24, 69, 127 ; Otho, 24
Gilpin, George, 74, 151, 156, 160
Glemham, Sir Henry, 132
Goldsborough, Dr. Godfrey, 14
Gommershall, Mr. 156; Mrs. 156
Goodwin, Sir Francis, 117; John, 171 ; Dr. William, 143, 149 ;
——— , 1
Gorges, Sir Arthur, 92; Lady, 92 ;
  Sir Ferdinando, 38, 42; Sir Thomas, 45, 120, 142, 143
Gonfaloniere della Chiesa, 72
Gosnall, ———, 130, 138
Gowrie, Earl of, 159
Grace Dieu, 7
Grand, Mons. Le, 91
Grant, Dr. Edward, 120
Graveling, 79

Gravesend, 59
Gray, Sir John, 139, 171
Green, Mr. 117; ——, 102
Gresham, Mr. 186
Greville, Fulke, 37, 59, 142, 143
Grey, Thomas Lord, 3, 24, 38, 42, 49, 75, 81, 85, 89, 131, 134, 142, 156, 180
Griffith, ——, 180
Grulwendoncks, ——, 66
Groine, the, 58
Guiana, 24

Hague, The, 44, 99, 151, 170
Hainhault, 81
Hamden, Sheriff, 50
Hampshire, 77, 101, 111, 115, 116, 137
Hampton Poile 114
Hanse Towns, 150
Harefield House, 150, 164
Harlington, 150
Harrington, Sir Henry, 57; Sir John, 63, 171
Harris, Serjeant, 177
Harrison, Mr. 164, 166
Harvy, ——, 97
Haughton, Sir Richard, 53
Havanna, The, 180
Hawkins, Dr. 106; Young, 172
Hay, Dr. 130
Hayward, Dr. John, 47
Heale, Serjeant, 71, 94, 101, 102, 152; Mr. 71
Heine, Capt. 78, 125
Heneage, Michael, 100
Henningham, Sir Arthur, 50
Herbert, Henry Lord, 79, 82, 83; Lady, 79, 83, 87; Dr. John, 6, 24, 27, 52, 73, 75, 94, 101, 112, 151; William Lord, 57
Hertford, Earl of, 102, 112, 117, 146, 150; Frances 2nd Countess, 10; 3d Countess, (see Prannel, Mrs.)
Hertfordshire, 7, 49, 59, 61, 115, 121, 152, 166
Hervey, Sir Gerrard, 20, 44, 99, 122; John, 99; Sir William, 12, 43
Heydon, Sir John, 63, 89, 92
Hickes, Sir Baptist, 139
Highgate, 7
Hill, Richard, 52

Hinchinbrook, 112
Hobart, Henry, 177
Holborn Bridge, 161
Holcroft, Capt. 118
Holland, the States of, remarks on, and allusions to, *passim*
Hollock, Grave, 82
Holyhead, 49
Honeywood, Capt. 85
Hooker, Mr. 178
Howard, Thomas Lord, 3, 18, 56, 59, 92, 115, 166; William Lord, 10, 102
Howson, Dr. John, 112, 143, 178
Hume, Sir George, 150, 157
Humphrey, Dr. Lawrence, 122
Hunsdon, George Lord, 68, 71, 79, 98, 100, 147, 152, 166
Huntingdonshire, 150
Hussey, John Lord, 100

Inquisition, the, in Rome, 71
Ireland, *passim*
Irish, game of, 34
Isabella the Infanta of Spain, 17, 24, 70, 84, 100, 139
Italy, 99

James VI. of Scotland, 39, 52, 66, 97, 157, 162, 180
James, Dr. 100
Jegon, Dr. John, 173, 179
Jermyn, *see* Germin
Jersey, Island of, 89, 146
Jones, Capt. 166
Joyeuse, Duke de, 50, 71
Junius, 164

Kent, 31, 101, 152, 166
Keyes, Capt. 161
Kildare, 12th Earl of, 65; Countess of, 27, 40, 65, 79, 109; 13th Earl of, 39
Killegrew, Sir Henry, 97, 120
Kilmallock, 36
King, Dr. John, 143, 149
King's Bench, the, 115, 135
Kinsale, 119, 123
Knchworth, 5, 19, 44, 48, 64, 73, 88, 98, 103, 109, 116, 118, 120, 124, 137, 148, 150, 169, 172
Knevet, Sir Henry, 133; Sir Thomas, 142

Knightley, Sir Richard, 146
Lady, 146
Knollys, Sir Francis, 38; Lettice, 156; Robert, 164; Sir Thomas, 38; Sir William, 114, 115, 117, 133, 164, 171

Lake, Sir Thomas, 173; Dr. 173
Lambert, 100
Lambeth, 32, 97, 126, 179
Lancashire, 53
Landriani, General, 85
Lascelles, Sir Thomas, 61
Latware, Dr. 115
Lea, Sir Henry, 149; Sir Richard, 149
Ledsam, Dr. 47
Lee, Sir Anthony, 64; Sir Henry, 64, 114; Sir John, 172; Captain Thomas, 104, 105
L'Estrange, Sir Nicholas, 126
Leicestershire, 4, 8
Leix, the Woods of. 73
Lennard, Sir Henry, 32
Lenox, Duke of, 97, 122
Le Sieur, ——, 151
Levant, the, 73, 83, 109
Lewisham, 133
Lewson, Sir Richard, 32, 39, 132, 136, 141, 143; Sir Walter, 32, 160
Lile, Capt. 161
Limerick, 31
Lincoln, Earl of, 50
Lincolnshire, 4, 101
Lindley, Sir Henry, 63
Lisbon, 49, 51
Little Britain, 69, 76, 88, 92, 98, 99, 147
Littlecote, 115, 117
Littleton, John, 106, 115
Little Wood Street, 9
Loftus, Dr. Adam, 36
London, *passim*
Long, Capt. 4
Lorraine, 95
Loughfoile, 17, 57, 75, 131
Lough Sidney, 115
Louth, Lord of, 79
Louvre, the, 71
Lovelace, Sir Richard, 63; Sir William, 63
Lovell, Mrs. 4

Low Countries, the, *passim*
Lucas, Mr. 118
Lytton, Rowland, 5, 10, 15, 19, 25, 27, 42, 53, 59, 70, 73, 77, 93, 99, 106, 108, 118, 121, 123, 127, 133, 137, 140, 147, 150, 154, 158, 176; Mrs. 5, 74, 109, 116, 118, 125; Anne, 33; William, 93, 121, 124

Macarthy More, Florence, 68
MacDermond, 160
MacFeof, Fellom, 101
Macguire, ——, 145
Machugh, Feffe, 2
Mactoole, Fellom, 101
Macwilliams, Henry, 52; ——, 52
Madrid, 71
Malbic, Capt. 177
Manners, Francis, 133; ——, 108
Mansfield, Sir Robert, 37, 89, 92, 119, 151, 161
Mantua, Duchess of, 95
Manwood, Sheriff, 166
Mar, Earl of, 108
Marseilles, 71
Marsh, Mr. 159
Marshalsea, the, 39, 69, 122
Marston Moor, 10
Martin, 112
Massam, 108, 122, 133
Masterson, Capt. 60
Mathew, Dr. Toby, 1, 120; Mrs. 121; Toby, 1, 2, 10, 120, 133
Maurice, Grave, 69, 75, 81, 82, 84, 86, 93, 151
Mayence, Duke of, 68
Maynard, Henry, 16, 59
Meklin, Gregory Ivanowich, 89, 96, 99, 108
Meluing, 135
Mermaid Tavern, 178
Merrick, Sir Gilly, 60
Merton College, 27, 179
Michelhorn, Sir Ed. 151
Middleburg, 16, 32, 142, 145, 151
Middleton, Capt. 172
Milan, 39
Mildmay, Sir Anthony, 2, 5, 10, 45, 64, 108; Mary, 45; Sir Walter, 2

CAMD. SOC.

Milles, Black, 74, 160
Mitcham, 19
Moffatt, Dr. 47
Moirie, the Fort of the, 92
Mompesson, 102, 120
Mook, Levinus, 154
Moscow, 89, 151, 160
Monson, Sir William, 141
Monteagle, Lord, 82, 108
Montpensier, Duke of, 50
Moore, Sir Tho. 34; Lady, 34
Mordaunt, Louis Lord, 112
Morison, Sir Richard, 63
Morley, Lord, 32
Morton, Corbet, 5
Moryson, Sir Richard, 100
Mosley, Sir Nicholas, 29, 62, 132
Mount, Dr. William, 170
Mountjoy, Lord, 3, 23, 26, 50, 58, 65, 75, 79, 81, 86, 92, 94, 96, 101, 115, 119, 122, 127, 130, 134, 145, 156, 164
Mountperson, ——, 120
Mowbray, Francis, 157, 167, 177
Munster, 23, 26, 28, 36, 39, 46, 66, 68, 75, 127, 130, 145, 160

Nantes, 6
Nasse, The, 34
Neale, Dr. Richard, 133
Nevers, Duke of, 126
Neville, Sir Henry, afterwards Lord Abergavenny, 104; Lady, 104; Sir Henry, Ambassador in France, 24, 26, 44, 69, 73, 75, 91, 94, 108, 113, 133, 188; Edward, 32
Newgate, 164
Newport, Mr. 180
Newry, the, 119, 127, 130, 145
Nicholls, Serjt. Augustine, 177
Nieuport, 82; battle of, 84
Nooth, the Lord of, 23
Nombre de Dios, 180
Nonsuch, 19, 22, 61
Norfolk, 101
Norris, Lord, 2, 9, 51, 60, 112, 114; Lady, 51; Sir Edward, 9, 16, 74, 80, 93, 109, 111, 117, 120, 125, 130, 134, 141, 168, 169; his Lady, 79, 80, 114; Francis, afterwards 2nd

2 B

Lord Norris, 47, 100, 149; Sir Henry, 60, 63; Sir John, 2, 117; Sir Thomas, 2, 28, 30, 36, 51, 57, 63; his Lady, 2, 160
North, Roger, 2d Lord, 4, 50, 92, 97; Dudley, 3d Lord, 136, 139, 141, 156, 160; his Lady, 136, 156, 160; Sir John, 4; his Lady, 4, 6, 27
Northampton, Helena Dowager Marchioness of, 45, 143, 157, 170
Northamptonshire, 4, 11
Northumberland, Henry 9th Earl of, 9, 58, 60, 82, 107, 109, 110, 112, 126, 131, 132, 140, 157, 170; Countess of, 152; Algernon 10th Earl of, 157
North-west passage, 157
Norton, John, 113, 147
Norway, 57
Nottingham, Charles Earl of, 27, 38, 56, 58, 60, 62, 68, 97, 157, 166, 169, 170, 179; Countess of, 179
Nottinghamshire, 52

Oatlands, 150
O'Conor Sligo, 73
O'Donnell, ——, 73, 75, 131, 159
Ogle, Capt. 131; Henry, 54; Launcelot, 54
Oldenburgh, 84
Oldenbarneveldt, *see* Barneveldt
O'Moors, the, 73
O'Neale, Terlogh, 131
Ore Orgh, 75
Ormond, Earl of, 26, 42, 46, 66, 73
Ortelius, his Thesaurus Geographicus, 27, 33, 42
Orwell, Capt. 106
Ossory, Lord of Upper, 73
Ostend, 6, 19, 48, 81, 84, 93, 99, 112, 115, 119, 142, 156, 176
O'Sullivan, 130
Overall, Dr John, 132, 143
Owen, Thomas, 37
Oxford, John Earl of, 3; Edward Earl of, 16, 64; Countess of, 16, 64
Oxford, city, 10, 80, 103, 111, 149, 149, 155, 160, 166, 179

INDEX.

Oxfordshire, 4, 15, 53, 58, 64, 87, 92

Packer, ——, 130
Packington, Sir John, 29
Paget, William, 156
Painter, the post, 1
Palavicine, Lady, 112
Palmer, Sir Henry, 37
Paris, 5, 6, 27, 66, 71, 79, 109, 110; siege of, 11
Parker, Sir Nicholas, 42; Mr. 32
Parkins, Dr. Christopher, 14, 33, 34, 35, 72, 118
Parma, Duke of, 72
Parry, Sir Thomas, 24, 108, 127, 130, 134, 138, 144, 146, 148, 168
Paston, Sir William, 126
Pates, ——, 24
Paulet, Sir Amias, 40; Sir Anthony, 80; William, 126
Pelham, Sir Edward, 132; Sir John, 19; Lady, 19, 150; Sir William, 132
Pembroke, Henry 2nd Earl of, 60, 92, 100; Countess of, 100; William 3d Earl, 100, 171
Percy, Sir Charles, 39; ——, 108
Perins, Mr. 143
Perkins, Dr. William, 160
Peyton, Sir John, 4, 179; Lady, 179
Philip II. of Spain, 3, 16, 17, 21, 40; III. of Spain, 24, 27, 39, 40, 47, 71, 88, 91, 180
Phillips, Sir Edward, 143; Sir Robert, 143; Lady, 143; ——, 177
Picardy, 7
Piedmont, 96
Plaifair, Dr. 160
Plymouth, 10, 39, 101, 122, 142, 143, 145, 166, 167
Poland, 14, 96
Poore, Sir Henry, 42
Pope, Mr. 76
Popham, Sir John, 23, 112, 115, 117, 163
Porto Rico, 21, 89
Portsmouth, 6, 142, 143, 146, 150
Portugal, 39, 40, 47, 88, 144
Poulter, Mr. 118

Poultney, Mr. 143
Powell, Thomas, 10
Prannell, Henry, 97; Mrs. 97, 100, 112
Preston, Sir Amias, 119
Puddle Wharf, 98, 120
Purefoy, John, 112
Purlen, or Purton, Capt. 85

Radcliffe, Sir Alexander, 39, 62,
Raleigh, Sir Walter, 3, 7, 14, 18, 21, 59, 69, 70, 89, 146, 171
Ramsey, Sir Thomas, 120; Lady, 120, 122
Reading, 117
Redman, Dr. William, 157
Remington, Sir Robert, 53
Reynolds, Dr John, 27
Rich, Robert Lord, 3, 65; Lady, 65, 76
Richards, Capt. 161
Richardot, Jehan, 73
Richardson, Father, 179
Richmond, 22, 45, 89, 150, 157, 170
Rivas, Govr. of Flanders and Sluce, 85
Robinson, Dr. Henry, 10; Mr. 25
Roche, Lord, 160
Rochelle, 64
Rodney, Sir George, 100, 112
Rudwaye, Mr. 179
Rohan, Viscount de, 91
Rolles, ——, 24, 26
Rowe, 71
Rotheram, Sir John, 96
Russell, John Lord, 87; Lady, 79, 83; Elizabeth, 87; Sir William, 2, 59, 60, 62, 150; ——, 102, 161
Rutland, 2nd Earl of, 100; Edward 3rd Earl of, 79; Roger 5th Earl of, 38, 42, 49, 51, 82, 102, 108, 171
Rutlandshire, 171
Rycot, 2, 114, 149

Sadler, Sir Thomas, 118; Ralph, 118
St. Denis, 82
St. George's Field, 61
St. Helena, 142

St. James's, 61; Park, 133
St. John, Oliver Lord, 5, 19, 150; Oliver, 126; Elizabeth, 126; Sir Oliver, 130, 134; ——, 116; House of, 120; Street, 64
St Malo, 97
St. Paul's, 10, 44, 70, 74, 88, 90, 97, 102, 120, 127, 162, 175, 176; Cross, 62, 163
St. Peter's Hill, 88
St. Lawrence, 23
Salines, Count de, 85
Saltingstall, Alderman, 98
Sandwich, 6
Sandys, Lord, 108; Lady, 160
Sapina, Don Carlo de, 85
Sartogenbosch, 66
Sas, 81
Savage, Sir Arthur, 31; Sir John, 53; Sir Thomas, 135; Lady, 53
Savile, Henry, 27, 106; Mr. 140, 179
Savoy, 88, 96; Duke of, 66, 71, 91
Saunders, Robert, 139, 171; Mr. 139, 141, 156, 158, 164, 170
Say and Sele, Richard Lord, 126
Scory, 58
Scott, Capt. 85; Sir John, 47, 106, 170
Scotland, 12, 57
Scudamore, Sir James, 18, 53; Lady, 18; Philip, 4; Mrs. 102
Sebastian, King of Portugal, 24, 40, 47, 52, 88, 96
Serres, Jean de, 32
Seymour, Edward, 97; Mrs. 97
Sherbourne, 41, 171
Sherley, Sir Anthony, 32, 92; George, 4, 33; Sir Thomas, 32, 132, 144
Shrewsbury, Gilbert Earl of, 9, 52, 60, 112, 146; Countess of, 177
Sidney, Sir Henry, 100; Sir Philip, 40; Sir Robert, 7, 24, 30, 81, 82, 86, 108, 146, 156, 171, 173; Lady, 170
Sigismund III. King of Poland, 24
Sims, Col. 144
Simnes, Capt. 46
Skidmore, Mrs. 102

Skinner, Alderman, 170; Mr. 170
Sligo, 101
Slingsby, Sir Henry, 135
Sluce, 67, 75, 79. 85, 92
Smith, Sheriff, 106; Mrs. 106;
    Ann, 170; ——, 179
Smithfield, 78, 126
Snelling. ——, 7
Somerset House, 68
Somersetshire, 4, 101
Soubise, Mons. de, 91
Southampton, 132; Henry Earl
    of, 3, 18, 29, 30, 38, 49, 51,
    75, 89, 104, 106; Countess
    of, 18. 27; Dowager Countess
    of, 13, 43
South Sea, the, 89
Southwell, Sir Robert, 27; Lady,
    27, 41, 47
Spain, *passim*
Spencer, Sir John. of Althorpe,
    52; Sir John. 43, 50, 109;
    Elizabeth, 43, 50, 109; Dr.
    John, 143; Thomas, 101; Sir
    William, 18
Spenser, Edmund, the poet, 41
Spiring, Francis, 170
Squire, ——, 26, 28, 29, 47
Stafford, Edward Lord, 125; Sir
    Edward, 52, 94, 112, 139;
    Sir Rhead, 117
Stanhope, Dr. Edward, 69; Sir
    John, 18, 21, 52, 89, 100, 112;
    John, 52, 54, 55; Michael, 100
Stanley, Edward, 172; John.
    21. 24, 26, 27, 28, 29; Sir
    William, 85
Star Chamber, the, 65, 77, 135,
    144, 145, 179
Starkie, ——, 177
Stoke, 118
Strange, Lady, 91, 151
Stuart, Lady Arabella, 177;
    Prince Charles, 97
Stukeley, Mrs. 53, 109, 116, 120
Suffolk, 61, 101
Surrey, 31, 101, 152
Sussex. 31, 101, 152; Robert
    Earl of. 58
Sutcliffe, Dr. Mathew, 119
Sutton, Mr. 120
Swale, Dr. 72
Sweden, 24
Swiss League, The, 159

Tanfield, Lawrence, 143, 177
Taisborough, Sir Thomas, 173;
    Lady, 167
Terceras, the, 21
Terringham, Young, 45
Therfield, 7
Thomond, Earl of, 31, 127
Thornborough, Dr. John, 163
Throgmorton, Sir Thomas, 135;
    Young, 10
Tilbury, 56, 59
Tipperary, 26
Tirone, Earl of, 17, 21, 27, 36,
    49, 57, 60, 66, 75, 80, 105,
    119, 127, 131, 138, 145, 151,
    172, 176, 180
Tirrell, ——, 164, 170, 176
Tottenham, 46, 59, 60
Tower, the, 21, 24, 64, 78, 97,
    133
Tresham, ——, 108
Trevallin, 2
Trevor, Sir Rich. 2; Mr. 37
Tripoli, 69
Trot, Mr. 143
Turkey, 91
Turner, ——, 177
Tyburn, 7, 25, 104, 179
Tyrrell, Capt. 85

Underhill, Sir Hercules, 161
Unton, Sir Henry, 4; Lady, 4, 33

Valentine, 155, 175
Valladolid, 159
Valois, Marguerite de, 71
Van Bergh, Count Frederick, 85
Vanifer, Capt. 161
Veillar, Don Louis de, 85
Velasco, Gen. 86
Vendosme, Duke of, 71, 81
Venice, 24, 40, 69
Venner, Mr. 163
Vere, Sir Francis, 3, 14, 21, 24,
    45, 56, 58, 81, 82, 84, 85, 112,
    126, 131, 132, 134, 140, 142,
    151, 156, 161, 167; Horace
    Lord, 3
Vernon, Sir John, 18, 27
Verreyken, Louis, 66, 67, 70, 73
Vervins, the Peace of, 91
Vroom, Henry Cornelius, 170

Wachendoncke, 68

Wainman, Capt. 111; Sir Rich.
    117
Walachia, Vaivode of, 96
Walcheren, Isle of, 16
Wallop, Sir Henry, sen. 5, 46,
    60, 70; Lady, 60; Sir Henry,
    5, 60, 75, 87, 109, 127, 134,
    137, 147, 150; Lady, 5, 79,
    102, 109, 115, 116, 170; Sir
    Oliver, 46; Winifred, 70, 77,
    109, 111, 115, 150
Walpole, 28
Walsingham, Sir Francis, 49,
    143; Lady, 143
Wanstead, 15
Warburton, Capt. 167
Warcop, Mr. 113
Ward, Sir Richard. 117
Wards, Court of, 23, 31, 160
Warwick, 53; Ambrose Earl of,
    87; Countess of, 87
Watson, Dr. Anthony, 136
Wendie, Sheriff, 166
Westminster, 41, 70, 78, 121
Wexford, 75, 86
Weymouth, Capt. 132
Wharton, Lord, 173; Young, 173
Wheeler, 151, 160
Whiddon, Capt. 111, 120, 138,
    141, 175, 176
Whitehall, 29, 33, 70, 162
Whitelock, Capt. 131
Whitgift, Dr. John, 97, 126
Wight, Isle of. 59
Wilford, Sir Thomas, 59, 126
Wilkinson, ——, 144
William, Grave, 82
Williams, Alexander, 6, 9, 11,
    13, 92, 128; Mrs. 1, 74, 111,
    152, 155; Capt. 17
Willis, Simon, 151, 154
Willoughby, Ambrose, 139;
    Peregrine Lord (of Eresby),
    112
Wilton. 3
Wimbledon, 57, 61
Winchester, 160; William 3rd
    Marquis of, 9, 32. 41; William
    4th Marquis of, 32, 116
Windsor, Ge. 108, 115, 117;
    Henry Lord, 3, 38, 82
Wingfield, Sir Edward, 39; Sir
    Richard, 101; Sir Thomas
    Maria, 2, 36; House, 110, 113

Winwood, Ralph, 41, 81, 108, 109, 115, 121, 123, 127, 137, 138, 140, 144, 148, 152, 156, 158, 160, 161, 164, 167, 174, 176, 178
Wisbeach, 80
Witheringtons, the, 10
Withipole, Sir Edward, 61
Wittenberg, Duke of, 71
Woode, Mr. 109
Woode, Deane, 106

Woodhouse, Sir William, 38, 41, 46, 47, 50, 57
Woodstock, 114
Wotton, Sir Edward, 59, 108, 171, 172
Worcester, Edward Earl of, 60, 79, 83, 112; Countess of, 170
Wroth, John, 24, 156; Sir Robert, 134
Wroughton, Sir Thomas, 4, 33

Xarife Muley Hamet, 91, 93

Yaxley, Captain, 85
York, 63
Yorke, Sir Edward, 42
York House, 87
Yorkshire, 61

Zeland, 145
Zouch, Lord, 14, 108, 139, 157,

## ERRATA.

P. 89 note, for Sir William Heydon, read Sir John.

P. 108, note *, the reference to p. 104 is incorrect, the " Sir Harry Neville " in this page being the lately appointed ambassador to France (see the Index).

Printed by J. B. Nichols and Sons, 25, Parliament Street.

# REPORT OF THE COUNCIL

OF

# THE CAMDEN SOCIETY,

ELECTED 2nd MAY, 1860.

---

THE Council elected on the 2nd of May, 1860, regret to report the deaths, during the past year, of the following Members:—
   The Right Hon. the EARL OF ABERDEEN.
   The Rev. Dr. BANDINEL.
   Sir HENRY BUNBURY, K.C.B.
   GEORGE GODFREY CUNNINGHAM, Esq.
   Miss RICHARDSON CURRER.
   HENRY CURWEN, Esq.
   Mrs. HALL.
   CHARLES WILLIAM HALLETT, Esq.
   THOMAS MASON, Esq. F.S.A.
   Sir JOHN E. SWINBURNE, Bart. Pres. Soc. Ant. Newcastle.
   Mr. ALDERMAN WIRE.

It will be seen that this List contains the names of some of the earliest and most distinguished Members of the Society. The EARL OF ABERDEEN, who was President of the Society of Antiquaries when the Camden Society was established, gave it the advantage of his public support at a very early period; and the names of the Rev. BULKELEY B. BANDINEL, Bodley's Librarian at Oxford; Sir HENRY BUNBURY; G. G. CUNNINGHAM, Esq.; Miss RICHARDSON CURRER; CHARLES WILLIAM HALLETT, Esq.; THOMAS MASON, Esq.; and Sir JOHN EDWARD SWINBURNE, will all be found in the First Annual List of the Members of the Camden Society.

Although the number of Members whose loss the Society has thus to regret is not much above the usual average; yet the List has been so greatly reduced of late years that the proportion is a large one, and the Council would urge upon the Members to lose no opportunity of bringing the Society under the notice of such of their friends as are interested in the study of any of the branches of our Civil, Ecclesiastical, or Social History.

The Council having understood that Gentlemen desirous of joining the Camden Society have been deterred from giving in their names by the expense of procuring the publications of past years, have recently directed that New Members should be allowed to purchase the publications of past years, so far as they can be supplied, at the rate of ten shillings for each year's books, with the exception of those of the last two years preceding their admission, the price of which has been fixed at thirty shillings. The impression of each work now published by the Society is strictly limited to six hundred.

The following Articles have been added to the List of Suggested Publications during the past year.

I. A Series of Descriptions of Pope Alexander VII. and his Cardinals, from the MS. Notes of Dr. John Bargrave. To be edited by the Rev. CANON ROBERTSON.

II. A Series of News Letters, written by John Chamberlain, Esq. to Sir Dudley Carleton during the reign of Elizabeth, from the Originals in the State Paper Office. To be edited by MISS WILLIAMS.

III. Notes of Speeches in the Parliament of 1610, from MSS. in the British Museum. To be edited by S. R. GARDINER, Esq.

IV. Cromwell and Barrington Correspondence, from the Originals in the possession of Allan Lowndes, Esq. of Barrington Hall, Essex. To be edited by JAMES CROSBY, Esq. F.S.A.

V. An account of Sir John Mason, in the time of Elizabeth; and a Discharge of Dethick, Garter, for Expenses of the Funeral of Mary Queen of Scots.

VI. List of the Walloons resident in England in the time of James the First, with other Documents of a similar character. To be edited by W. DURRANT COOPER, Esq. F.S.A.

VIII. Early English Poems, from a MS. in the possession of the Dean and Chapter of Windsor. To be edited by B. B. WOODWARD, Esq F.S.A., Librarian to Her Majesty.

Several of these are short works, and are intended for publication in the next volume of the Camden Miscellany.

The Books of the present year are two in number:

I. Narratives of the Days of the Reformation, and the contemporary Biographies of Archbishop Cranmer; selected from the Papers of John Foxe the Martyrologist. Edited by JOHN GOUGH NICHOLS, Esq F.S.A.

II. Correspondence of King James VI. of Scotland with Sir Robert Cecil and others during the Reign of Queen Elizabeth. Edited by JOHN BRUCE, Esq. V.P.S.A.

The former of these Volumes has met with due commendation from the Reviewers. Edited with the fullness and care which distinguish all Mr. Nichols's works, it cannot fail to take its place among the most reliable authorities for one of the most important periods in our history.

The latter volume will be not less serviceable to the historical inquirer. Derived from the collections of the Marquess of Salisbury at Hatfield, it lays open for the first time the real Secret Correspondence between King James and Sir Robert Cecil, and will be found to be full of valuable information with reference to transactions at the close of the reign of Queen Elizabeth.

Both works will do credit to the Society, and are manifest evidences of its continued importance and usefulness.

Mr. Collier, who has served the Society as Treasurer for sixteen years, has been desirous for some time past to relinquish the duties of that office, on the ground of increasing years. Mr. Collier having again pressed his retirement upon the Council, Mr. Blaauw has kindly consented to assume the post, and will be proposed for election at the first meeting of the New Council. The Council need scarcely recommend to the Society the propriety of passing a vote of grateful recognition of Mr. Collier's long and valuable services, which will still however be continued to the Society as one of the Council.

Another change is also about to take place in the conduct of the affairs of the Society, in the retirement of Mr. Thoms from the management of the accounts, an alteration rendered necessary by the pressure of other official engagements. The Society will, however, retain his valuable services as Honorary Secretary. Any inconvenience which might have resulted from this change has been obviated by the kindness of Mr. John Gough Nichols, who has offered to take upon himself the whole responsibility of the correspondence in connection with the Subscriptions. The Council have gladly availed themselves of this offer, and have to intimate that all payments of subscriptions and correspondence respecting the accounts should in future be addressed to Mr. John Gough Nichols, and that post-office orders should be made payable at the office in Parliament Street.

The Council would not endeavour to conceal from the Society that its position, although perfectly secure, being without debt, and having an investment of £1,016 3s. 1d., is not so satisfactory as it has been. New Members do not join the Society so rapidly as the old ones fall off, and the income and consequent means of usefulness have decreased. The sphere open to the Society seems clear, and the publication of such books as those already mentioned, and Chamberlain's Letters during the reign of Elizabeth, which will be the first volume of the next year, supply ample proof that the disappearance of the Camden Society would be a great loss to historical literature.

It is to be hoped that such publications will tend to recruit the number of Members, and restore the income of the Society to its old amount.

By order of the Council,

JOHN BRUCE, Director.
WILLIAM J. THOMS, Secretary.

17 *April*, 1861.

# REPORT OF THE AUDITORS.

WE, the Auditors appointed to audit the Accounts of the Camden Society, report to the Society, that the Treasurer has exhibited to us an account of the Receipts and Expenditure from the 1st of April, 1860, to the 31st of March, 1861, and that we have examined the said accounts, with the vouchers relating thereto, and find the same to be correct and satisfactory.

And we further report that the following is an Abstract of the Receipts and Expenditure during the period we have mentioned.

| RECEIPTS. | £. | s. | d. | EXPENDITURE. | £ | s. | d. |
|---|---|---|---|---|---|---|---|
| By Balance of last year's account.. | 96 | 3 | 7 | Paid for printing 600 copies of "Carew Letters" .... | 57 | 6 | 6 |
| Received on account of Members whose Subscriptions were in arrear at the last Audit.......... | 73 | 0 | 0 | Paid for printing and paper of 750 copies of "Narratives of Reformation" ........................ | 186 | 17 | 0 |
| The like on account of Subscriptions due 1st May last (1860) .. | 307 | 0 | 0 | Paid for binding 500 copies of "Milton Papers" .... | 17 | 0 | 0 |
| The like on account of Subscriptions due 1st May next............. | 15 | 0 | 0 | The like of "Carew Letters" and "Narratives of Reformation"........................................ | 39 | 17 | 0 |
| One year's dividend on £1016 3s. 1d. 3 per Cent. Consols, standing in the names of the Trustees of the Society, deducting Income Tax.. | 29 | 4 | 4 | Paid for Paper........................................ | 41 | 18 | 6 |
| | | | | Paid for Transcripts................................. | 12 | 4 | 0 |
| | | | | Paid for Miscellaneous Printing..................... | 5 | 18 | 6 |
| | | | | Paid for delivery and transmission of 500 copies of "Carew Letters" and of "Narratives of Reformation," with paper for wrappers, warehousing expenses, &c. .............................. | 19 | 7 | 6 |
| | | | | Paid for Advertisements.............................. | 4 | 12 | 6 |
| | | | | One year's payment for keeping Accounts and General Correspondence of the Society .................. | 52 | 10 | 0 |
| | | | | Paid for postage, carriage of parcels, and other petty cash expenses.................................. | 3 | 7 | 4 |
| | | | | | 440 | 18 | 10 |
| | | | | By Balance.............. | 79 | 9 | 1 |
| | £520 | 7 | 11 | | £520 | 7 | 11 |

And we, the Auditors, further state, that the Treasurer has reported to us, that over and above the present balance of £79 9s. 1d. there are outstanding various subscriptions of Foreign Members, and of Members resident at a distance from London, which the Treasurer sees no reason to doubt will shortly be received.

HENRY STONE SMITH,<br>WILLIAM SALT.

17th April, 1861.

www.ingramcontent.com/pod-product-compliance
Lightning Source LLC
Chambersburg PA
CBHW021729220426
43662CB00008B/765